THE EXPERTS' BOOK OF
Sewing
Tips & Techniques

The Experts' Book of Sewing Tips & Techniques

From the Sewing Stars of America—Hundreds of Ways to Sew Better, Faster & Easier

CONTRIBUTING EDITORS:
MARYA KISSINGER AMIG, BARBARA FIMBEL,
STACEY L. KLAMAN, KAREN KUNKEL, AND
SUSAN WEAVER

Rodale Press, Inc.
Emmaus, Pennsylvania

OUR MISSION

We publish books that empower people's lives.

RODALE BOOKS

On the cover: Sewing machine courtesy of Bernina of America

If you have any questions or comments concerning this book, please write to:
Rodale Press, Inc.
Book Readers' Service
33 East Minor Street
Emmaus, PA 18098

THE EXPERTS' BOOK OF SEWING TIPS & TECHNIQUES EDITORIAL STAFF

Editors: Marya Kissinger Amig, Stacey L. Klaman, Susan Weaver
Cover and Interior Designer: Patricia Field
Photographer: John Hamel
Technical Illustrator: Charles Metz
Illustrators: Len Epstein, Mario Ferro, Barbara Field, Glenn Hughes, Frank Rohrbach, Jackie Walsh
Studio Manager: Leslie Keefe
Copy Editor: Carolyn Mandarano
Editorial Assistance: Stephanie Wenner
Manufacturing Coordinator: Melinda B. Rizzo

RODALE BOOKS

Editorial Director, Home and Garden: Margaret Lydic Balitas
Senior Editor, Craft Books: Cheryl Winters Tetreau
Art Director, Home and Garden: Michael Mandarano
Copy Director, Home and Garden: Dolores Plikaitis
Office Manager, Home and Garden: Karen Earl-Braymer
Editor-in-Chief: William Gottlieb

Library of Congress Cataloging-in-Publication Data
The experts' book of sewing tips & techniques : from the sewing stars of America—hundreds of ways to sew better, faster and easier / contributing editors, Barbara Fimbel ... [et al.].
    p. cm.
  ISBN 0–87596–682–9 (hc : alk. paper)
  1. Machine sewing. 1. Fimbel, Barbara.
TT713.E96 1995
646.2'044—dc20   95–248

Distributed in the book trade by St. Martin's Press
2 4 6 8 10 9 7 5 3 1 hardcover

Contents

Introduction

What sewer wouldn't jump at the chance to cross the country on a sewing-information spree? Imagine being able to attend every lecture, seminar, workshop, and convention your heart desires. You have all the time in the world to ask your favorite sewing stars for their best tips, techniques, and industry secrets and the most burning sewing questions on your mind. Perhaps you want to know the most effective way to organize your sewing room. Or how to press a seam without leaving marks on the right side of your fabric. Maybe you're about to purchase your first serger and need professional advice. Though a trip like this would be a dream come true for many, most of us can't afford to travel at whim, let alone have the time to make it happen. That is why this dynamic book was developed.

For more than a year we worked with a team of editors who interviewed more than 100 of the nation's top sewing experts and manufacturers to solicit their advice on how to help you sew faster, better, and easier. The results are in the information-packed pages that follow. They are filled with years of experience and wisdom, along with a few anecdotes for good measure.

Leafing through *The Experts' Book of Sewing Tips & Techniques* is like having each expert sit beside you at your sewing machine, offering per-sonal instruction on how to tackle various aspects of garment and home decoration construction. Though you'll want to keep this book next to your sewing machine, you'll soon discover how much fun it is to read when you're not sewing. And the more you read, the more you'll want to sew. Each time you pick up this book to browse through the pages, you'll find useful information or a variation on a skill that you will want to try the next time you sit down at your machine.

The timesaving methods, bright ideas, efficient techniques, and smart shopping suggestions are sure to become part of your growing repertoire of skills. The experts quickly move you up to professional speed as they show you how to resolve recurring problems, perfect techniques, and employ new tricks.

If you find it difficult to maximize your sewing time, the first chapter is the place to start. It is devoted to arranging an effective sewing space, since organization is the key to efficient sewing. If you want to know specific information, such as the secret to constructing a better button-hole or the best stabilizer to use with specific kinds of fabric, follow the book's easy A to Z format. The fabric key that follows will be helpful in identifying the batting, stabilizer, interfacing, freezer paper, and right and wrong side of fabric representations, so that it will be easy to position your fabrics together correctly.

Working on this book has provided us with the opportunity to confirm a

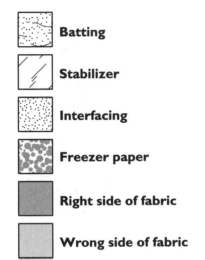

Batting

Stabilizer

Interfacing

Freezer paper

Right side of fabric

Wrong side of fabric

long-simmering suspicion of ours— that sewers are a very gracious and generous group of people, eager to share their knowledge to empower others. Each sewer our editors talked with was delighted to answer questions and share secrets. So we are indebted to all of those experts who contributed to this book. Their combined talents have produced a superb collection of inspirational, innovative, and indispensable tips, tricks, and little-known facts. You can read more about these remarkable pros in "The Sewing Experts," beginning on page 314.

The Rodale Sewing Editors

Organizing Your Sewing Space

Your work space and equipment don't have to be top of the line to be effective. Learn to work with what you already have. Take a sewing inventory and organize a space tailored to your needs. With a little extra know-how, you can make your existing equipment and tools perform more efficiently. Creating and utilizing a well-designed space will bring immense satisfaction and more pleasure to sewing.

Creative Setup

Easily accessible storage space and adequate work surfaces are essential to any efficient sewing room. Instead of purchasing specially designed cabinets, consider using recycled office furniture. Look in your local newspaper's classified section for upcoming business closings, auctions, or sales. Here are a few creative ways to use your new-found furniture.

- **Tall bookcases with adjustable shelves.** With the ability to adjust shelf height, you can easily organize your fabric collection into large containers and your sewing supplies into colorful baskets, labeled boxes, or other holders for quick identification.

- **Two-drawer file cabinet.** Use this as a sturdy base for your desk or sewing table, or place it underneath the fold-out end of your sewing machine cabinet. The spacious drawers hold patterns, sewing information, or leftover fabric.

- **Desk.** One with a large, smooth top makes a roomy sewing surface. As you sew, the table will prevent the weight of any heavy or large projects from pulling on the machine stitches. It will also keep your projects from picking up lint from the floor. If your desk has a compartmentalized drawer, use it to keep extra bobbins, spare machine needles, small scissors, and a seam ripper handy.

- **Small bookshelves.** Shelves that fit on the back of your desk or sewing table can create space for your sewing library, most frequently referenced sewing information, or most-used sewing supplies. Simply brace one or two shelves within arm's reach, and you'll never have to move from your work area while you sew.

- **Other office equipment.** For even greater efficiency, use a secretarial chair for easy turning and good back support, bulletin boards for tacking sewing information, and floor or desk lamps to ensure ample lighting as you work.

Tammy Young

Organizing Your Sewing Space

Organizing Your Sewing Space

Make a Work Triangle

I find that the most efficient use of my sewing room space is with my iron and ironing board, serger, and conventional machine set up in a work triangle. This configuration is ideal because my equipment is easily accessible, and I can conveniently use both machines as often as I need them.

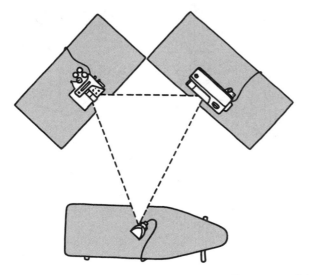

Peggy Bendel

Room to Move

If you're thinking about designing a new sewing room but have limited space, don't construct too many built-in storage cabinets. Instead, invest in tall wire drawers on wheels and bookcases with movable shelves. They have worked well in my sewing room, which is nicknamed the "bowling alley" because it is 8 feet wide × 39 feet long. I can easily move the wire drawers next to my work area when needed, then push them back when I'm finished. The movable shelves of my bookcase make rearranging a breeze.

Robbie Fanning

Mark It

I keep an extra-fine point, felt-tip pen with my sewing tools. It comes in handy to label and mark a variety of items and saves me time in the long run. I like to use a Sharpie brand because it is relatively permanent—can be removed with alcohol. I use my marker to

- label a presser foot if its identity is not readily apparent.

- identify type, size, and brand of thread on wound bobbins. This is especially helpful when I have six or more white bobbins at a time.

- indicate the slit that holds the tail of thread in place on a spool.

- write on template plastic.

- put my name on any sewing notions that I take to a sewing class.

Carol Laflin Ahles

Deck the Walls

I store my thread in shadow boxes and printer's boxes. You can find these old boxes in many shapes and sizes at flea markets or antique stores. New boxes of the same style can be found in gift and hobby shops that sell miniatures. These boxes make terrific room decorations, too!

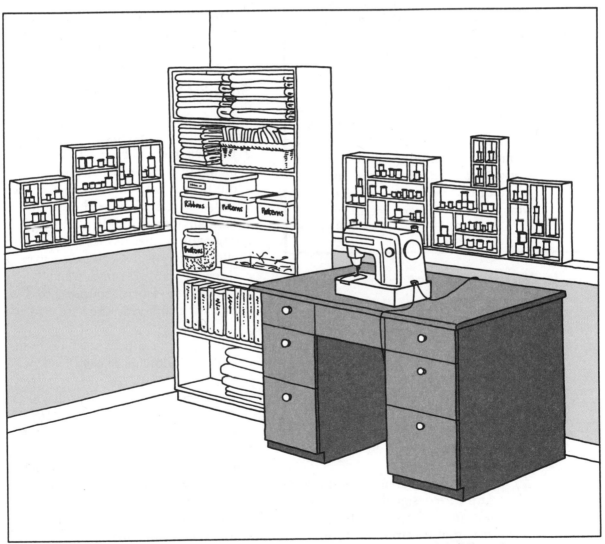

Libby Lehman

SMART SHOPPER

Don't store your fabrics in those pretty printed paper bags that some fabric stores use. The bags are actually made from fabric printing leftovers. When fabric is printed with a heat-transfer process, the pattern is first printed onto paper, then onto the fabric. The paper is peeled off and recycled into shopping bags. This eco-wise idea is fine for transporting fabric goods but not for long-term storage. If you keep your fabric in the bag, eventually the dye will transfer onto your fabric. So, remember to add your fabric to your stockpile as soon as you get home. But don't throw the bag away. Use it as wrapping paper for your special gifts!

Kendra Brandes

What a Racket

Organize threads on a rack by color, so you'll know at a glance whether you have topstitching thread, decorative thread, and/or regular sewing thread in a specific color.

Linda Griepentrog

Space Saver

My favorite space saver is a piece of furniture designed specifically for sewers—a drop-leaf table. It's so versatile that it can be used three ways. When the leaves are fully extended, this table can be used for cutting out projects. When one leaf is extended, the table turns into a handy crafting surface next to which you can place a kitchen stool. And when both leaves are down, this table can be used as a narrow sideboard.

Tammy Young

Sneaky Storage

If you aren't lucky enough to have a room exclusively dedicated to sewing, don't despair! There are plenty of storage spaces throughout your home that can cleverly disguise your fabric stash. The trick is to be thoroughly organized. Begin by separating natural fiber fabrics from synthetics. Then sort by color or season and separate knits from wovens. Finally, tie the fabric groupings together with ribbon so they are easy to grab at once.

Now you're ready to stash them in one of the following places.

- Use a shelf or two in your linen closet or bathroom if you tend to hoard more fabric than linens or towels.

- Fill up half of a guest room closet with fabric hung on large wooden or plastic hangers. Use the lower drawers of a dresser or night table for your sewing notions and other sewing supplies.

▣ An antique trunk has lots of fabric storage space and will make an attractive addition to your den, family room, or living room.

▣ Under-the-bed storage should be saved for fusibles and fabrics with natural fibers. Don't put these sensitive fabrics in your attic, where insects love to nest, or in your basement, where the humidity tends to fluctuate.

Janis Bullis

On a Roll

Recycle the cardboard tubes from paper towel rolls to organize your ribbon collection. Wrap ribbons around the tubes to eliminate wrinkles, and secure them with straight pins. If you sort by color and type, you'll always have a complete inventory right at your fingertips.

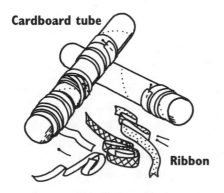

Cardboard tube

Ribbon

Elizabeth M. Barry

My Favorite Floor Covering

If you are planning to redo your sewing room floor, opt for vinyl. You'll be surprised at how much sewing use you'll get out of it! I prefer 6- or 12-inch-square tiles so I can square up my fabric, especially when working with quilt blocks. Not only do I use my vinyl floor to lay out and cut fabric and patterns but I also use it to tape my quilt blocks together so they don't shift when I layer and baste them. I even use the tiles to calculate pattern repeats! Best of all, this floor is a snap to maintain—I just use a broom to sweep up the mess!

Annie T. Tuley

Organizing Your Sewing Space

Sharp Shears

Tie a ribbon around the handles of your sewing shears to remind your family that they're for fabric cutting only!

Elizabeth M. Barry

A Label of Love

One sewing room essential that I can't live without is my portable tape recorder. As I sew, I like to listen to books on tape. As a special remembrance, I often stitch a label into the garment that I'm working on with the name of the book I'm listening to. For example, my daughter's long, romantic flannel nightgown has a label with *Anne of Green Gables* written on it because that is what I listened to while sewing.

Robbie Fanning

I Can See Clearly Now

Carpenter's cabinets with clear plastic drawers are great for storing sewing notions because you can clearly see where everything is lo-cated. I've stacked four of them on the desk in my sewing area, and all are within arm's reach. The compartments are great for small sewing notions, decorative threads, buttons, elastic, and other supplies. You can find these cabinets in several sizes in your local hardware or building-supply store.

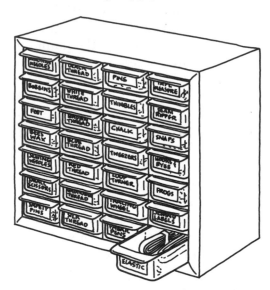

Peggy Bendel

Double or Triple Up

I find it helpful to double up or even triple up on small sewing notions such as scissors, seam rippers, tape measures, and pincushions. I place one set at my ironing board, another beside my sewing machine, and the third next to my favorite chair.

Lynn L. Browne

Pinked Advantage

I often find that pinking shears are more than ravel-resistant seam finishers. Pinked edges are less bulky than overcast or serged finishes. They soften a seam allowance and lessen the chance of a ridge showing through on the outside of a garment after pressing.

I use pinking shears to

- trim, grade, notch, and clip enclosed seam allowances, such as inside collar seams, in one step.

- cut the outside edges of interfacings before fusing them to a garment.

- snip long lengths of ¼-inch-wide sections of fusible web after I've rolled it into one long tube. The pinked edges of the strips will disappear when fused between two layers of fabric for a soft finish.

- cut fanciful appliqués that have been fused with paper-backed fusible web.

Betty Ann Watts

Stock Up

When stocking your sewing room, don't skimp on bobbins or sewing machine and serger needles! Purchase an extra supply of each from mail-order notions suppliers. Wind the bobbins with the colors of thread that you use most often so that you never have to stop and wind one as you sew. Keep the sewing machine needles close by so that you can simply switch to another type or a fresh one when you encounter stitching problems.

Peggy Bendel

Keep It Cool

Prevent your glue sticks from drying out or molding by storing them in the freezer. After using a glue stick and before placing it in the freezer, place a few drops of water on the tip to prevent it from drying out.

Annie T. Tuley

Organizing Your Sewing Space

It's in the Bag

Utilize reclosable plastic bags for inexpensive, flexible, see-through storage of sewing machine feet, thread, machine needles, safety pins, patterns, ribbons, and other notions.

Gail Brown

Pet Peeves

In all my years of sewing, very few things have managed to get the better of me. Running out of bobbin thread tops the list. Having thread disappear from my needle while in the middle of sewing is frustrating, so before I start a project, I wind two bobbins of thread. This way, I always have a spare at my fingertips when I need it.

Another pet peeve of mine (and my husband's) is finding little pieces of thread all over my home. To help limit those thread ends, I place a piece of contact paper, sticky side up, to the left of my sewing machine. After stitching, I cut thread ends over the contact paper.

Virginia K. Jansen

Cut in Place

Instead of scissors, I like to keep a small rotary cutter and 6-inch-square cutting mat that quilters use next to my sewing machine. Then I can save time by accurately measuring and trimming seams, clipping corners, and trimming thread ends without having to get up.

Peggy Bendel

Quick Pickup

If you accidentally spill small items like seed beads, retrieve them quickly by placing a nylon stocking over the nozzle of your vacuum cleaner. The beads will stick to the stocking for quick and easy cleanup.

Kenneth D. King

The Best Sewing Tools

The three tools I can't sew without are a clear, 2 × 18-inch quilt ruler, a water-soluble marking pen for light-color fabrics, and a chalk wheel for dark fabrics. I use them to mark hemlines, stitching lines, pivot points, and a number of other places.

Mary Griffin

Sort Your Stash

At least once a year, go through your fabric stash and give away fabrics you'll never use. Donate them to schools, churches, and charity groups. Or include them in a garage sale, pricing them as low as 10 cents a yard. Passionate bargain hunters won't be able to resist. And you'll have space to stock more!

Gail Brown

Tool Time

I find a magnetic tool rail, available at kitchen-accessory stores, an invaluable part of my sewing room setup. Installed at arm's distance, it conveniently holds various sizes of scissors and shears, threaded hand-sewing needles, a thimble, the wire threader and tweezers for my serger, assorted screwdrivers, a tracing wheel, seam gauge, and my seam ripper.

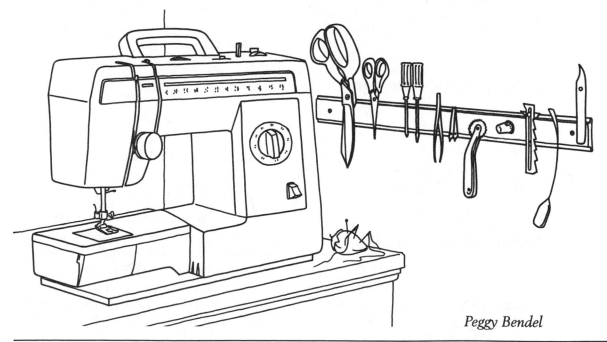

Peggy Bendel

Appliqué

Appliqué is one of the most versatile forms of surface embellishment. It can be done by hand with tiny blind stitches or with decorative stitches, such as the feather or blanket stitch. By machine, appliqué can be done with a straight stitch to produce a traditional look, or it can be quickly and dramatically worked with bold satin stitching.

Your Own Template Library

When your project is completed, store used templates in plastic sleeves in a loose-leaf binder. You'll be able to find those templates in a flash, should you ever want to use them again. Use a separate sleeve for each project, and label all templates with the name of the design and number them, preferably in order of assembly. I like to organize by shape or by project.

Margit Echols

Organized by project **Organized by shape**

Coloring-Book Designs

Children's coloring books are hard to beat as a source for appliqué designs. The design shapes are clear, and the bold lines provide sharp definition.

Julia Bernstein

Ultradurable Templates

Use scraps of linoleum flooring or vinyl tile to make nearly permanent templates for often-used shapes.

Stacey L. Klaman

It's in the Bag

For less mess when cutting small pieces, work over an open paper grocery bag. Folding the top edge of the bag back on itself about an inch will keep the bag open nice and wide. All of your scraps will fall into the bag for instant cleanup!

Barbara Fimbel

Be a Quick-Change Artist

To mark plastic templates, use a sticker, gummed label, or masking tape. Be sure the ink you use is waterproof and smudge-proof. When your project is complete, you can remove the label and save the template for another use.

Karen Costello Soltys

Fast Fuse-Basting

If you want to temporarily tack your appliqué pieces to your garment before machine sewing them in place, you can do so quickly and easily with fusible web. Follow the manufacturer's directions to iron the fusible web to your appliqués. Then remove the paper backing from the web and place your appliqués, fusible side down, on your garment. Glide a medium-hot iron over the appliqués for about three seconds. If you want to move your appliqués, simply peel them off and reposition them. The fusible web will remain on the appliqués.

Freudenberg Nonwovens
Pellon Consumer Division

Handy Hoops

When hand appliquéing, you'll find that an embroidery hoop allows you to view, stitch, and handle your fabric easily. Follow these steps for easy appliquéing.

Step 1: On a flat surface, pin only those appliqué pieces to your garment that will fit inside your hoop.

Step 2: Baste the appliqué pieces in place with a contrasting color thread, making sure you don't baste too close to the edge where you will sew permanent stitches. Remove the pins when you have finished basting.

Step 3: Put the fabric into your hoop carefully. Smooth out any wrinkles, and make sure fabric layers haven't shifted before you tighten the hoop.

Step 4: Hand sew the appliqués in place. When you are finished, remove the basting stitches.

Gay Quinn

SMART SHOPPER

Pop into your favorite photocopy shop to save time enlarging and reducing designs. Group as many pieces as possible that need the same size change onto an 8½ × 11-inch sheet of paper. Give the final size you want to the salesperson, who will figure out the percentage of enlargement or reduction. Enlargements may spill over to an extra sheet or two of paper, but the cost is still minimal.

Elizabeth M. Barry

Appliqué

Universal Match

For machine appliqué, you don't have to search for thread in a dozen exotic colors! Gray thread is a neutral that blends well with many hues. Use gray thread in the same color value—lightness or darkness—as the fabric you are appliquéing.

Elizabeth M. Barry

See-Through Rulers

To measure the placement of pieces on a project, buy a couple of heavy, clear plastic or acrylic rulers. One small ruler (2 × 6 inches) and a large one (2 × 18 inches) will do fine. The rulers should be marked in ⅛-inch increments and have a heavier line indicating every inch; some are marked with bias lines as well. If you have a choice, select a thicker ruler to give a better edge for marking and for guiding rotary cutters. You can find these rulers at office-supply, craft-supply, and quilt stores.

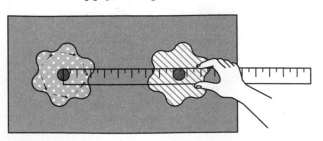

Barbara Fimbel

Nonskid Surface

To keep your fabric from slipping as you trace around a template, place a sheet of fine-grade sandpaper under the fabric.

Judi Abbott

Goof-Proof Your Templates

When working with a template that's not reversible, label the right side clearly with THIS SIDE UP. You'll never have to worry about placing it correctly.

Barbara Fimbel

A Better Bond

When working with any iron-on appliqué, complete the fusing process from the back, following the manufacturer's directions. Pressing from the back gives the most permanent bond because the heat of the iron is closest to the fusible web.

Patricia De Santis

Snag-Free Sewing

When hand appliquéing, pin appliqués from the underside of your fabric. That way you'll never catch your thread on the ends of the pins.

Sonja Dagress

Hand Basting Basics

A longer needle means fewer pull-throughs when basting by hand, so use the longest needle you can find. Use a doll-making or soft-sculpture needle or any other needle that is fine and sharp.

Charlotte Biro

One Good Turn

When using a nonfusible inter-facing as a stabilizer for an appliqué that will be sewn to delicate fabrics, such as silk, make sure you sew the wrong side of your fabric to the inter-facing and leave the opening for turning along the straightest part of the appliqué. Your appliqué will be easier to turn and will look much neater.

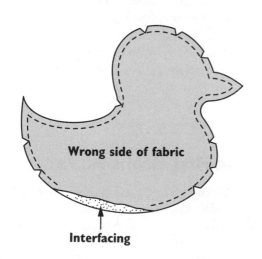

Wrong side of fabric

Interfacing

Robin Rose

From the Kitchen to the Sewing Room

When turning appliqué shapes right side out, use the point of a chopstick to get into the tightest corners. There's no sharp point—as you'd have with a scissors blade—to tear, fray, or puncture your fabric.

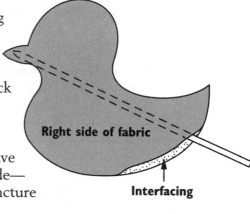

Right side of fabric

Interfacing

Barbara Fimbel

Turnabout Is Fair Play

Sometimes a pattern requires the reverse of an appliqué piece. But why create two templates if one will do? To save time and avoid error, make your templates reversible. Use a transparent mate-rial, such as heavyweight plastic or acetate. Use a piece of masking tape and label the front RIGHT SIDE, as shown on the left. Then use another piece of tape and mark the flip side REVERSE, as shown on the right. This marking will remind you to reverse your pieces as necessary before you cut your appliqué pattern.

RIGHT SIDE

REVERSE

Judi Abbott

★ Bright Idea ★

WHO SAYS YOU HAVE TO BASTE? Instead of pinning appliqués in place and basting them by machine, use a fabric glue such as Sticky Stuff. Just dab small drops of glue on the wrong side of your appliqué at least ⅛ inch in from the outer edge so that the glue doesn't ooze out when you press the appliqué in place. Turn your appliqué over and gently press it in place on your garment. Let the glue set before machine sewing your appliqué.

Barbara Fimbel

Now You See It, Now You Don't

One way to create perfectly shaped appliqué pieces is with a water-soluble stabilizer.

Step 1: Trace your appliqué shape onto the stabilizer. Then cut it out, allowing for a ⅛-inch seam allowance outside the marked line.

Step 2: Lay the stabilizer on the right side of your fabric, and machine stitch on the marked line.

Step 3: Cut out the appliqué shape, leaving a ⅛-inch seam allowance outside of the stitching. Clip any curves.

Step 4: Slit the stabilizer and turn the fabric right side out. Place your appliqué on your garment and sew it in place as desired.

The water-soluble stabilizer will hold the seam allowance in place for either hand or machine stitching, and the stitching will disappear like magic in the first washing. Or you can remove it by ironing the completed appliqué between two damp paper towels or pressing cloths.

Jacquelyn Smyth

A Seamless Look

Having trouble choosing between two threads for appliquéing? To make sure thread blends in with the fabric, always choose thread that's a shade darker, rather than a shade lighter, than the fabric.

Julia Bernstein

Fuse First Means No Fray

If you plan to use a thin fabric or fabric that frays easily for an appliqué shape, iron a piece of fusible interfacing to the back of your fabric before you cut it out.

Jan M. Steltz

Press-In Padding

 If you want to pad an appliqué piece without having the fleece shift as you machine sew, try using low-loft fusible fleece on the wrong side of your appliqué. Just reverse your template and trace it on the non-fusible side of the fleece. Cut out the fleece and trim ⅛ to ¼ inch off the outside of the piece, depending on the width of your satin stitching. Place the fusible side of the fleece against the wrong side of your appliqué piece, and press with an iron according to the fleece manufacturer's directions.

Marya Kissinger Amig

Basting in a Jiffy

You can baste your appliqué pieces to your garment or project in a jiffy when you use this fusible thread technique.

Step 1: Trace your template onto the wrong side of your appliqué fabric.

Step 2: Wind fusible thread onto your bobbin. Then with the wrong side of your appliqué fabric facing up, machine stitch around your appliqué piece one needle width to the outside of your tracing line.

Step 3: Cut out the appliqué piece, leaving a ¼-inch seam allowance to the outside of the fusible thread. Finger press the seam allowance to the wrong side of the appliqué piece.

Step 4: Position the appliqué piece on your garment or fabric and press with an iron. The fusible thread will hold the appliqué in place until you complete your hand or machine stitching.

Susan Huxley

Outside Right, Inside Left

When you machine appliqué, remember that when pivoting at an outside corner, finish your satin stitching with the needle in the right position; when pivoting at an inside corner, finish stitching with the needle in the left position.

Marya Kissinger Amig

★ Bright Idea ★

YOU CAN CREATE ONE-OF-A-KIND DE-SIGNS BY USING DIFFERENT TEXTURE MA-TERIALS or trinkets in your appliqué projects. For example, use corduroy for a puffy cat tail, lamé for a crown, a piece of lace on the bottom of a little girl's dress, or tiny brass ornaments for decorations on a Christmas tree.

Jan M. Steltz

Appliqué

No-Fail Machine Appliqué

Here's a speedy way to appliqué using fusible interfacing.

Step 1: Trace around the appliqué template with a pencil on the wrong side of the fabric, as shown in **Diagram 1.**

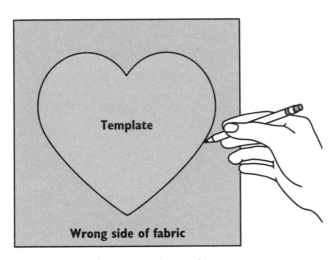

DIAGRAM 1

Step 2: Slip a piece of lightweight fusible interfacing underneath the fabric, with the fusible side toward the right side of the fabric and the wrong side of the fabric facing up, as shown in **Diagram 2.**

DIAGRAM 2

Step 3: Machine stitch on the pencil line.

Step 4: Cut out the shape and clip the curves. Make a slit in the interfacing, as shown in **Diagram 3,** and turn your fabric right side out through the slit.

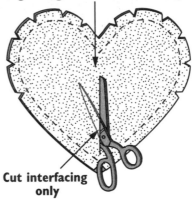

DIAGRAM 3

Step 5: Position the appliqué on your garment and press it in place. The fusible backing will hold the piece in position for topstitching or for a machine satin stitch, and the appliqué will be smooth and perfectly shaped.

Charlotte Biro

Intricate Appliqué Made Easy

You'll find that intricately shaped appliqués are easier to machine sew if you trim seam allowances and clip V-shaped

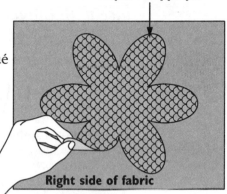

Sequined appliqué

Right side of fabric

notches into the curves as close to the pressed fold as possible. This method lets the fabric give more, and the seam allowance will lay flat. First press the raw edge under with a steam iron, then trim it and clip V-shaped notches into any curves. Before sewing the shape in place on your garment, use Fray Check or a glue stick to secure threads and prevent fraying.

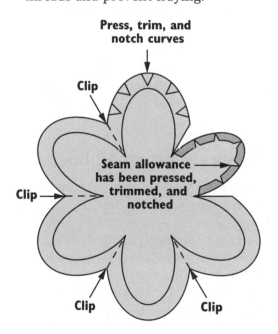

Press, trim, and notch curves

Clip

Seam allowance has been pressed, trimmed, and notched

Clip

Clip

Clip

Elizabeth M. Barry

Easy On, Easy Off

Here's how to make a removable appliqué. Follow the same technique mentioned in "Now You See It, Now You Don't" on page 22,

tracing the appliqué template onto lightweight muslin instead of onto water-soluble stabilizer. With right sides together, machine stitch the muslin to your appliqué fabric, slit the muslin and turn the fabric right side out. Then apply a pressure-sensitive adhesive, such as Stikit Again & Again, to the muslin side of your appliqué. Presto! Your appliqué is removable. This works great for sequined appliqués or other elegant embellishments that should be removed before cleaning or for appliqués that you might want to recycle later.

Jacquelyn Smyth

Stitch without Puckers

When I machine appliqué, I like to use Perfect Sew water-soluble liquid stabilizer as an adhesive. I apply it to the edges of the wrong side of my appliqué pieces, then stick the pieces to my garment. After drying and pressing, I can easily accomplish decorative stitching without puckers or skipped stitches. Perfect Sew is available from Palmer/Pletsch, P.O. Box 12046, Portland, OR 97212; (800) 728-3784.

Stacey L. Klaman

Battenberg Lace

Battenberg lace was originally made by hand with handmade decorative tapes. Today, you can produce the same antique-looking lace with the use of your sewing machine and machine-made tapes. Because of its versatility, Battenberg lace adds an elegant touch to your garments or home decorating projects.

Inspiring Designs

Inspiration for Battenberg designs doesn't have to come only from pattern books. I love to use Celtic embroidery shapes, pretty script embroidery alphabets, and shapes taken from nature. If the design you want is not the right size, enlarge or reduce it on a photocopier. Look around—designs are everywhere!

Karen King Carter

Baste Straight

Always baste or pin Battenberg tape along the straight outer edge. This leaves the gathering thread along the inner edge free so you can create curves in your design.

Barbara Fimbel

Shrink-Proof Your Tape

Unless you are certain that your Battenberg tape is preshrunk, preshrink it by washing it. Many of these fabric tapes can shrink considerably in the final stages of your technique as you dissolve the water-soluble stabilizer, ruining your design.

Barbara Fimbel

Fit to Be Dyed

White or natural Battenberg tape can be dyed with fabric or silk dyes. Follow the dye manufacturer's directions to mix the dye with water. Place the tape on a stack of paper towels and color it with a small paintbrush. Let the tape dry thoroughly, then press it. Then rinse the tape to remove any excess dye, dry, and press.

Judi Abbott

Marvelous Mounting Board

A piece of foam core makes a terrific portable, flat surface on which you can anchor your water-soluble stabilizer. Pinning your Battenberg tape to the stabilizer will then be a breeze. If you like, you can cover or paint one side of the board in a dark color for working with light-color tapes.

Elizabeth M. Barry

Use a Bolt Board

A fabric bolt board makes a perfect work surface because it is simple to maneuver and portable. After covering the board with batting and muslin, you can easily pin your water-soluble stabilizer and Battenberg tape in place. Ask your favorite fabric store to save you an empty bolt board from 45-inch-wide fabric. Cover one side with light-weight quilt batting and then cover the entire board with unbleached muslin. Staple the muslin to the board through the batting. The batting will hold the pins in place, and the muslin will protect your work from the fuzziness of the batting.

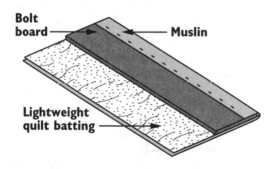

Karen King Carter

A Pearl of a Cotton

Winding pearl cotton onto your bobbin works nicely for large-scale Battenberg projects. But if you want a lighter, more delicate effect, use size 30 or 50 cotton thread in both the needle and the bobbin. If you use size 30 thread, use a size 11 Metalfil needle.

Karen King Carter

It's a Match

If you prefer to make your Battenberg lace before dyeing it, make sure you use cotton thread and not rayon when sewing the in-filling stitches. The rayon may react differently than the tape when dyed, creating uneven bands of color.

Julia Bernstein

Battenberg Notecards

Save not-so-perfect Battenberg motifs you've made, and glue them to brightly colored paper for use as greeting cards or bookmarks. You can hide messy stitches by manipu-lating the piece while gluing it.

Gay Quinn

Battenberg Lace

Add a Satiny Sheen

Shiny rayon threads, such as Sulky's #30 or #40, add sheen to Battenberg infilling stitches.

Sulky of America

Give Yourself a Hand

If you're among the many people who truly enjoy hand sewing, here is the traditional technique used to make Battenberg lace. Remember, practice makes perfect, so try a couple of practice pieces first.

Use a purchased pattern or create your own design. If you design your own pattern, make sure you purchase the lace tape first since the widths vary. Try to pin your tape to the purchased pattern or your own design with as few stops and starts as possible. An undulating curved line is the hallmark of Battenberg.

Supplies

- Solid-color cotton fabric, 4 inches larger than your pattern
- White Battenberg tape
- White crochet cotton, size 30 for use with wide Battenberg tape or size 60 for use with narrow Battenberg tape
- Contrasting color sewing thread for basting
- Purchased pattern (optional)
- Iron-on transfer pen
- Sheet of tracing paper
- Fine tapestry needle
- Liquid seam sealant or clear craft glue

Step 1: If you are using a purchased pattern, place a sheet of tracing paper over your pattern. Trace the pattern onto the paper with the iron-on transfer pen. If you are creating your own design, draw it directly onto the tracing paper with the iron-on transfer pen. Then place the ink side of the tracing paper onto the fabric and press the paper with a hot iron. The pattern will transfer to the fabric, as shown in **Diagram 1.** (If you're using a dark-color tape, use a light-color fabric that is not white or ivory.)

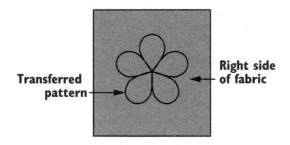

Transferred pattern

Right side of fabric

DIAGRAM 1

Step 2: Baste the outer edges of the tape to your pattern design with contrasting color sewing thread, as shown in **Diagram 2.** Each time you begin or finish basting, leave an extra inch of tape at the end for finishing later. Pull the gathering threads, called draw-threads, along the inside edge of the

tape to form the curves in your design and to keep the tape flat. Make sure any excess drawthreads don't get caught on the right side of your work by tucking them between two pieces of tape that overlap. Where two pieces of tape overlap, baste through the center of both of them.

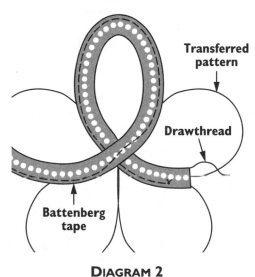

Transferred pattern

Drawthread

Battenberg tape

DIAGRAM 2

Step 3: Beginning where the tapes overlap and sewing only into the tapes, not the fabric, work all of the infilling stitches using crochet cotton and a fine tapestry needle. To start, do not tie a knot in the end of your crochet cotton. Anchor the thread in the middle of a tape by taking a small stitch and tying the two ends of the crochet cotton into a square knot. Make three long stitches across the area to be infilled, anchoring each stitch along the edge of the tape. Cover the infilling stitches

with a tight line of buttonhole stitches, as shown in **Diagram 3.** Remember to begin and end all stitching where the tapes overlap.

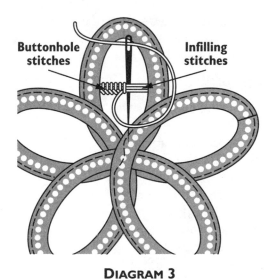

Buttonhole stitches

Infilling stitches

DIAGRAM 3

Step 4: Finish any short raw edges of the tape after you have created the infilling and buttonhole stitches in each area of your design. To do this, trim each 1-inch tail of tape to ⅛ inch. Then apply a few drops of liquid seam sealant or craft glue to the raw edge to prevent it from fraying. Fold down the tail and sew it to your design. Using a running stitch, sew together any areas where two layers of tape overlap, being careful not to catch the fabric.

Step 5: When you have finished your design, remove the basting stitches.

Kaethe Kliot

Battenberg Lace

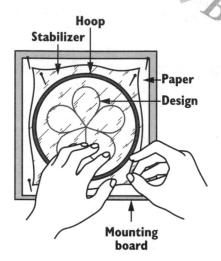

Battenberg by Machine

Making Battenberg lace by machine may seem more difficult than making it by hand. Frankly, until you're comfortable doing it, it is. But if you persist, the lace making will become lots of fun and very rewarding.

Supplies

- Tracing paper for tracing your pattern
- Battenberg tape
- Machine embroidery thread to match the tape
- Purchased pattern (optional)
- Water-soluble stabilizer
- Mounting board
- Quilter's straight pins
- Embroidery hoop
- Glue stick
- Embroidery scissors

Step 1: If you are using a purchased pattern, trace the pattern onto the paper. If you are creating your own design, draw it directly onto the paper. With the design faceup, pin the sheet of paper to the mounting board with the pins.

Step 2: Place a sheet of water-soluble stabilizer tautly in an embroidery hoop that is larger than your design. Pin the stabilizer to the mounting board outside the hoop, as shown in **Diagram 1**.

Diagram labels: Hoop, Stabilizer, Paper, Design, Mounting board

DIAGRAM 1

Step 3: Arrange and pin the Battenberg tape over your design, as shown in **Diagram 2,** pulling the drawthread as necessary to keep the tape flat. Hide any excess drawthreads on the wrong side of your work where two tapes overlap.

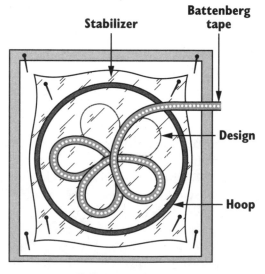

Diagram labels: Stabilizer, Battenberg tape, Design, Hoop

DIAGRAM 2

Step 4: When you've laid out your complete design, tuck the end of the tape underneath another section of the tape to hide the raw edge. Leave your work in the hoop. Remove one or two pins at a time, and use a glue stick to attach the tape to the stabilizer, as shown in **Diagram 3.** (Once you become a pro at laying out your design, you can use spray glue, such as KK-100, instead of pins.) Remove your work from the mounting board.

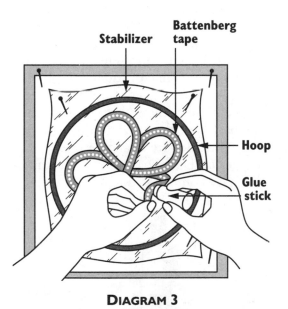

DIAGRAM 3

Stabilizer

Battenberg tape

Hoop

Glue stick

Step 5: Thread your machine and bobbin with machine embroidery thread. Attach a darning or spring foot to your machine or remove the presser foot altogether. Lower or cover the feed dogs and set your ma-

chine for a straight stitch. Place the hoop with your design under the needle and lower the presser foot lever. Let the needle go into the tape and come up. Pull the tail of the bobbin thread so that it comes up to the right side of your work. Then sew a few stitches in place to anchor your thread. Stitch around the outer edges of the tape. Where two edges of tape come together, use a straight zigzag stitch. That is, move the hoop from side to side to catch the very edge of the tape while the machine is still set for a straight stitch.

Step 6: Make an incision in the stabilizer in one area of your design with the scissors. Then carefully cut away the stabilizer. You will create Richelieu bars in this open area of your design before moving on to another area. (See "Ready Richelieu Bars" on page 32.) If you prefer, use machine infilling stitches of your choice in this and other open areas of your design.

Step 7: Remove your completed work from the hoop. Trim away the excess stabilizer and save the scraps for another project. Submerge your finished work in water for about two minutes or until the stabilizer has dissolved. Iron your work dry using a press cloth and the paper pattern as a blocking guide.

Sulky of America

Hoopla

Before you start creating Battenberg lace on a sewing machine, purchase a good sewing machine hoop. As you sew, the hoop will hold together the layers of fabric and water-soluble stabilizer needed to create Battenberg lace. I prefer an 8-inch-diameter hoop that has a small indentation in one spot and a screw to tighten the hoop. The indentation allows the hoop to be slipped under the presser foot. The screw, used with the appropriate screwdriver, will ensure that the stabilizer doesn't slip or pucker.

When I make Battenberg lace, I prefer to use Solvy or Aquasolve water-soluble stabilizer. Regardless of what type of stabilizer you choose, it must be cut at least 2 inches larger than the hoop in all directions to fit comfortably.

Karen King Carter

Ready Richelieu Bars

If you don't have time for hand sewing, you can quickly create delicate Battenberg Richelieu bars or infilling stitches by machine. You need a little patience to get started.

Step 1: To mark the open area of your Battenberg design for richelieu bars, use a water-soluble marking pen and mark dots on the edges of the tape opposite one another.

Step 2: To sew one Richelieu bar, position your needle over one dot. Manually place the needle into the tape and pull it up. Pull the tail of the bobbin thread so that it comes up to the right side of your work. Then sew one stitch in your design to anchor the thread. With the needle in the up position, move the hoop to draw the thread across the open area to the dot on the opposite side of the tape. Anchor the thread in place by taking one stitch into the tape at this end. This is a "walk" stitch. Now create another walk stitch right next to the first stitched line that runs back to the first dot and then forward again to the opposite dot. Be sure to anchor each line of stitches in place. You will have a total of three walk stitches. Using a narrow zigzag stitch, sew back over the previous three rows of stitches. Be sure to anchor the stitches in the opposite side of the tape. You have completed one Richelieu bar.

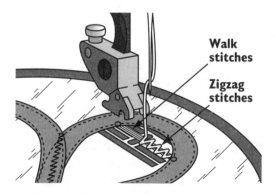

Walk stitches

Zigzag stitches

Step 3: Take tiny stitches along the edge of the tape until the needle is di-

rectly under the dot that marks the next Richelieu bar. Repeat Step 2 to sew the second bar. Continue in this manner until all of the Richelieu bars in one area have been completed. Then move to the next area and repeat the sequence.

Sulky of America

Bob Bob Bobbin Along

If your sewing machine has a removable separate bobbin case, buy a spare bobbin for use with pearl cotton and set it aside just for Battenberg lace. You'll save time by setting the bobbin tension on the spare for use with pearl cotton only. But if your machine has a drop-in bobbin, don't despair! You'll just have to adjust your thread tension each time you use pearl cotton. Although your stitches will look a bit different with a change in thread tension from time to time, you will still be able to produce beautiful Battenberg lace.

Karen King Carter

Thread Is a Matter of Choice

For machine-made Battenberg, I use size 30 or 50 cotton thread in the needle because of its softness. I don't like the sheen of rayon thread or the stiffness of polyester or poly/cotton thread. Cotton is stronger than rayon, so it won't break as readily in the bobbin.

In the bobbin, I use pearl cotton made for sergers. It is softer, making it easier to handle. Look for it on a cone in the thread section of your favorite notions shop.

Karen King Carter

Bedding

Bedrooms can double as sitting rooms, workplaces away from the office, sewing and craft areas, or even gyms. The key to a successful and well-coordinated bedroom begins with the bedding. Sewing your own bedding provides you with a custom look not found in any department store or linen shop.

No-Shift Bed Skirt

For a perfectly fitted, no-shift bed skirt, start with a purchased fitted sheet instead of making the deck commonly used with bed skirts. Here's what to do.

Step 1: Before beginning your bed skirt, cover the box spring with a fitted sheet. It doesn't matter whether or not this sheet matches your bedroom decor because it will be hidden by the mattress.

Step 2: Draw a dashed line with an air-erasable marking pen around three sides of the sheet where the sides and top intersect, as shown in **Diagram 1.**

Step 3: Remove the fitted sheet from the box spring and set it aside. Gather or pleat your skirt panels and hem them as you have planned. Then, with right sides together, pin the panels to the fitted sheet along the marked line. Sew the skirt panels to the sheet with a ¼-inch seam allowance.

Step 4: Fit the sheet with the attached skirt panels onto the box spring, as shown in **Diagram 2.** Not only will you end up with a perfectly fitting bed skirt that looks elegant but you will also have cleverly concealed under-the-bed storage space.

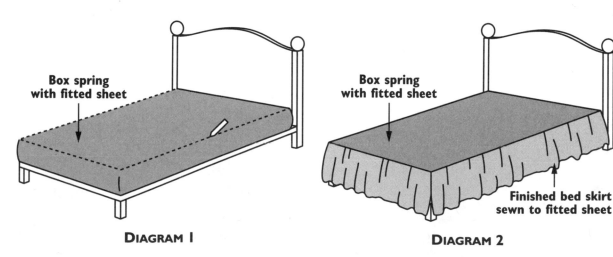

Box spring with fitted sheet

DIAGRAM 1

Box spring with fitted sheet

Finished bed skirt sewn to fitted sheet

DIAGRAM 2

Barbara Fimbel

Quick-Change Bed Skirt

Nonadhesive 1-inch-wide Velcro tape comes in handy in creating a nonshifting bed skirt. The Velcro lets you remove the bed skirt without wrestling with the mattress.

Step 1: Cover your box spring with a fitted sheet. Draw a dashed line with an air-erasable marking pen around three sides of the sheet where the sides and top of the sheet intersect, as shown in Diagram 1 of "No-Shift Bed Skirt."

Step 2: Pin the hook side of the Velcro tape to the sheet, ¼ inch above the dashed line. To avoid a gap between the Velcro and the fitted sheet at the corner, cut the Velcro just before rounding the corner. Then place the cut end of the Velcro tape flush against the pinned end and continue, as shown in **Diagram 1.** Repeat the sequence to pin the Velcro tape to the remaining side of the sheet.

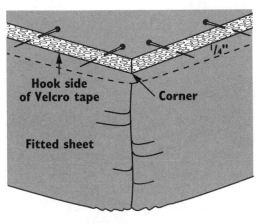

DIAGRAM I

Step 3: Remove the sheet from the box spring and sew the tape in place. Then fit the sheet back onto the box spring, and measure from the inner edge of the Velcro to the dashed line marked on the sheet, as shown in **Diagram 2.**

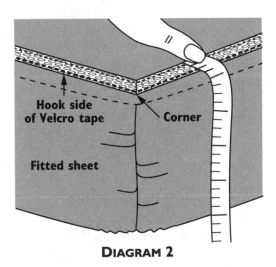

DIAGRAM 2

Step 4: Before constructing your bed skirt panels according to your pattern, add the measurement taken in Step 3 to the finished length of the skirt. This added length will accommodate the ¼-inch space above the dashed line and the width of the Velcro tape.

Step 5: Stitch the loop side of the tape to the wrong side of the top of the bed skirt panels. Attach the bed skirt to the fitted sheet by pressing the two Velcro strips together.

Judi Abbott

Hang It All!

Curtain rods are not just for windows anymore. Use them to hang a bed skirt around any bed with heavy posts. Simply sew a casing along the top edges of your skirt. Then attach curtain rods and hardware to the inside of each bed post, and hang the bed skirt the same way you would hang a curtain! This innovative technique will save you the time and trouble of removing the mattress in order to take off the skirt for washing. But don't try this on a priceless antique bed.

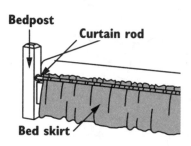

If the side rail on your bed comes up high enough around the box spring, consider mounting a support bracket for your curtain rod midway along each side of the bed. I recommend this especially if the bed skirt fabric is heavy.

Charlotte Biro

Deckless Bed Skirt

On most beds with wooden rails, you can attach the bed skirt directly to the wood with self-adhesive Velcro tape. First double-check the measurements of your comforter or bedspread to make sure it is long enough to hide the top of the bed skirt.

Step 1: As shown below, attach the hook side of the self-adhesive Velcro tape to the top of the wooden rails, following the manufacturer's directions.

Step 2: Make either a pleated or gathered bed skirt, according to your pattern directions.

Step 3: Sew the loop side of the Velcro tape flush with the wrong side of the top of the completed bed skirt.

Step 4: To attach the bed skirt to the bed, begin at one end of the wooden rail and press the loop side of the Velcro tape to the hook side of the tape. To remove the adhesive tape from the wooden rails of your bed, use a glue solvent like Goo Gone. Be sure to follow the manufacturer's directions, so the adhesive doesn't leave any marks.

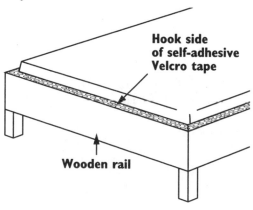

Carolyn Hoffman

It's a Snap!

To hold your duvet or comforter in place at the corners of its cover, try this trick.

Step 1: Turn your duvet or comforter cover wrong side out. From fabric that matches the cover, cut eight 4-inch squares. Four will be used at the corners of your duvet or comforter, and four will be used at the corners of its cover.

Step 2: With the wrong side of a square facing up, turn up ¼ inch on all four sides and press, as shown in **Diagram 1**. Repeat for the remaining squares.

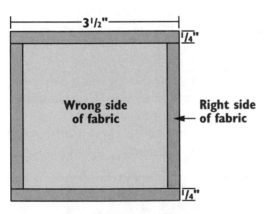

DIAGRAM 1

Step 3: With the wrong side facing up, fold each square in half and sew all of the edges together using a ¼-inch seam allowance. You now have eight tabs.

Step 4: As shown in **Diagram 2**, center the ball half of a snap along one short side and ¼ inch from the bottom edge of each of four tabs. Center the socket half of a snap along one short side and ¼ inch from the bottom edge of each of the remaining tabs.

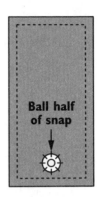

DIAGRAM 2

Step 5: Sew one tab with the ball half of a snap to each corner of your duvet or comforter, as shown in **Diagram 3**. Making sure that the ball half of the snap matches the socket half, sew one tab with the socket half of the snap to each corner of the wrong side of the duvet or comforter cover.

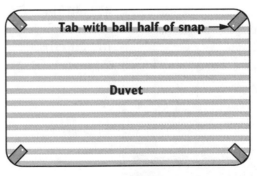

DIAGRAM 3

Step 6: Insert the duvet or comforter into the cover, then snap each corner together. You'll never have to worry about your duvet or comforter shifting again!

Julia Bernstein

What a Sham!

If you have leftover fabric from your curtains, duvet cover, or bed skirt, why not make a simple set of shams to create an ensemble? They're quick, easy, and use very little fabric.

Step 1: Measure the length and width of your pillow. If you want a wrinkle-free appearance, do not add a seam allowance. If you'd rather have a looser fit, add a ½-inch seam allowance to the length and width.

Step 2: Using your measurements, cut one sham front piece. Cut the sham back piece 3 inches longer than the sham front, as shown in **Diagram 1.** Fold the sham back piece in half crosswise and cut it in half.

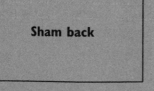

DIAGRAM 1

Step 3: To hem each sham back. turn under ½ inch along one long side and press. Turn under another ½ inch and press again. Topstitch each hem in place, as shown in **Diagram 2.**

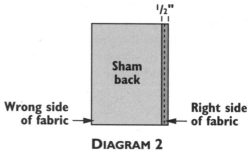

DIAGRAM 2

Step 4: With right sides together, pin one sham back to the sham front, making sure the raw edges are even along the top, bottom, and sides. Then, with right sides together, overlap and pin the remaining sham back piece to the sham front. Sew the sham front to the back using a ½-inch seam allowance, as shown in **Diagram 3.** Clip the corners, turn the sham right side out, and press it. Insert your pillow into the sham.

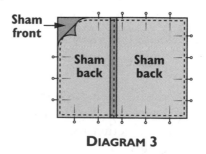

DIAGRAM 3

Stacey L. Klaman

Tape That Skirt!

When gathering long strips of fabric, such as the panels on a bed skirt, consider using gathering tape. The time and aggravation you save by not gathering the panels by hand or machine more than make up for the small cost of the tape.

Barbara Fimbel

Buying Off the Bolt

When heading out to the fabric store, consider selected seconds for bedding projects. Imperfections in fabric don't affect its wear. Ask the salesperson what's wrong with the fabric. It may be as simple as the color not being up to the fabric company's standard. This means money in the bank for you!

Jane F. Cornell

SMART SHOPPER

How do you begin to choose colors and fabrics for your bedroom? Start with a sheet shopping spree. Visit your local department store or flip through your favorite mail-order catalog for the latest look in luxurious linens. Consider how various colors and patterns will work in your room. It's easy to enlarge a small room with light colors and few patterns. Conversely, you can make a large, airy room feel warm and cozy with dark colors and a variety of patterns. The minute you fall in love with a pattern that works for your room, you'll be off and running with a color scheme and some fabric options.

Barbara Fimbel

Bias

Bias is the diagonal line of a fabric. It is formed where the lengthwise and crosswise grains meet. It provides the greatest amount of stretch and therefore is often used as binding around curved areas. You can easily eliminate neckline facings and interfacings in lightweight and sheer fabrics by adding bias binding. And you can use bias binding for neat seam finishes or as decorative edgings on place mats and home decorating projects.

Two-in-One Bias

Here's an easy step-by-step method for making two-tone bias strips for ties, sashes, trims, and other decorative accents. We recommend using a silky fabric because it is quick and easy to turn right side out.

Step 1: Cut two bias strips, each from a different fabric, the desired length and width of the edge of your project to be covered plus ¼ inch for the seam allowance.

Step 2: With right sides together and raw edges even, pin one strip on top of the other.

Step 3: Fold the strips in half lengthwise, and stitch ¼ inch from the long edge through all four layers of fabric, as shown in **Diagram 1**.

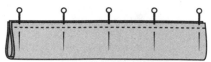

**Two bias strips folded
lengthwise and sewn together**

DIAGRAM 1

Step 4: Turn the strips right side out using a needle and thread, a tube turner for fabric, or a safety pin, as shown in **Diagram 2**. The tube turner or safety pin must be attached only to the inner tube and must lie between the two tubes. You'll end up with two tubes sewn together and the seam allowances enclosed within one tube.

Strip being turned right side out

DIAGRAM 2

Step 5: Press the bias strips flat so that the seam is centered between the two tubes, as shown in **Diagram 3**.

Two bias strips

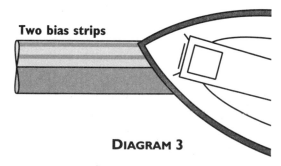

DIAGRAM 3

Step 6: If you plan to attach the bias strip to your garment as a trim, align the garment's edge with the seam between the tubes. Fold one tube to the front and one to the back, then pin the tubes to the garment. Sew the unseamed edges of the tubes to the garment, making sure to catch both layers on either side of the garment.

Ronda Chaney and Lori Bottom

Beautiful Bias Edge

Do you have trouble applying double-fold bias tape to the curved edge of fabric? If so, try my worry-free method.

First, steam press the bias tape into your desired shape before sewing it in place. Next, sew only one side of the tape in place. Finally, fold the tape over the edge of the fabric and sew it in place directly over the previous row of stitching.

Janis Bullis

Superfast Binding

Did you know that you can attach bias binding superfast with a bias binder attachment for your sewing machine? You'll not only save time but will also produce a neat edging with professional results. Use this attachment to duplicate a Hong Kong finish, bind the edges of a garment, or finish the edges of a quilt with no handwork at all.

There are two types of attachments available—a spiral bias binder and a flat bias binder. The spiral bias binder attaches purchased ½-inch single- or double-fold tape, as shown in **Diagram 1**. The flat bias binder attachment allows you to make your own bias binding. It is designed to fold and attach flat bias tape, binding, or trim, as shown in **Diagram 2**.

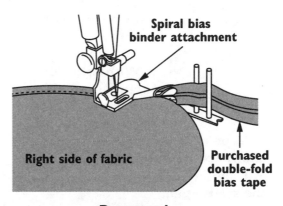

Spiral bias binder attachment

Right side of fabric

Purchased double-fold bias tape

DIAGRAM 1

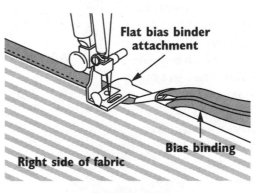

Flat bias binder attachment

Right side of fabric

Bias binding

DIAGRAM 2

Bernina of America

★ Bright Idea ★

WHEN YOU NEED LONG LENGTHS OF BIAS STRIPS, save time by making one continuous strip and cutting it as you go.

1. Fold a square of fabric in half on the diagonal and press it. Open the square and cut it in half along the diagonal, as shown in Diagram 1.

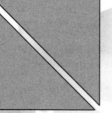

Cut square on diagonal
DIAGRAM 1

2. With right sides facing, overlap the triangles and stitch from point A to point B using a ¼-inch seam allowance, as shown in Diagram 2. Press the seam open.

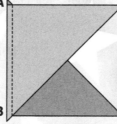

DIAGRAM 2

3. Mark the desired width of your bias strip on the diagonal of the wrong side of the fabric until the piece is marked, as shown in Diagram 3. Trim any excess beyond the last marked line.

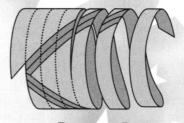

DIAGRAM 3

4. With right sides together, fold the bottom of the fabric to the top, making sure to offset the sides by the width of one bias strip.

5. Using a ¼-inch seam allowance, sew the top and bottom together to create a tube.

DIAGRAM 4

Press the seam open. Your fabric will be twisted, as shown in Diagram 4.

6. Beginning at one end, cut the bias in a spiral following your marked lines, as shown in Diagram 5. You now have one long, continuous bias strip. Use a bias tape maker to quickly create bias tape.

DIAGRAM 5

Karen Kunkel

It's a Stretch

The bad news is that bias seams will always stretch. The good news is that there are some ways to minimize the stretch, as listed here.

- Don't hand baste bias seams before sewing.

- Use a shorter machine stitch length and stitch with the grain of the fabric.

- Stitch all of the seams in your project in the same direction.

- Before hemming a garment cut on the bias, allow it to hang for three or four days to allow the fabric's fibers to stretch naturally.

Marian Mongelli

garment or home decorating project, just remember to cut away the seam allowance that will be encased in the binding before you begin to sew.

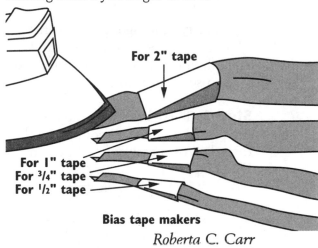

For 2" tape

For 1" tape
For ³/₄" tape
For ¹/₂" tape

Bias tape makers
Roberta C. Carr

Great Tape

Creating bias strips from the same fabric as your project or from a contrasting one is easy to do with a bias tape maker. This timesaving little tool can be purchased where sewing notions are sold or from mail-order notions catalogs. It comes in different widths to create ¹/₂-, ³/₄-, 1-, and 2-inch finished strips. Simply follow the manufacturer's directions for cutting your fabic and inserting it through the tape maker. The width of your bias binding will be perfect every time. If you are planning to add binding to a

SMART SHOPPER

To find the true bias on your fabric for cutting bias strips, purchase a clear acrylic or plexiglass 45/90-degree triangle at an art-supply store. Align the longest edge of the triangle with the lengthwise grain of the fabric. With an air-erasable marking pen, mark the desired width of your bias strips along the diagonal, or the bias, of your fabric. Then cut out your strips. For speedier cutting that does not require a marking pen, place the fabric on a cutting mat and use your triangle as a guide to rotary cut your bias strips.

Karen Kunkel

Buttons and Buttonholes

Is there anyone you know who doesn't have a button collection stashed away in her sewing room? These little gems come in every shape and color imaginable. Whether you use them as functional closures or decorative accents, buttons allow you to personalize your sewing.

Button It Up

Thirty years ago, a tailor named C. J. Santopietro taught me this method for sewing on buttons, and I've used it ever since.

Step 1: Thread a needle and double the thread, but don't knot it. Run the thread across beeswax, as shown in **Diagram 1.**

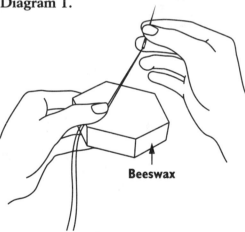

Beeswax

DIAGRAM 1

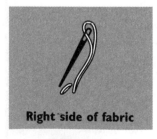

Right side of fabric

DIAGRAM 2

Step 2: Working from the garment's right side, anchor the thread in the garment by making two tiny stitches in an X-shape where you want to sew on the button, as shown in **Diagram 2.**

Step 3: Elevate the button above the fabric with the fingers of your left hand, then sew through the holes in the button and into the fabric several times until the button feels secure, as shown in **Diagram 3.** (If you are left-handed, use your right hand.)

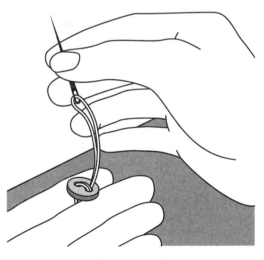

DIAGRAM 3

Step 4: Take the last stitch through a hole in the button, but not through the fabric.

Step 5: Wind the thread tightly around the slack thread between the button and the fabric to create a stiff shank, as shown in **Diagram 4.** Pass the needle back and forth through the thread shank twice at different angles.

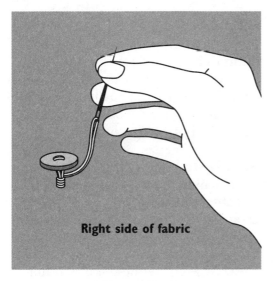

Right side of fabric

DIAGRAM 4

Step 6: Clip the thread close to the shank. The button will never pop off, and the inside of the garment is master-tailor neat, with no knot showing!

Peggy Bendel

Color Cues

When sewing buttonholes in multicolored fabric, consider button placement before choosing thread color. Depending on the placement, each buttonhole may need to be sewn in a different color. When the buttonhole will span two contrasting fabric colors, match the thread to the fabric color that will show when the garment is buttoned, not the color that will be hidden.

Ann Price Gosch

The Great Button Cover-Up

When making a fabric-covered button, use the end of a pencil eraser to attach your fabric to the button teeth. It saves time and your fingernails!

Dianne Giancola
Dritz Corporation

Dental Floss to the Rescue

Rough edges on metal-shank buttons rub and cut through all-purpose thread, resulting in lots of lost buttons. I remedy this problem by using unwaxed dental floss to sew metal shank buttons to a garment. The buttons stay put and won't cut through the floss.

Clotilde

SMART SHOPPER

Instead of purchasing new buttons for every garment you make, why not recycle them from old garments? Look through your closet for clothes that you no longer wear to see if the buttons are worth saving. Garage sales, flea markets, and church bazaars are also great sources for garments and buttons. Look at the garments for their buttons rather than for their wearability. You may even get lucky and find some real antiques!

Karen Kunkel

Buttons and Buttonholes

Use Your Machine

When I have lots of buttons to sew, I attach them by machine. The buttons are firmly attached, and the method is fast and easy. Use this only for buttons with holes.

Step 1: Drop or cover the machine's feed dogs so you can stitch in one place. Use a button sewing foot, which helps hold the button and the fabric in place, as shown in **Diagram 1**. If you don't have this foot, remove the presser foot.

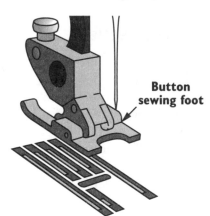

Button sewing foot

DIAGRAM 1

Step 2: To create a thread shank, place a straight pin or round toothpick on top of the button. Use a piece of transparent tape to hold the pin or toothpick and button in place on the garment, as shown in **Diagram 2**.

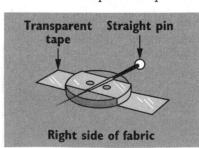

Transparent tape **Straight pin**

Right side of fabric

DIAGRAM 2

Step 3: Select a zigzag stitch and adjust the width to accommodate the button's holes, and set the stitch length to zero. Turn the sewing machine handwheel manually to be sure the needle clears the button, then stitch the button slowly.

Step 4: To lock the thread ends, set the machine for a short straight stitch and stitch in one hole several times to create a knot. Clip the thread, leaving a long tail.

Step 5: Remove the pin or toothpick and the tape. Pull up the button so the top of the thread is snug to the top of the button and the shank is exposed. Wrap the thread ends around the shank several times using a hand-sewing needle, then bring them to the wrong side, as shown in **Diagram 3**. Tie off the thread.

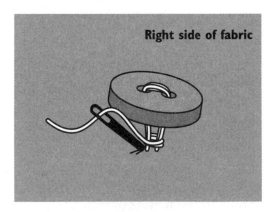

Right side of fabric

DIAGRAM 3

Karen Kunkel

Think Shank

Here's a neat trick that will help you to create a shank when attaching a button with holes. Place one or two toothpicks under the button to raise it above the fabric, as shown. Then sew the button to your garment. Before tying off the thread, remove the toothpicks and wind the thread underneath the button to create a shank. This makes buttoning and unbuttoning a garment easier.

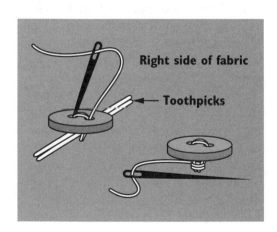

Right side of fabric

Toothpicks

Janis Bullis

A New Twist

Use a piece of floral wire to group matching loose buttons. Thread the wire through the buttons' shanks or holes and twist the ends together. You'll always have a matched set of buttons at your fingertips.

Elizabeth M. Barry

A Different Shank

When I sew a button to a garment that I know will be worn a lot, I make a stronger shank. I start by using four to six strands of crochet thread to sew the button to the garment, making sure the button is elevated above the fabric, as shown in **Diagram 1**.

Then, working between the button and the fabric, I make a row of buttonhole stitches along each set of threads that form the shank, alternating back and forth as I sew, as shown in **Diagram 2**. This makes a very sturdy shank for coats and blazers. Another plus is that your button will stand up and not flop over.

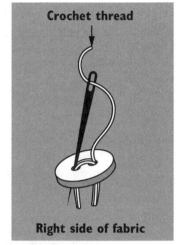

Crochet thread

Right side of fabric

DIAGRAM 1

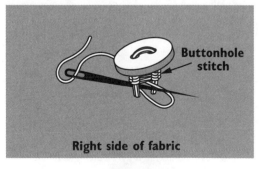

Buttonhole stitch

Right side of fabric

DIAGRAM 2

Claire Shaeffer

Buttons and Buttonholes

Stabilize Accordingly

If you add extra stability to buttonholes stitched on knit fabric, it will help them to keep their shape for a long time. To do so, cut a strand of embroidery floss or crochet thread 6 inches longer than twice the length of your buttonhole. Then place the strand over your buttonhole placement mark, forming a loop at one end and two tails at the other. Sew your buttonhole over the strand. Tug on both ends of the strand and tie the ends together, as shown (top). Clip the excess thread and tuck the knot under the bar tack, as shown (bottom).

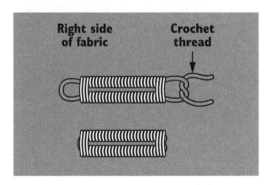

Karen Kunkel

'Ear the Good News

Do you ever have trouble finding just the right pair of earrings to match your newly sewn garment? For a surefire solution, convert your favorite buttons into earrings with a Button Ons kit. The kit contains reusable findings that are compatible with buttons that have shanks. You can find them in the notions section of your local sewing store or in a mail-order catalog of sewing supplies.

Clotilde

Take Cover

Here's an easy way to assemble fabric-covered buttons that won't fray around the edges. Cut a circle of fabric ¼ inch larger than the button. With a large-eye needle and heavy-duty thread, sew a running stitch ¼ inch from the outer edge of the circle, as shown. Tie a knot in the thread end and trim the excess. Center the button cap on the fabric circle and pull up on the thread to gather the fabric around the cap. Snap on the button back. There is no need to worry about the raw edges of the fabric escaping!

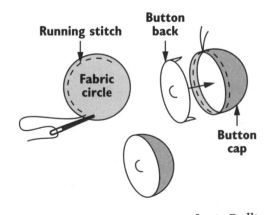

Janis Bullis

Double Your Security

To ensure that your buttons will stay securely fastened to your garment, try ThreadFuse in your bobbin when you sew them on by machine. Then place your garment wrong side up on your ironing board. Cover the area where the buttons were sewn with a nonstick press cloth and fuse the bobbin thread. Instant security!

Janet Klaer

Buttonholes Made to Last

Increase the life of your buttonholes by preventing raveled edges with a liquid seam sealant such as Fray Check. Before cutting your buttonholes open, simply apply the liquid sealant over the stitching on the wrong side of the fabric and let it dry. A word to the wise: If you use a water-soluble marking pen for buttonhole placement, be sure to remove the markings before applying the liquid seam sealant; otherwise, it may set the markings.

Nancy Nix-Rice

Linked Up

Don't run the risk of losing precious antique or expensive designer buttons in the laundry or at the dry cleaner. Protect them with simple-to-make button "cuff links." Just hand sew each antique or decorative button to an inexpensive flat shirt button. Then, depending on where you'll use your cuff links, sew additional buttonholes opposite the existing ones on the front, back, placket, or wrist cuff of your garment. Button the decorative button of the cuff link through the top buttonhole and the flat button through the bottom one. Before laundering your garment, remove the cuff links. Your decorative buttons will be saved from ruin.

Antique button

Flat button

Elizabeth M. Barry

★ Bright Idea ★

WHO SAYS BUTTONS HAVE TO MATCH? Why not mix and match several different buttons on one garment for a designer look? Try it with bejeweled buttons or buttons with different shapes, colors, and sizes.

For added impact, sew additional buttons between the buttonholes on the front of a blouse, shirt, or dress. You'll never need to worry about accessorizing your outfit!

Karen Kunkel

All in a Line

I always sew vertical buttonholes, not horizontal ones, on the front band of a blouse to ease fabric stress. The secret to buttonhole placement is to mark the first one just below the strain of your bust. Use this key location as your starting point to measure and mark the rest of your buttonholes above and below this one.

Clotilde

Check It Out

After sewing on a button, whether by hand or machine, apply a small drop of liquid seam sealant, like Fray Check, to the sewing thread on the inside of your garment. This will help to secure the thread ends and keep them from becoming undone.

Dianne Giancola
Dritz Corporation

One-of-a-Kind Buttons

Looking for just the right accent for a plain jacket or simple dress? Having trouble finding the perfect button to complete a project? Why not decorate a fabric scrap and use it to make one-of-a-kind buttons? You can decorate the fabric as simply or as elaborately as you like. Sometimes I sew rows of decorative stitching or twin needle tucks. Other times I dupli-cate a pattern already in the fabric's print. I have also been known to simply add a tassel or two after my buttons are covered. One of my favorite designs is a stitched snowflake button cover. Here's what you'll need for one snowflake button cover.

Supplies

- 6-inch square of fabric
- 6-inch square of fusible interfacing
- Decorative thread to match, coordinate, or contrast with the fabric
- Satin stitch or embroidery foot for your sewing machine
- Size 90/14 stretch or 80/12 embroidery machine needle
- Covered button form
- Vanishing or water-soluble marking pen
- Tracing paper
- Pinking shears

Step 1: Following the manufacturer's directions, fuse the 6-inch square of interfacing to the wrong side of the 6-inch square of fabric.

If your fabric is dark, use a dark-color interfacing, and if your fabric is light, use a light-color interfacing. This way, the metal button form won't shine through the fabric.

Step 2: Cut the interfaced square of fabric in half. You will use one half to test the stitch and the other half for decorating and covering the button.

Step 3: Place the embroidery needle in your machine, and thread your machine with decorative thread. Select a dense satin stitch motif on your sewing machine. I like the diamond shape. Set the stitch length to 0.3 to 0.5 and the width to the largest amount.

Step 4: Stitch a single motif on the test fabric. Then stitch a second motif just below the first, as shown in **Diagram 1.** Remove the fabric, pull the threads through to the wrong side of the fabric, and clip them.

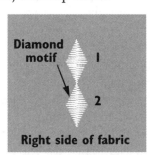

DIAGRAM 1

Step 5: Rotate the fabric 90 degrees and center the needle between the first and second motif. Stitch a third motif, as shown in **Diagram 2.** Remove the fabric, pull the threads to the wrong side of the fabric, and clip them.

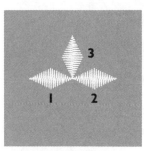

DIAGRAM 2

DIAGRAM 3

Step 6: Rotate the fabric 180 degrees and repeat Step 5 for the last motif, as shown in **Diagram 3.**

Step 7: With the marking pen and tracing paper, trace the correct size button form from the back of the button package and cut it out.

Step 8: Center and trace the button form pattern over your snowflake design with the water-soluble marking pen. Cut the button form shape out of the fabric with pinking shears to eliminate raveling, as shown in Diagram 4.

DIAGRAM 4

Step 9: Follow the manufacturer's directions for covering the button form with the fabric.

Follow these tips to ensure a snug fit. When covering your button form with a colorfast and washable lightweight fabric, wet it with warm water first. If you're using a heavier fabric, run a hand gathering stitch around the circle ⅛ inch from the cut edge. Center the form on the fabric circle and pull up the stitches around the form. Then finish putting the button together according to the manufacturer's directions.

Jan Saunders

Buttons and Buttonholes

Bejeweled Buttons

My favorite trick of the trade is to transform inexpensive earrings into one-of-a-kind designer buttons. Try making matching pins or shoe ornaments for a coordinating look.

You can find these supplies in most hardware or bead-supply stores. Here's how to make a pair of buttons.

Supplies

- Pair of post or clip-on earrings that do not have a hollow or rough bottom and that are large enough to cover the flat-head buttons
- Two ¼- to ⅜-inch flat-head buttons with a shank
- Small needle-nose pliers
- Wire cutters
- Rubbing alcohol
- Sandpaper
- Metal file
- Metal adhesive

Step 1: Use the pliers to grip and remove the backing from the clip earrings. Use the wire cutters to snip off the welded post, as shown in **Diagram 1**. Remove any glue with rubbing alcohol.

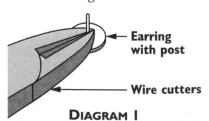

DIAGRAM 1

Step 2: Prepare the earring backs by lightly sanding the surface, as shown in **Diagram 2**.

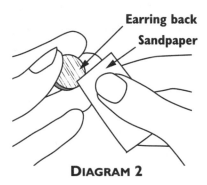

DIAGRAM 2

Step 3: Using the file or sandpaper, gently rub the top of the buttons so the earrings will adhere properly. Test the surface with your finger; the top should feel rough.

Step 4: Apply a small drop of adhesive to the center of the back of one earring. Using the needle-nose pliers to grip the shank of the button, center and press the button top on the back of the earring, as shown in **Diagram 3**. Repeat this sequence for the remaining earring and button. Let your new buttons dry for four to six hours before using them.

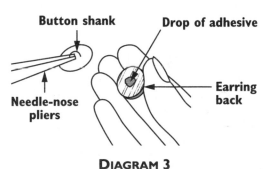

DIAGRAM 3

Barbara Wright Sykes

Button Don'ts

Here are a few little-known button facts that will help you to perfect the details of your garment.

- Don't sew stay buttons (flat, little clear buttons) to the facing of a garment. This immediately tells everyone that your garment is homemade.

- Don't sew a button at the fullest point of the bust, especially if your blouses tend to strain at this point.

- Don't begin sewing buttons from the facing side of your garment. The stitches look especially messy at a neckline. Take your stitches through the right side of your garment only.

Claire Shaeffer

Buttonholes with Muscle

Strengthen your buttonholes and use your fusible interfacing scraps all at the same time. Keep a box of leftover pieces of woven or knit interfacing near your button collection. Whenever you make a buttonhole, cut a small square of interfacing with the lengthwise grain running in the same direction as the buttonhole. Fuse the interfacing square to the wrong side of the fabric at the buttonhole placement mark before sewing the buttonhole. Sew the buttonhole and trim away the excess interfacing.

Lisa Shepard
Handler Textile Corporation

Safe Cutting

If you find cutting open buttonholes to be nerve-racking, especially if you don't have a steady hand, try this trick. Place a straight pin through the bar tack at the inside edge of each end of the buttonhole. The pins will prevent you from accidentally cutting through the ends of the buttonhole. Use a craft knife or scissors to cut open the buttonhole.

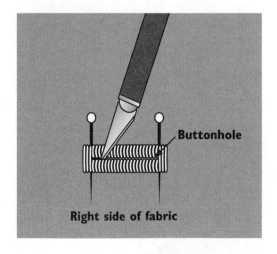

Buttonhole

Right side of fabric

Dianne Giancola
Dritz Corporation

Shortcut Button Pillow

If you are long on style but short on fabric, time, and money, you can still make a smashing decorator pillow with button accents in less than an hour. Follow these easy steps.

Supplies

- A fabric remnant large enough to cover a pillow
- Leftover cording from your sewing basket
- A solid-color pillow to coordinate with your fabric remnant
- Four or five large and unusual buttons
- Thread to match the fabric

Step 1: Measure the length and width of your pillow and add a 1/2-inch seam allowance to each side. Using these dimensions, cut out one pillow front and one pillow back from your fabric remnant.

Step 2: With right sides together, sew the pillow front and pillow back together along three sides, using a 1/2-inch seam allowance, as shown in **Diagram 1.**

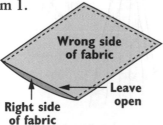

DIAGRAM 1

Step 3: Turn under a 3/4-seam allowance along the remaining side and hem the edge. Turn the pillow cover right side out and press.

Step 4: Sew the buttons close to the hemmed edge along the right side of the pillow front, as shown in **Diagram 2.**

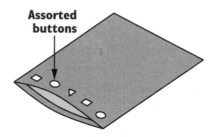

DIAGRAM 2

Step 5: To make sure the button loops are large enough to go around the pillow and each button, insert your pillow into the cover. Then make loops from leftover lengths of cording. Attach the loops to the inside hem of the pillow back opposite each button, as shown in **Diagram 3.**

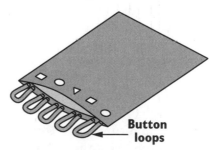

DIAGRAM 3

Step 6: Referring to **Diagram 4,** insert your pillow and button it up!

Pillow

DIAGRAM 4

Jackie Dodson and Jan Saunders

Buttoning Up Buttonholes

Here are my best tips for stitching buttonholes. If you follow these suggestions, you'll find it a breeze to sew buttonholes on all of your garments and home decorating projects.

⊕ I like to machine sew buttonholes with embroidery thread. It has a wonderful sheen because it is made from a better grade of cotton. One of my favorites is #60. I find the lightness of this thread to be especially nice on lightweight fabrics.

⊕ Use a water-soluble stabilizer or spray starch on washable silk or lightweight fabrics. It will help to prevent snags in the fabric as you sew a buttonhole. Apply the stabilizer to the wrong side of the fabric where you will sew your buttonhole.

⊕ Don't use a very dense satin stitch when you make buttonholes. They should blend in with the fabric, not stand out.

⊕ Always make a test buttonhole on a piece of scrap fabric first. Stand back and check to see that your choice of color and stitch density is correct.

⊕ Cut open the test buttonhole to be sure the button goes through easily.

Claire Shaeffer

Button, Button, Where's the Button?

Take a lesson from the ready-to-wear industry. When purchasing buttons for a garment, buy an extra one to sew to an inside seam of your finished garment. You'll never have to worry about losing and matching a button because you'll always be carrying a spare.

Elizabeth M. Barry

Closures

Button it! Snap it! Zip it! Loop it! An all-important part of any project, closures have become more than just functional necessities. They now can double as decorative accessories as well.

Loop It Closed

Here's a superfast way to make several loop closures from one continuous length of purchased cording or braid.

Step 1: Make a loop placement guide by cutting a sheet of paper 1½ inches wide and the length of the garment where the loops will be sewn.

Step 2: Draw a line the length of your guide and ⅝ inch in from one long edge, as shown in **Diagram 1**.

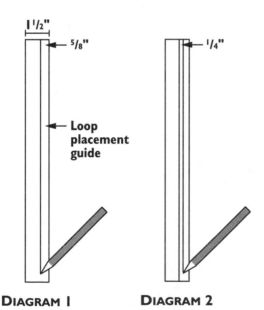

DIAGRAM 1   **DIAGRAM 2**

Step 3: Measure the width of your cording or braid. As shown in **Diagram 2**, draw a second line on your guide to the right of the first one, spacing it the width of your cording or braid.

Step 4: Now draw horizontal lines on your guide to indicate the size and placement of the loops on your garment, as shown in **Diagram 3**.

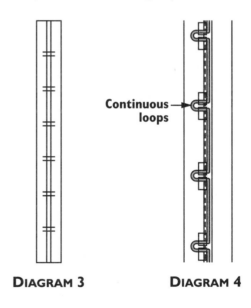

DIAGRAM 3   **DIAGRAM 4**

Step 5: Form the loops with the cording or braid, tape them to your guide, and machine baste them in place between the two placement lines, as shown in **Diagram 4**. Check to see if the loop size is correct by inserting a button through each one. If the button doesn't fit, take out the basting stitches and reposition the loops on your guide. Then baste the loops in place again.

Step 6: To attach the loops to your garment, fold back the guide so that the loops are flush against the garment. Leaving the tape intact, pin and sew the loops in place, as shown in **Diagram 5**. Remove the guide and the tape, and continue assembling your garment.

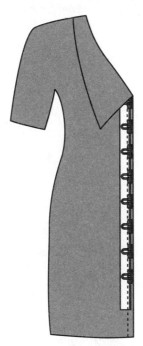

DIAGRAM 5

Karen Kunkel

It's a Snap to Close

Snap tape, typically used on children's clothing, is a cinch to apply. Try it on home decorating projects such as duvet covers, pillow shams, or even slipcovers. Place the socket section of the tape on the wrong side of the fabric and the ball section of the tape on the right side of the fabric. Use a zipper foot to help you edge stitch through all layers with ease.

Cheryl Winters Tetreau

Button Loops That Don't Give an Inch

Do your button loops grow and stretch as you use them? To create loops that will stay true to size, always cut narrow strips on a true bias. Then when you seam the strips, use a stitch length of 20 stitches per inch. Finally, dampen the strips and, keeping them taut, pin them to the ironing board until they're dry.

Claire Shaeffer

★ Bright Idea ★

WHEN YOU'RE HAND SEWING SNAPS OR HOOKS AND EYES and can't find a thread color to match the fabric, unravel a few threads from the straight or cross grain of a leftover piece of fabric. Thread it onto a needle and use it to sew your closures.

Karen Kunkel

Closures

Perfect Placement

To line up the two halves of a snap so they meet precisely for closure, first sew the ball half of the snap in place. Then rub the tip of the ball with tailor's chalk and finger press it against the other half of the garment. The chalk will automatically mark the placement area for the other half of the snap.

Stacey L. Klaman

Thread Loops

Thread loop closures are used with buttons at a neckline opening for a flat and inconspicuous finish. With a little practice, you'll become an expert at making them in no time at all.

Step 1: Sew the button in place flush along the neckline opening of your garment. Mark the position for the thread loop along the neckline opening opposite the button by aligning a straight pin with the top and bottom edge of the button, as shown in **Diagram 1.**

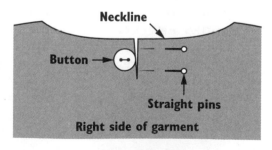

DIAGRAM 1

Step 2: Knot the end of a single strand of matching thread and come up from the underside near the edge of the opening at the top pin marker. Leaving a loop large enough to slip easily over the button, take a stitch at the bottom pin marker, as shown in **Diagram 2.** Remove the pins.

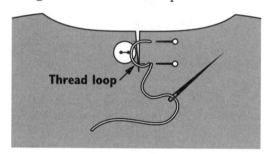

DIAGRAM 2

Step 3: Work back and forth in this manner, making sure the loops are the same size, until you have four loops, as shown in **Diagram 3.**

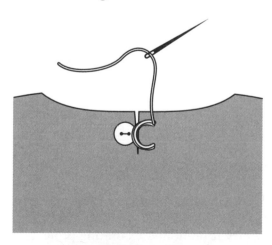

DIAGRAM 3

Step 4: Working from one end of the loops to the other, sew a buttonhole stitch over the strands of thread, making sure your stitches are close together, as shown in **Diagram 4.** Secure the single strand of thread tightly on the underside of your garment.

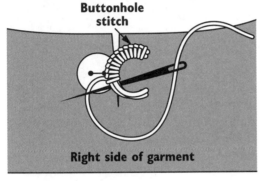

Buttonhole stitch

Right side of garment

DIAGRAM 4

Karen Kunkel

the length of the strip ⅛ inch in from the fold, as shown in **Diagram 1.** Pull gently on the strip while stitching to prevent the stitches from breaking.

Step 3: Trim the seam allowance so that the strip is ⅜ inch wide. Using a loop turner, turn the strip right side out, as shown in **Diagram 2.** The seam allowance stuffs the strip and transforms it into a corded loop.

DIAGRAM 1

¹/₂"

⅛"

Fold

³/₈"

Loop turner

DIAGRAM 2

Marian Mongelli

Easy Corded Loops

It won't cost you a penny to add expensive-looking corded button loops to your evening wear with this technique. The secret is that the seam allowance becomes the cording.

Step 1: Cut true bias strips 1 inch wide and the desired length needed to go around the button. Don't make the bias strip too long, or it will be difficult to turn.

Step 2: With right sides together, fold the strip in half lengthwise. Sew along

SMART SHOPPER

To transfer pattern markings and closure placement marks to fabric quickly and easily, try Pattern Pals—pressure-sensitive peel-off stickers that eliminate the need for chalk, carbon, or pens. They are ideal for marking snaps, buttons, darts, notches, pockets, and more. To order Pattern Pals, send a self-addressed stamped envelope and $3 to 705 Hyde Park Road, Silver Spring, MD 20902.

Dorothy R. Martin

$$$

A Professional Finish

How can you tell the difference between a professionally finished garment and one that is homemade? Look at the detailed handwork on the closures. To duplicate the polished look from the ready-to-wear industry, use a buttonhole stitch when you sew snaps, hooks and eyes, or frog closures onto your garment. It is neat and looks expensive.

Laurel Hoffmann

Use Your Foot

If you find that your sewing machine needle often shreds the threads of the hook portion of Velcro, switch to a zipper foot. The foot will hold the hook portion of the tape in place so you can sew along the ⅛-inch hook-free border.

Janis Bullis

★ Bright Idea ★

EVER WISH THAT SNAPS AND HOOKS AND EYES CAME IN AS MANY SHADES AS YOUR FABRIC? Well, they can. Use nail polish to paint silver and black snaps and hooks and eyes. It's a great way to custom color match your fabric.

Karen Kunkel

Simple Buttonhole Stitch

Don't know how to make a buttonhole stitch? It's easy if you follow these simple illustrations and directions. Bring your needle up through the fabric at point A. Then, in one motion, insert your needle down into the fabric at point B and bring it up at point C, as shown in **Diagram 1**. Pull the thread to complete the stitch. Continue in this manner to complete the number of stitches necessary, as shown in **Diagram 2**.

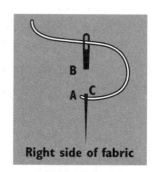

Right side of fabric

DIAGRAM 1

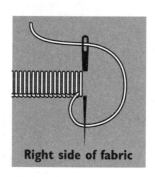

Right side of fabric

DIAGRAM 2

Karen Bolesta

It's a Snap to Stay Undercover

To ensure that your snaps remain hidden, place each half of the snap ⅛ inch from the finished edge of your garment.

Karen Kunkel

Let's Go with Velcro

Velcro can be used instead of snaps as a closure. The fuzzy side of the tape is the loop portion and should be sewn to the facing of your garment. The stiff side is the hook portion and should be sewn to the right side of your garment.

Janis Bullis

Stitching Is a Snap

Have you ever stitched a snap to your garment to find the snap wouldn't stay closed because you had used too much thread? Or have you laundered your garment and found your snaps dangling by a few threads? Follow this simple tip to make stitching a "snap."

Place the ball part of the snap on the underside of the overlap at the desired position. Take six whipstitches through one hole, then carry the thread under the snap to the next hole. When you have completed stitching the ball half of the snap, place the socket half on the topside of the underlap so that it is lined up with the ball half. Remember to make the stitches through the facing and interfacing only so that the stitches will not be visible on the right side of the garment.

Karen Kunkel

Collars

Collars can be any shape and depth, from high and round to flat and square. A collar accents a garment and complements the shape of your face. The shape of the collar's outer edge determines its style, while the inner edge determines how it will look when worn. Collars are a focal point of a garment, so they should be well made.

The Perfect Roll

Does it bother you when the undercollar seam shows through on the right side of your jacket collar? If so, you're not alone. To eliminate this problem, I always cut the upper collar a little bit wider to allow for the roll. Then, after I sew the upper collar and undercollar together but before I stitch the collar to the neck edge, I take it in my hands and roll it as if the collar were already stitched to the jacket. The fullness of the upper collar is automatically taken up in the roll. Finally, I baste the open edges of the upper collar and undercollar together before sewing the collar to my jacket. This is particularly useful when working with thicker fabrics like wool.

Marian Mongelli

Pinked to Perfection

I don't like the ridge of interfacing that may show through on the right side of jacket collars. So I fuse interfacing to the upper collar rather than to the undercollar. Also, I fuse interfacing to the jacket front facing, or upper lapel, not to the body of the jacket.

Janis Bullis

Spare Ribs

If you have a piece of leftover ribbed knit fabric, use it to make a quick-and-easy yet polished-looking collar for knit (and some woven) garments that have a crew neckline. Here's what you do.

Step 1: Cut two lengths of ribbed knit fabric two-thirds the circumference of the crew neckline on your garment and twice the finished width you want, plus ½ inch.

Step 2: With right sides together, fold one length of the fabric in half crosswise. Use an embroidery foot on your sewing machine, and set the machine for a very narrow zigzag stitch. Sew the short ends of the fabric together with a ¼-inch seam allowance, as shown in **Diagram 1.**

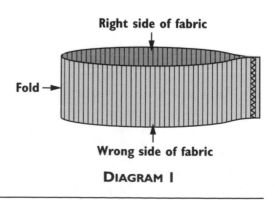

Right side of fabric

Fold →

Wrong side of fabric

DIAGRAM 1

Step 3: Now fold the same piece of fabric in half lengthwise with wrong sides together, making sure to keep the circular shape, as shown in **Diagram 2.**

DIAGRAM 2

Step 4: With raw edges even, pin and sew the ribbed knit to the neckline on your garment with a ¼-inch seam allowance.

Step 5: Use the remaining length of fabric to make matching cuffs for your garment. Simply cut the length of ribbing into two pieces, each measuring two-thirds the circumference of the cuff opening, then repeat Steps 2 through 4.

Gaye Kriegel

Rolling Along

When tailoring a jacket, I keep the roll line of a lapel firm with ⅜-inch-wide fusible tape. It is available in straight and bias grain. For this technique, I use the straight grain tape and fuse it onto the length of the roll line. Then I sew the collar and lapel as usual.

Roberta C. Carr

How to Handle Peter Pan

I cut the upper collar and undercollar pieces of a Peter Pan collar on the bias. The bias-cut collar pieces mold smoothly around the neckline, so they are easier to attach.

Eunice Farmer

Hot under the Collar

If your upper collar and undercollar pieces are cut from the same pattern, pin the outer edges together before you sew so that the undercollar extends ⅛ inch beyond the upper one. The result? The undercollar will be smaller than the upper one, allowing the whole collar to roll under and stand away from the garment slightly.

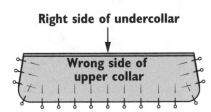

Right side of undercollar

Wrong side of upper collar

Clotilde

Disappearing Seams

To camouflage seam allowances in a crisply pressed collar made from a light-color fabric, fuse lightweight interfacing to the upper collar and undercollar before sewing them together.

Linda Griepentrog

Collars

Edge It in Lace

Do you like the look of a lacy collar but find that the lace always gets caught in the seam allowance as you sew? That will never happen if you use this technique.

Step 1: Trace your upper collar pattern onto your fabric with a water-soluble marking pen, adding a 1-inch seam allowance to the edges of the collar where you want to apply the lace, as shown in **Diagram 1.** Cut out the collar pieces.

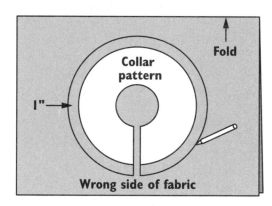

DIAGRAM 1

Step 2: With wrong sides together, baste the upper collar and undercollar together along the raw edges with a ½-inch seam allowance.

Step 3: Pin the lace, right side up, in place along the collar ⅝ inch from the edge, as shown in **Diagram 2.** Turn under the raw edges of the short ends of the lace.

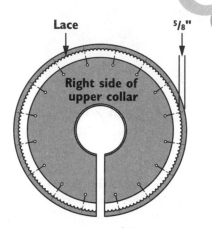

DIAGRAM 2

Step 4: Baste the lace to the collar.

Step 5: Thread the sewing machine and bobbin with machine embroidery thread, and satin stitch the lace in place around the collar through all thicknesses, as shown in **Diagram 3.**

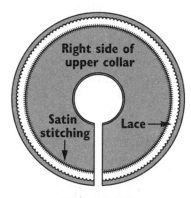

DIAGRAM 3

Step 6: Lift up the lace and trim the fabric close to the satin stitching.

Step 7: Sew the collar to the garment according to the directions on your pattern.

Glynda Black

"Seam"-ly Collar

Here's a frustration-free method for sewing the collar of a shirt or blouse by eliminating one collar seam and reducing fabric bulk.

Step 1: Place the stitching line of the long straight edge of the shirt collar pattern piece on the fold of the fabric, as shown in **Diagram 1**. Cut out the collar.

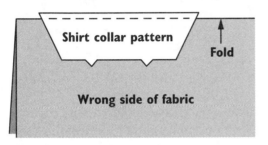

Shirt collar pattern

Fold

Wrong side of fabric

DIAGRAM 1

Step 2: Unfold the collar. Along one side of each end, trim ¼ inch starting at the neck edge and tapering to nothing at the collar point, as shown in **Diagram 2**.

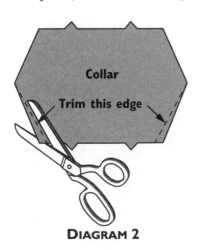

Collar

Trim this edge

DIAGRAM 2

Step 3: Fold the collar in half with right sides together and the long straight edges even, and then stitch the end seams. The seam will automatically be pulled slightly to the wrong side of the garment when the collar is completed.

Nancy Nix-Rice

Get Right to the Point

How do you press the points of a collar? Simple! Begin by melding the seam—pressing both sides of the stitching line flat. Then press the seam open over a Tailor Board. This allows you to not only get right to the collar point but also provides 12 different-shaped pressing surfaces.

Roberta C. Carr

Sheer Pleasure

To finish a collar made from sheer or lightweight fabric, I create a hairline seam. To do this, I place a strand of matching pearl cotton or crochet thread over the seam line and stitch it in place with a very narrow zigzag stitch. Then I trim the seam allowance close to the stitching.

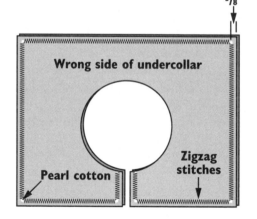

5/8"

Wrong side of undercollar

Pearl cotton

Zigzag stitches

Karen Kunkel

Collar Finesse

You can master the art of professional-looking collars with a little extra know-how.

◉ Directional stitching helps to maintain the shape of any collar. When sewing the upper collar and undercollar together, sew from the middle of the back of the collar around to the front. Then go back and sew again in the opposite direction to

complete the collar, as shown by the arrows in **Diagram 1.**

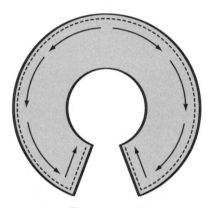

DIAGRAM 1

◉ Pinking shears simultaneously trim and notch the seam allowance of a collar with curved edges, as shown in **Diagram 2.** Not only do you save time but you also eliminate the danger of clipping through the seam allowance when making notches with straight shears.

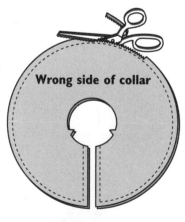

Wrong side of collar

DIAGRAM 2

⊕ Collar edges will be sharper if you press the seams open before turning the collar right side out, as shown in **Diagram 3.**

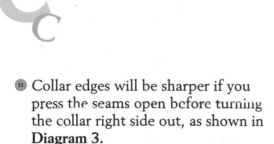

**Collar seams
pressed open**

Right side of upper collar

DIAGRAM 3

Fred Bloebaum

Sharpen It

If you find sharp collar points impossible to make, try this trick. When you get to within ½ inch of the collar point, shorten the stitch length and take one or two diagonal stitches across the collar point. The short stitch length strengthens the point and allows you to trim close to your stitching.

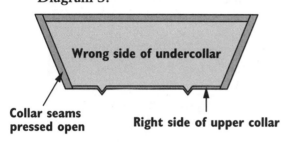

Right side of upper collar

Short stitch length

Wrong side of undercollar

Clotilde

 ★ **Bright Idea** ★

EXPERIMENT WITH CUTTING THE INTER-FACING FOR YOUR COLLARS ON THE BIAS OR CROSSWISE GRAIN. The layers work together beautifully to produce a perfect roll. Be sure to test fuse the interfacing before applying it to your fabric. Once fused, the interfacing will make the fabric feel slightly crisper and firmer. Make sure the care requirements for the fusible interfacing are the same as those for your fabric.

Lisa Shepard
Handler Textile Corporation

Elegant Lace Collars

Do you hate to see your seam allowances showing through collars and cuffs made from lace or crocheted fabrics? You can hide those unsightly seam allowances by lining your collars and cuffs with organdy or organza fabric. Your garment pieces will take on a lovely opaque cast and still retain their lacy look.

House of Fabrics
So-Fro Fabrics

Color Theory

One of the most important secrets in successful sewing is learning to have an eye for color. Finding the right color can change your wardrobe from ho-hum ordinary to showstopper stunning! The color of your fabric deserves just as much attention as the pattern you choose. Once you know your ideal colors, it is important to make those colors and your pattern work in perfect harmony. Then you can begin to plan and build your wardrobe using color principles.

The Blink Test

When I help someone choose the right color for fabric, I consider skin tone and hair color. My goal is to choose colors and prints that enhance the person and reflect a positive outlook, not detract from or overwhelm the person. So I use the blink test. The point of the test is to see if you and the fabric look harmonious together. It's easy and lets you see yourself as others do.

Stand 10 feet away from a full-length mirror and drape the fabric you're considering over your body. Close your eyes for a second or two and then open them. What is the first thing you see? Do you disappear? If so, then the color or print is too overwhelming for you. If the color gives you the blahs, it is probably too neutral or too dull. But if the color complements your own coloring and the print is flattering to your shape, then you have a winner.

Jan Larkey

Color Yourself Lovely

The secret to successful dressing is to balance the color of your clothes harmoniously with the color of your complexion and features. The clothes you wear should look like they belong with you. To guarantee your clothes will always be in sync with the rest of you, follow one of these simple strategies.

● Repeat your most attractive personal coloring—hair, eye, skin, or cheek color—in your clothing.

For example, if your eyes are blue or green, choose clothes that are neutral, smoky blue, or olive green. If your hair is blond, balance your overall appearance with camel, tan, ash, or ivory-color garments.

- Reflect your clothing color on or near your face with makeup and accessories. For example, use lip or blusher colors to bring out the coral, pink, or red colors in your clothing. Pick up shades of browns or blues from your wardrobe with similar colors of eye shadow or eyeliner. For hard-to-match colors, try earrings, scarves, or hair accessories.

Judith Rasband

Optical Illusions

Take advantage of the following ways color can create optical illusions to enhance your appearance.

- Cool colors, such as blue, green, and violet, will slim down your figure.

- Warm colors, such as red, yellow, and orange, will enlarge or accentuate your figure.

- Dull colors tend to recede, so they will disguise your true size.

- Contrasting color schemes can make your figure appear larger than it is, while subtle or blended color schemes will make your figure appear smaller.

- Bright colors stand out and will increase your size.

Butterick Company

Core Colors

Learn to build your wardrobe around several core colors. As the clothes in your closet begin to coordinate with one another, you won't need to sew as often. And it makes packing for travel easy.

Anita Collins

Spool Inspiration

Want to find new outfits hiding in your closet? Open up that neglected scarf drawer for inspiration! Choose a multicolored scarf that coordinates with several outfits you own. Select a spool of thread to match each color in the pattern of your scarf, then set your scarf aside. Group the spools of thread into two or three different color combinations. Carry the thread combinations you like best to your closet, and use them to discover new ways to mix and match your wardrobe separates.

Nancy Nix-Rice

SMART SHOPPER

Do you have a stockpile of fabric but little time to sew it up? That unused fabric eventually becomes out-dated—which means wasted dollars! Here are some hard-and-fast rules to help you plan your fabric purchases wisely and inspire you to sew.

1. Stick to a wardrobe plan. Sewing random pieces will leave you with a closet full of garments that don't co-ordinate. Select fabrics in colors that are subtle and neutral. Then add accent colors to complete the look. Three basic colors plus two accents work well.

2. Shop early in the season for the best color selection. Know which fabric stores have the best assort-ment, quality, price, and sale items.

3. Don't shop when stressed or hurried.

4. Remember the rule of three. Don't buy fabric unless it coordi-nates with at least three existing pieces in your wardrobe.

5. If you fall in love with a fabric, purchase enough yardage to make three matching pieces, such as a jacket, a skirt, and pants. You may not be able to find more later on, and you've just formed a wardrobe cluster. Select coordinating fabric at the same time for matching tops.

Anita Collins

Look 10 Pounds Thinner in Minutes!

Try any or all of these strategies to help you look ten pounds thinner now.

⊕ Match the color of your hosiery to your shoes, skirt, or pants. This eliminates any visual break below your waist, making you appear taller and thinner.

⊕ Taper the side seams of your straight skirts 1 inch from the hips to the hemline. This will create a slimming silhouette.

⊕ Wear bold and large earrings. Draw attention to your face rather than to your hips or other figure challenges with earrings that are about the size of a quarter.

Nancy Nix-Rice

Unleashing the Power of Color

When you know how to unleash the power of color, you'll be able to maintain a fresh, healthy appear-ance any time of day or night. Here are a few simple rules to remember.

⊕ Keep unwanted eyes away from your most unflattering areas by wearing detractor colors such as black, navy, brown, and gray.

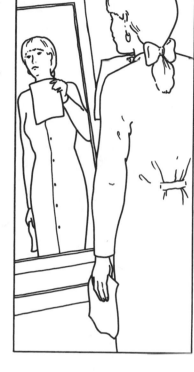

- Use color to accentuate the areas of your body that you are most pleased with.

- Create visual interest with blocks of color that accentuate the positive and downplay the negative.

- Use similar-tone coloring for an overall slenderizing effect.

Diana L. Carswell

How Cool Are You?

Selecting flattering colors for your wardrobe is easy if you know your color temperature. Are you warm or cool? Clothes and makeup should echo your personal color undertones to even out skin color.

Unsure of your undertone? Hold a 10 × 15-inch rectangle of both gold and silver lamé (or foil paper) under your chin while standing in front of a mirror. If the gold is a winner, then you have warm undertones, and yellow-based colors are your best bet. If the silver looks better, you are cool and should choose blue-based colors for your wardrobe.

Nancy Nix-Rice

Curtains and Drapes

If you are planning to redecorate a room, windows are the ideal place to begin. For a small investment, you can make a dramatic change to your decor with curtains, drapes, and other window treatments. Because they are often the focal point of a room, windows deserve careful thought and special attention. You don't have to spend a fortune on fabric to achieve a professional look.

Take Time to Measure

Never assume that all windows in one room are exactly the same size, no matter how identical they appear. Houses can settle, and builders can make errors. Measuring each window might take five extra minutes, but it can save you lots of grief later.

Gay Quinn

Measure for Measure

When measuring windows, always use a rigid ruler, such as a yardstick, to take small measurements and a metal tape for larger ones. Metal tapes that lock in place are particularly handy for awkward spaces. A wooden carpenter's rule works fine, too, as long as the folding sections stay securely in place.

Barbara Fimbel

Just Go and Freshen Up

How do you clean drapes that have a taped heading? Although you can't wash them because the tapes will lose their stiffness, you can freshen them. Working with one panel at a time, place it in the dryer with a damp towel. Set your dryer on NO HEAT, and tumble for about 20 minutes. Use a fresh towel for each panel. You'll be surprised by the amount of dust the towel collects! Remove the panel immediately and rehang it. Creases will disappear as the panel hangs. If you prefer, go over the panel lightly with a hand-held steamer.

Richard M. Braun

A Hot Tip for Baseboard Heaters

Cut drapery lengths so they fall above baseboard heaters for safety and to let heat enter the room. If the color contrast of the fabric and heater is jarring, paint the heater a color that complements your drapes.

Julia Bernstein

Consider Your Carpet

If you're planning to redecorate a room to include wall-to-wall carpet and drapes, take drapery measurements after the carpet has been installed. There could be a significant difference between the height of the bare floor and the carpeted one. If you must measure before the carpet is in place, lay a sample of the carpet and its pad on the floor under the window, then measure.

Richard M. Braun

Weights Make Straight

For a professional look, I use drapery weights in the hems of my drapes so they will hang straight and produce an even hemline. Before inserting the square weights into my drapes, I help hide them by covering them with a lightweight, neutral fabric such as muslin.

Peggy Bendel

Standard Procedure

Did you ever get stuck in the fabric store trying to decipher the window measurements you wrote down weeks earlier? If so, then follow these standard measuring procedures. It could mean the difference between wasting time and money on the wrong amount of fabric and saving it on the correct amount. Refer to the diagram when measuring your windows, and write those measurements on an index card so you can take them to your fabric shop.

- Measure the width first, the length second, and the depth third.

- Measure from left to right to the nearest ⅛ inch. Round off to the higher number except when purchasing items like shades, which could catch on the frames if they are too wide.

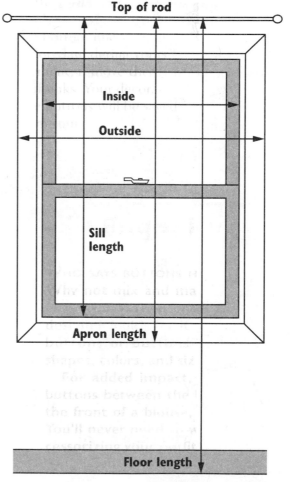

Barbara Fimbel

★ Bright Idea ★

DRAPES MADE OF LOOSELY WOVEN FAB-
RICS TEND TO STRETCH WHEN HUNG. To
compensate for this, I measure
my fabric so that the finished drapes
will hang I inch above the floor. To
ensure that they hang evenly, I hem
the sides of my drapes first. Then I
turn under ½ inch along the bottom
and press. Finally, I insert a lightweight chain weight along the hemline, then fold it up and sew the hem.

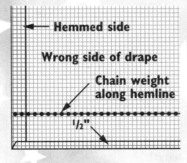

Elizabeth M. Barry

Don't Tread on Me

Unless you want puddled drapes,
remember to allow about ½-inch
clearance between the floor and the
lower edge of your drape. This
leaves room for electric cords and allows the vacuum cleaner to reach right
to the wall.

Charlotte Biro

What about the Neighbors?

Your curtains and drapes may
look great from the inside, but
what about from the outside? You
want your neighbors to have an attractive view, too! So whenever possible, line your curtains and drapes.

Claire Shaeffer

Take It from the Top

Do you love the look of swags,
valances, and scarves but are unsure about how to measure for
these window treatments? Here are
two hard-and-fast rules to get you up
and running.

⊙ Drape swags and scarves across the
top of a window so the shortest point
of the scallop is not less than 4 inches
from the top of the windowpane, as
shown in **Diagram 1.**

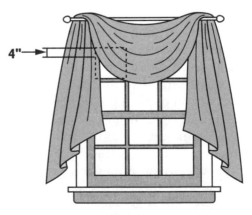

DIAGRAM 1

● Mount the valance rod for your window topper at least 4 inches in front of your drapery rod, as shown in **Diagram 2**. And be sure the return on the valance rod clears the sides of your drapes by 2 inches.

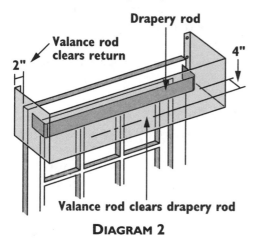

DIAGRAM 2

Gay Quinn

Allow for Shirring

If your curtains will be shirred, add ½ inch to the lengthwise window measurement to compensate for any loss in length due to shirring.

Judi Abbott

Drapery Insurance

If you send your drapes out to be professionally dry-cleaned, you'll want to make sure they return with their original measurements. Give

your cleaner the length and width of each panel, and have her write it down on your receipt for her reference. If she won't, find a cleaner who specializes in home furnishings. A little sleuthing can save you from having to make a new set of drapes!

Judi Abbott

Ironing Is Sheer Madness

Unless you still enjoy ironing ruffled cotton organdy, rehang freshly laundered sheer curtains right from the spin-dry washing cycle. The curtains will slip onto the rods more easily, and any wrinkles will disappear as they dry.

Julia Bernstein

SMART SHOPPER

When making curtains, it is important not to skimp on fabric—expensive or inexpensive. Whether your curtains will hang inside the window frame or extend to the outside, the rule of thumb is to triple the window width measurement. The fuller your curtains, the more professional they will look. But if the price of your favorite fabric puts you over your budget, find a less expensive fabric and purchase enough yardage. Don't sacrifice the fullness for the fabric.

Peggy Bendel

How Simple Can You Get?

Here's a curtain that you can make from a bed sheet in a half hour—guaranteed! Purchase a flat sheet with a top hem that is open along the sides. If the hem is stitched closed, you will need to make an opening along the center of the hem to insert a curtain rod.

Fold the hem in half lengthwise to find the center. At one short end, remove as many stitches as needed between the folded edge and the bottom of the hem to insert the curtain rod, plus an additional ¼ inch. Then repeat the process for the remaining short end. To form the casing for the rod, topstitch lengthwise across the hem ⅛ inch in from either end of the opening, as shown. Insert the rod and hang your curtain! You can even use this method to make a shower curtain.

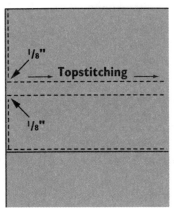

⅛"
Topstitching
⅛"

Julia Bernstein

Varying Window Heights

If you have windows of varying heights along different walls in the same room, here's a strategy for dealing with them. When the difference is a couple of inches at most, use the highest window as the stan-

dard for measuring to the floor. Raise the rods on the other windows so that all of the hems are the same distance from the floor.

If your windows have markedly different heights, try swags, scarves, or other soft treatments. They are particularly good at fooling the eye and presenting a more uniform appearance.

Carolyn Hoffman

From Table to Window Valance

Here's a quick-and-easy way to turn an antique table linen into a terrific window topper.

Step 1: Mount a finished or stained wooden pole above your window.

Step 2: Cut a square tablecloth in half diagonally. You will have two 90-degree triangles. Fit the cut side of one triangle across the top of your window frame. If the cut side extends beyond the edges of the frame, the triangle is too large. Fold down the fabric along this side until the triangle fits across the frame. Cut off the excess fabric. If you wish, make a rolled hem or pink the raw edges along the cut side for a neat appearance. Save the remaining triangle for another window in the same room or another room, but repeat the process for fitting because window frames may vary in width.

Step 3: Take down the wooden pole from above the window. Draw a straight line from one end of the pole to the other with a pencil and a yardstick. Use a staple gun to staple the cut side of the triangle to the pole, making sure the point hanging down is centered in the window.

If you don't like the look of staples or if you have a hand-forged decorative rod, try self-adhesive Velcro. Following the manufacturer's directions, adhere the hook portion of the tape to the pole and the loop portion to the wrong side of your valance. Your valance can easily be removed for washing!

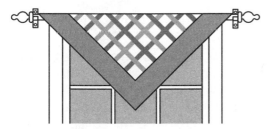

Charlotte Biro

From Table to Window Valance II

If you are reluctant to cut up a cherished tablecloth for a window topper as described in "From Table to Window Valance," a set of lace-trimmed napkins will also do the trick. They don't even have to match!

Arrange the napkins along a finished or stained wooden pole that has been mounted above your window so that they overlap one another. You can use as few or as many napkins as you wish, as long as the width of the over-lapped napkins equals the width of the top of the window frame.

You can secure the napkins together where they overlap by making tiny hand-tacking stitches with a needle and thread. Then use a staple gun to staple the napkins to the wooden pole from behind so that the staples cannot be seen from the front.

If you don't want to use staples or if you have a hand-forged decorative rod, try attaching the napkins to the rod with self-adhesive Velcro. Following the manufacturer's directions, adhere the hook portion of the tape to the pole and the loop portion to the wrong side of your napkins.

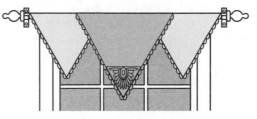

Charlotte Biro

Shear Sheers Slightly Shorter

If you plan to hang sheer curtains and drapes together, make the sheers 1 inch shorter than the drapes.

Jane F. Cornell

Here's to the Bishop

To make a bishop sleeve, the curtain panel should be tied below the pouf. Use a length of cording to tie the curtain. Screw a cup hook into the wall or window trim at the pouf and slip the cording onto it, as shown in **Diagram 1**. Arrange the upper part of the curtain over the cording to get the drape you desire.

If the fabric is not poufing as much as you'd like, stuff it lightly with loosely crumpled balls of tissue paper.

These curtains are particularly effective when puddled on the floor, as shown in **Diagram 2**. If you want yours to puddle, allow at least 6 inches of extra length when measuring your fabric.

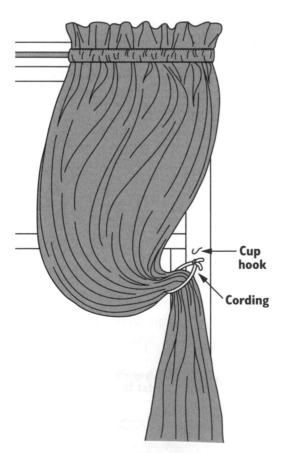

Cup hook

Cording

DIAGRAM 1

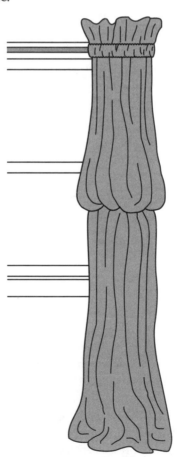

DIAGRAM 2

Jane F. Cornell

The Easiest Lined Panels

You can have lots of fun with these easy-to-sew curtain panels. From the basic design you can shirr the panels onto a rod, pleat them, or make them into tie-top curtains. Use one panel or two—it's up to you.

Step 1: Determine the finished length and width of your curtain panels according to the measurements of your window frame or area you want to cover. Make sure you add enough extra length for the casing or header of your choice, the hem along the bottom, and the hem along each side.

Step 2: Cut your curtain panels to the measurements from Step 1. Then cut your lining panel 1 inch shorter along the bottom edge and 1 inch narrower along both sides. Finish the hem on both panels as desired.

Step 3: With right sides together and raw edges aligned, pin and sew the curtain panel to the lining panel along each side, making sure the raw edges of the top of the panels are even. Turn the curtain right side out.

Step 4: Press the combined lining and curtain panel so there is about 1 inch of the curtain showing on either side of the lining, as shown in **Diagram 1**.

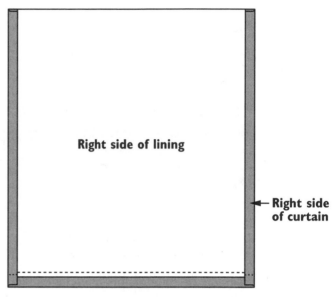

Right side of lining

◄— Right side of curtain

DIAGRAM 1

Step 5: Finish the top of your curtain panel as desired, treating the two fabrics as one, as shown in **Diagram 2**.

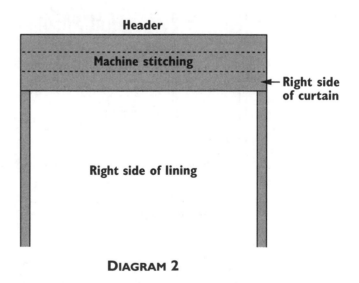

Header

Machine stitching

◄— Right side of curtain

Right side of lining

DIAGRAM 2

Charlotte Biro

Curtains and Drapes

Curtains for Kids

Here's a reversible window treatment that looks great in a child's bedroom. Make a pair of curtains from two coordinating fabrics that are of a compatible weight and have similar fabric care instructions.

Step 1: Measure the length and width of the inside of your window frame, as shown in **Diagram 1**. Add 2 inches to the length and 2 inches to the width.

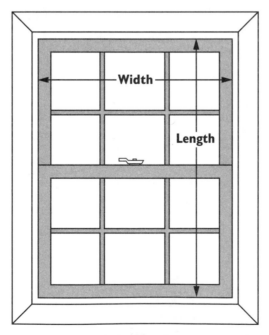

DIAGRAM 1

Step 2: From each fabric, cut one curtain panel according to the measurements from Step 1. Then cut each panel in half lengthwise.

Step 3: With right sides together and raw edges aligned, pin one curtain panel of each fabric together. Sew the panels together with a ½-inch seam allowance, leaving a 6-inch opening for turning, as shown in **Diagram 2**. Clip the corners and trim the seams.

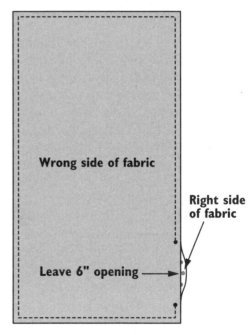

DIAGRAM 2

Step 4: Turn the completed curtain panel right side out. Turn under the seam allowance along the open edge and slip stitch it closed.

Step 5: Open just enough of the side seams below the top seam to insert a spring tension rod. Use a couple of tacking stitches or liquid seam sealant to keep the seam from opening farther.

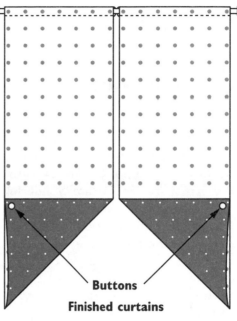

Buttons

Finished curtains

DIAGRAM 4

Step 6: Insert the tension rod in the opening. Create a casing for the rod by pinning the curtain panel across the width of the fabric below the rod, as shown in **Diagram 3**. Remove the rod and sew along the pinned line. Remove the pins and rehang the curtain panel.

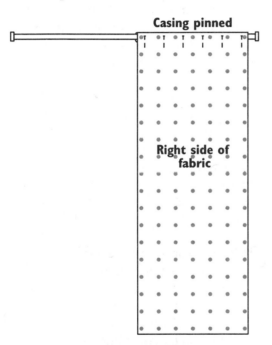

Casing pinned

Right side of fabric

DIAGRAM 3

Step 7: Repeat Steps 3 through 6 to sew and hang the remaining curtain panel.

Step 8: Referring to **Diagram 4**, fold the inside corners of each panel one-third of the way up and toward the outside of the curtain. Hand tack the

corners in place. Sew a button on top of each set of tacking stitches.

Gay Quinn

Make a Grand Appearance

To give shallow window frames and glass doors a wider, more open look, mount your window treatment outside of the frame.

Carolyn Hoffman

Catch the Drift

If you're sewing two widths of printed fabric together to make a single panel, sew from the bottom to the top. Mismatched patterns will be in the gathered heading rather than in a more obvious place.

Gay Quinn

Curtains and Drapes

SMART SHOPPER

When you are looking for quick window treatments that won't break the bank, head straight for the bedding department of your favorite store. Sheets are wonderful for windows because they come in wide widths, you can coordinate them with your bedding, they are less expensive than purchased curtains or drapes, fabric care is easy, and making window treatments from them is a snap.

Carolyn Hoffman

Fit to Be Tied

Here is an easy-to-sew curtain that can be made two different ways.

Step 1: Measure the length of your window frame.

Step 2: Cut a queen-size flat sheet to your lengthwise window measurement, adding a 1-inch hem allowance at the top and leaving the finished lower hem in place. Save the excess fabric for making fabric tabs to hang your curtains. Cut the flat sheet in half lengthwise and hem the raw edges.

Step 3: To make a double hem along the top of your curtains, fold down ½ inch and press it. Fold down another ½ inch and press again. Topstitch in place.

Step 4: From the excess fabric, cut enough 4 × 24-inch strips to cover the width of the curtain tops when placed 8 inches apart. Or you can cut 1½-inch-wide grosgrain ribbon, in a contrasting or complementary color, into 24-inch strips and follow the directions in Step 7.

Step 5: With the wrong side facing up, turn up ¼ inch on all four sides of each fabric strip and press, as shown in **Diagram 1.**

←¼"	**Wrong side of strip**

DIAGRAM 1

Step 6: With wrong sides together and edges aligned, fold each strip in half lengthwise and sew all of the edges together using a ¼-inch seam allowance, as shown in **Diagram 2.**

```
Finished strip
```

DIAGRAM 2

Step 7: Pin and hand sew the center of each strip ¼ inch down from the top of the hem on the wrong side of your curtains. Use small running stitches, and make sure they do not show on the right side of your curtains. The strips should be spaced 8 inches apart, as shown in **Diagram 3.**

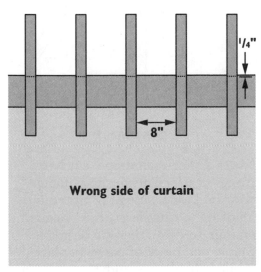

Wrong side of curtain

¼"

8"

DIAGRAM 3

Step 8: Install a wooden pole or metal rod directly above the window frame.

Step 9: Hang your curtains by tying the strips around the pole or rod, adjusting the spaces between the ties to create the illusion of pleats, as shown on the left in **Diagram 4.**

If you would rather not sew the fabric or grosgrain ribbon strips to the curtain, make 1-inch-wide vertical buttonholes, spaced 8 inches apart along the top hem of your curtains. Thread the fabric or ribbon strips through the buttonholes and tie them to the rod.

If you would rather have a single-panel curtain, as shown on the right in **Diagram 4,** don't cut the sheet in half as instructed in Step 2. Follow the rest of the directions for making two curtains.

Two-panel curtain   Single-panel curtain

DIAGRAM 4

Barbara Fimbel

Bright Idea

To keep dust from settling into my pouf valances, I spray the finished valances with Scotchgard, allow the fabric to dry thoroughly, and then gather the valances onto the rod. The Scotchgard finish helps to repel dust and keep the valances clean. When needed, I simply dust off the valances lightly with a clean dust mop.

Marya Kissinger Amig

For a Perfect Fit

When a curtain panel will be attached to rods at both the top and bottom, install the top rod first and hang the panel on it. Then slip the bottom rod into the bottom casing, pull the curtain down, and mount the hardware for the bottom rod accordingly. This ensures that the panel will be perfectly taut.

Barbara Fimbel

Discipline Your Drapes

When you have finished your pleated drapery panels and have hung them on their traverse rods, it's time to set the pleats so they remain permanent.

Step 1: Open the drapes as wide as possible. This makes the pleats as tight as they can be.

Step 2: Using your fingers like a rake, guide the pleats into even folds, as shown in **Diagram 1**.

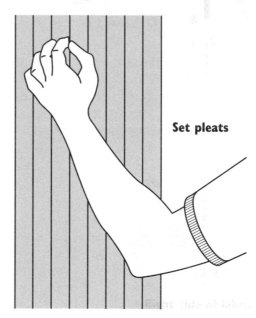

Set pleats

DIAGRAM 1

Step 3: For each drape, cut two pieces of paper or muslin 6 inches wide and long enough to fit around all of the pleats snugly but not tight enough to cause them to wrinkle. Staple one piece of paper in place around the drapes midway between the rod and the bottom edge of the panel, taking care not to catch the fabric in the staples, as shown in **Diagram 2**.

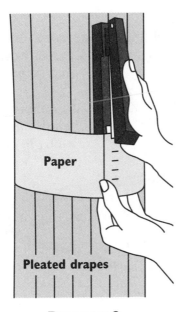

Paper

Pleated drapes

DIAGRAM 2

Step 4: Repeat Step 3 with a second piece of paper or muslin stapled just above the bottom edge of the drapes.

Step 5: Leave the paper or muslin wraps in place for about a week. Light steaming or natural humidity will aid in the setting process. Cut the paper or mulsin off, and you'll have perfectly mannered pleats!

Barbara Fimbel

SMART SHOPPER

By doing a little research in your favorite fabric store, you can save a lot of time creating window treatments. Among the drapery notions, you'll find fusible iron-on tapes that gather, shirr, and pleat, as well as fusible ring tapes that will help you to make Roman and balloon shades with ease. Look in the garment notions area for rolls of fusible web strips that can be used for fast and easy hemming, or cut your own strips from fusible web sold by the yard. You may want a stitched look for your window treatments, but these products can save a lot of time during construction.

Each fusible tape manufacturer has produced clear instructions, all of which vary slightly. Ask for these instructions when you make your purchase and follow them carefully. Some tapes can be machine washed and dry-cleaned, while some cannot be dry-cleaned. Instruction and creative tip sheets are also available for many fusible webs.

Julia Bernstein

Curtains and Drapes

HARDWARE FOR YOUR HOME

How you hang your curtains and drapes adds much to their final appearance. So choose your hardware with care. Here's a quick overview of some of the many options.

Barbara Fimbel

Type	Description	Ideal For	Appearance
Single rod	Plain rod with finials	Hanging sheer curtains under drapes	
Double rod	Two single rods combined with a 1-inch clearance between them	Hanging sheer curtains behind solid curtains or drapes; hanging curtains or drapes and a valance	
Continental rod	2½-inch- or 4½-inch-wide flat rod	Providing a gathered look to curtains and drapes that have no gathers	

Type	Description	Ideal For	Appearance
Clear plastic rod	Simple, clear rod that will not distract from the pattern of the fabric	Hanging sheer curtains or lace panels	
Traverse rods	Rod with a hidden track with rings that slide and cords for opening and closing drapes	Hanging drapes and valances	
Ringless traverse rods	Rod with a hidden track with slides, not rings, and cords for opening and closing drapes	Hanging pleated drapes	

(continued)

Curtains and Drapes

HARDWARE FOR YOUR HOME—Continued

Type	Description	Ideal For	Appearance
Wooden pole	Plain or fluted pole with one of a variety of finials; can be painted, stained, or covered with fabric; may or may not come with a set of matching rings	Hanging curtains with ties or loops	
Metal pole	Simple pole available in many finishes with one of a variety of finials; may or may not come with a set of matching rings	Hanging curtains with ties or loops	
Café rod	Simple rod available in many finishes from metal to wood; used with clip-on or sew-on rings	Hanging tie-on curtains; hanging curtains with rings; covering the lower half of a window or glass-pane door	

Type	Description	Ideal For	Appearance
Spring tension rod	Rod with tension springs inside to hold it in place in the window frame	Hanging lightweight curtains; hanging sheer curtain panels; hanging decorative shower curtains	
Holdbacks	Simple or elaborate arms that finish in a decorative head	Holding back panels of curtains or drapes; holding scarf and swag treatments at the top of a window frame	

Cutwork

In cutwork, some areas of fabric are embroidered and other areas are cut away to emphasize the design. The embroidery was originally done by hand. Later, satin stitches worked on the sewing machine were used. Today there are a variety of products, such as stabilizers, machine embroidery hoops, special scissors, and decorative threads, to make cutwork fun and easy.

Create Order in Your Work

Always complete the cutwork and satin stitching in one area to stabilize it before moving to the next area. Work from back to front. Work central design elements such as flowers and leaves before beginning the border areas.

Sulky of America

Mastering Machine Cutwork

Here's how to zigzag your way through elegant cutwork embellishments for tablecloths, curtains, and other household linens, or add a special touch to a dressy blouse.

Step 1: With a water-soluble marking pen, trace your design onto the fabric. Then mark your fabric with a straight line for an infilling stitch, such as a Richelieu bar, in the areas of your design that will eventually be cut away. Infilling stitches like Richelieu bars connect open areas of your design.

Step 2: Sandwich your design between two layers of water-soluble stabilizer on the bottom and one layer

on the top, as shown in **Diagram 1.** Then place your work in a 10-inch machine embroidery hoop.

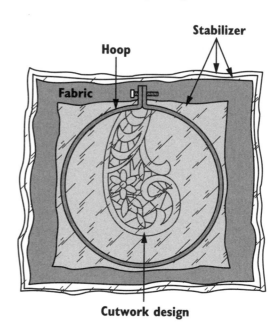

DIAGRAM 1

Step 3: Thread your machine and bobbin with white cotton embroidery thread. Lower or cover the feed dogs. Set the top tension slightly lower than normal, set the machine for a small stitch length, and attach a darning foot. Now you're ready for free-motion stitching.

Step 4: Straight stitch all of the pattern lines in your design except for the Richelieu bars, as shown in **Diagram 2**.

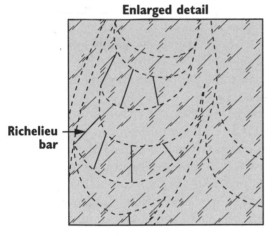

Enlarged detail

Richelieu bar

DIAGRAM 2

Step 5: Set your machine for a short, narrow zigzag stitch. Referring to **Diagram 3,** stitch again over the straight stitches. The straight stitches keep the fabric from stretching, while the zigzag stitches will keep the fabric from pulling away from the stitching when trimmed.

Step 6: Remove the hoop from the machine. With the work still in the hoop, use a seam ripper to make a small slit in the top layer of the stabilizer and the fabric within the area to be cut out. Then use embroidery scissors to cut away only the top layer of stabilizer and the layer of fabric.

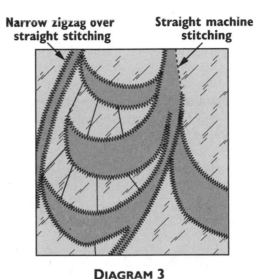

Narrow zigzag over straight stitching

Straight machine stitching

DIAGRAM 3

Step 7: Transfer the Richelieu bars from your original pattern onto the first layer of stabilizer. Thread the machine and bobbin with rayon thread, and set your machine for a straight stitch. You are now ready to sew the Richelieu bars that will connect the elements of your design.

Step 8: Begin at the edge of your design where one bar begins. Pull the bobbin thread to the right side of your work and sew one stitch in your design to anchor the bar. With the needle in the up postion, move the hoop to draw thread across the marked bar. Anchor the bar by taking one stitch into your design. You will have one long thread drawn across the open area of your design. This is a "walk" stitch.

Step 9: With the needle in the up position, "walk" back to your first stitch by moving the hoop and drawing the thread. Anchor your second walk stitch to your design right next to the first one. Repeat this step to create one more walk stitch, as shown in **Diagram 4.**

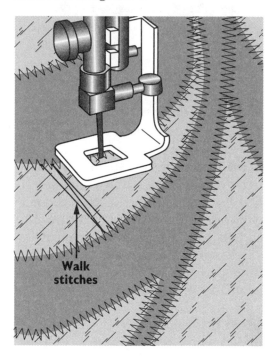

DIAGRAM 4

Step 10: Now set your machine for a very narrow zigzag stitch and satin stitch over the walk stitches, making sure that the zigzag stitches connect to your design at both ends of the bar.

Step 11: Set your machine for a short straight stitch and stitch along

the edge of your design to the next Richelieu bar.

Step 12: Repeat Steps 8 through 11 to sew Richelieu bars in the remaining areas of your design. To finish your work, you can use free-motion satin stitching, as described in Step 13, or you can use an appliqué foot, as described in Step 14.

Step 13: Leave your work in the hoop. Satin stitch around all of the cutwork openings on top of all of the previous stitches to enclose any raw edges. Keep your stitches perpendicular to the cutwork edge at all times.

Step 14: If you prefer to work with an appliqué foot, remove your work from the hoop. Make sure the feed dogs on your machine are up, and do not adjust the tension. The layers of stabilizer will help prevent tunneling (thread that forms a tunnel shape above the surface of the fabric) as you stitch. Set the machine for a zigzag stitch with a medium length and a width that will cover any previous stitching. Satin stitch around all of the cutwork openings on top of all of the previous stitches to enclose any raw edges.

Step 15: Cut away the bottom layer of stabilizer. Soak your work in cool water, and rinse it well to remove

all markings and any residue from the stabilizer. Roll your work in a towel to remove any excess water. Place your work right side down on a fresh towel. Iron it dry, removing all wrinkles.

Sulky of America

Throw Tradition to the Wind

Use colored thread in your cutwork projects instead of white or ecru to embroider. Or really pull out all the stops and use colored fabric with a contrasting thread.

Sulky of America

 Bright Idea

YOU CAN CREATE YOUR OWN ELEGANT LACE BY STITCHING CUTWORK EMBEL-LISHMENTS ON NETTING. Draw or trace your design and infilling stitches, or Richelieu bars, on a piece of water-soluble stabilizer. Then, working from the bottom up, build a fabric sandwich of blank water-soluble stabilizer, bridal tulle, English net, and the piece of marked stabilizer. Place your work in a 10-inch machine embroidery hoop, distributing the fabric gently and evenly until the fabric makes a drum sound when you tap on it. Follow Steps 3 through 5 of "Mastering Machine Cutwork," beginning on page 90. Then use embroidery scissors to cut away only the three top layers of your sandwich, leaving the bottom layer of stabilizer. To finish creating your personally designed lace, continue with Steps 7 through 15.

Karen King Carter

Darts

A dart is a stitched fold of fabric tapered to a point. Darts are used to shape a garment to the contours of the body at the bust, shoulder, elbow, waist, or hips. Whether straight, curved, or double-pointed, darts must fit precisely for a professional look.

Baste It, Don't Waste It

You'll save time if you baste the darts of the bodice of your garment, then try on the garment to check the fit of the darts before sewing. Make sure you wear the same bra or undergarment you intend to wear with the finished garment. Basting now will save you the trouble of ripping out your mistakes later.

Anne Marie Soto

Decorative Darts

For a clever decorative accent, sew your darts in reverse so they appear on the outside of your garment. Fold each dart with wrong sides together and stitch.

Marian Mongelli

Contour Darts

To correctly sew a contour dart (one that is pointed at both ends), start at the middle of the dart and sew to one end. Then go back to the middle and sew in the opposite direction to the other end, as shown in **Diagram 1.**

After stitching a contour dart, clip the dart crosswise at the widest point and then on either side of the widest point, as shown in **Diagram 2.** Be sure you don't clip through the stitching. The fabric will give as you press it, and the dart will lie smoothly. For reinforcement, sew a second row of stitches along the curve of the dart.

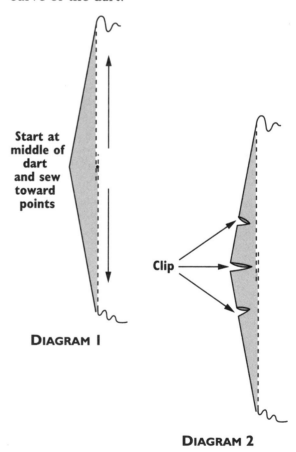

Start at middle of dart and sew toward points

DIAGRAM I

Clip

DIAGRAM 2

Karen Costello Soltys

Done Darts

To avoid tying off threads or backstitching at the end of a dart, shorten the stitch length to almost zero as you approach the point.

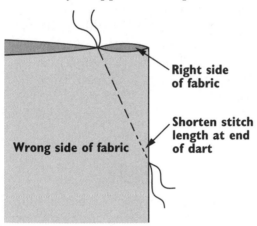

Right side of fabric

Shorten stitch length at end of dart

Wrong side of fabric

Linda Griepentrog

The Art of the Dart

Here are some timesaving tips to help you perfect the way you sew your darts.

- After cutting out your pattern, stitch the darts on all pieces first. Then you'll be ready for the next step in the construction process.

- Instead of marking darts with a fabric marker, pin and sew the dart immediately. This will lessen the chance of the pins falling out if you mark all darts at once.

- Stitch pucker-free darts by sewing the last few stitches parallel to the fold instead of parallel to the point.

Janis Bullis

Fine-Tune Your Darts

Here are two rules of thumb to remember when sewing the darts in the bodice of a dress or blouse or the waistline of a dress. An underarm dart on a bodice should end ¾ to 1¼ inches from the tip of the bust. A waistline dart on a bodice should end ½ to 1 inch below the tip of the bust.

Anne Marie Soto

Put a Dart in It

If the ready-to-wear jacket of your dreams is too boxy, you can alter it in a flash. Simply make two contour darts at the back of the jacket to absorb the excess fabric.

Without darts   **With darts**

Karen Costello Soltys

Add Darts Easily

If you wear a C-cup bra or larger, put darts into the side seams of the bodice of your blouse or dress so it will hang properly when you wear it. To do this, cut the front of the bodice about 3 inches longer than the pattern piece. Then sew the front and back of the bodice together along the shoulder seams. Try on the garment, and add darts to the side seams along the bustline by lifting enough fabric into the dart so that the side seam falls perpendicular to the hemline. Don't forget to adjust the length of the front of the garment so that it is even with the back before continuing. You'll be amazed at how much better your garment will look and fit.

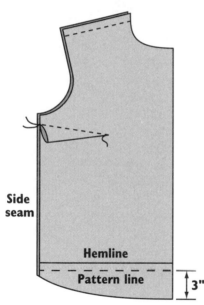

Side seam

Hemline

Pattern line

3"

Claire Shaeffer

Check Those Darts

If you baste your darts with the wrong sides together, then you can try on the garment, look in the mirror, and make any adjustments before permanently sewing the darts in place. Check to see if the darts need to be lengthened or shortened. If the darts are on the bust, make sure they are pointing to the fullest part of your bust. Then remove the basting stitches and repin the darts with right sides together, altering as necessary. It's always a good idea to try on the bodice one more time before sewing.

Anne Marie Soto

Darts Done Right

A correctly stitched dart should be barely visible on your garment. It must taper gradually to the point so there is no bulge. Place pins at right angles to the stitching line, with the pinheads toward the fold so you can easily remove the pins as you sew.

Marian Mongelli

Pressed to Perfection

Try these pressing techniques to ensure that darts will lie flat on the inside of your garment.

⊕ Press darts flat and in the same direction as they were stitched or toward the center of your garment.

⊕ Place the dart wrong side up over a tailor's ham, and press from the

wider end toward the point to give your dart shape.

- If your garment has deep-stitched darts, slash them first and then press them open.

- Use only the tip of your iron to press to the dart tip so that you don't press beyond the dart point.

Anne Marie Soto

Make Your Mark

When marking darts, use a paper clip at each seam allowance edge and a soap dot at the point.

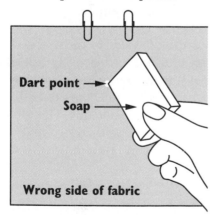

Linda Griepentrog

 Bright Idea

TO STITCH A PERFECTLY STRAIGHT DART, use 1/4-inch-wide quilter's tape as a guide. Simply fold, pin, and press the dart. Align one edge of the tape with the stitching line, and press the tape onto the fabric from the point of the dart to the cut edge of the fabric. Then stitch the dart along the edge of the tape.

Cheryl Winters Tetreau

Don't Forget the Dart

If you lengthen (or shorten) a pattern for slacks or a skirt, don't forget to adjust the length of the darts accordingly. You'll have a better-proportioned finished garment.

Karen Costello Soltys

Decorative Machine Stitching

There are an infinite number of ways to have fun with decorative machine stitching. Often a zigzag stitch is all it takes to produce stunning effects. Special threads and needles can enhance your design and increase your machine's capabilities.

Machine Stitch Everywhere You Can

I believe in never using a hand stitch when a machine stitch can be used. It's not only faster but also usually more durable. I've found expensive ready-to-wear garments a great source of inspiration. Here are my favorite machine stitching tricks.

- When cutting out your pattern, place the unnotched edge of waistbands, cuffs, ties, and front plackets on the selvage of the fabric, as shown in **Diagram 1.** Do not hem this edge. Then when sewing your garment together, simply stitch in the ditch on the right side of the fabric to secure this edge in place.

- Stitch in the ditch to secure neck and armhole facings, sleeves, and hems of lined garments, as shown in **Diagram 2.**

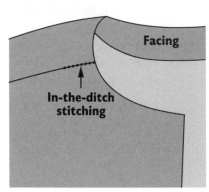

DIAGRAM 2

- To quick-finish faced necklines, armhole edges, sleeves, and skirt hems, sew four to six rows of parallel stitching ¼ inch apart in matching or contrasting thread, as shown in **Diagram 3.**

- Sew the right side of the notched edge of a cuff to the wrong side of the sleeve, making sure raw edges are even, as shown in **Diagram 4.** Turn the sleeve right side out. Then fold the cuff in half so that the wrong sides are facing. Turn under the seam

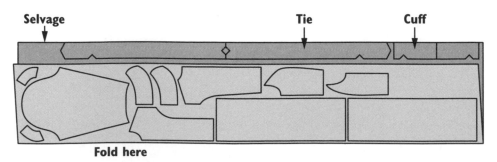

DIAGRAM 1

allowance along the unnotched edge of the cuff and edge stitch it in place from the right side of the sleeve, as shown in **Diagram 5.**

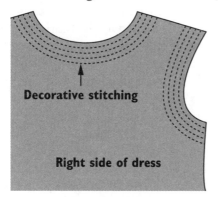

DIAGRAM 3

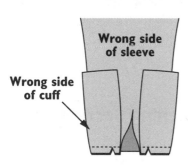

DIAGRAM 4

DIAGRAM 5

Betty Ann Watts

Net Results

Does your decorative thread slip down off the spool and wrap around the spool pin? If so, reduce your sewing speed to minimize friction and use a thread net, which will hold the thread in place and prevent slippage.

Sharee Dawn Roberts

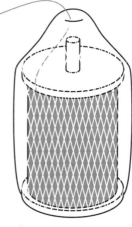

The Eyes Have It

When working with heavy decorative, metallic, or rayon threads in your sewing machine, try a top-stitching needle. Since the eye is proportionally larger than that of a standard machine needle, it offers the thread more room and lessens its chance of fraying.

Judi Cull

Automatic Appliqué

Who says you can't create decorative machine embroidery with an older model sewing machine that does not have computerized stitches? Just set the automatic buttonhole stitch in the forward position, and you can machine appliqué or create dozens of your own satin stitch designs.

Peggy Bendel

Decorative Machine Stitching

A Pattern Start for Wearable Art

Want to design wearable art but don't know where to begin? Start with a basic garment pattern that has an easy, comfortable fit and no binding armholes, detailed necklines, or fitting darts. For jackets, choose patterns that have drop, or kimono-style, sleeves and a minimum number of pieces. Fewer details on your pattern means your "canvas" will be easier to work with. Use the samples here to get you started. Once you've found a pattern that works for you, make it your master and use it over and over again.

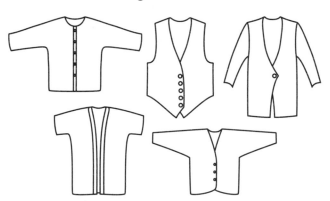

Jill Abeloe Mead

It's All in the Needle

Use large-eye or topstitching needles with metallic threads. They have a specially designed scarf and groove in front of an elongated eye,

helping to minimize the friction created with these threads. Choose the needle size that matches the weight of your fabric. If I'm using medium- to heavy-weight fabric, I use a size 90/14 needle. On heavyweight fabric, I use a 100/16 needle.

Metalfil needles work well with metallic threads and are similar in design to large-eye needles but have a Teflon-coated scarf to help reduce friction. However, Metalfil needles are only available in size 80/12.

The Schmetz machine embroidery needle is designed specifically for use with machine embroidery thread. It is ideal for rayon, silk, nylon, and tinsel threads but also works well with some lightweight metallic threads.

Sharee Dawn Roberts

Satin Stitching Secrets

The key to beautiful satin stitching begins with the basics.

⊞ Use a satin stitch foot. It has a groove on the bottom that allows raised stitching to flow smoothly under the foot without getting stuck.

⊞ Stabilize your fabric with tear-away stabilizer.

⊞ Use rayon or cotton embroidery thread, which will fill in satin

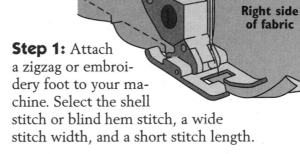

Right side of fabric

stitches for a thick, lustrous appearance.

Mary Griffin
Singer Sewing Company

Stop Thread Breakage

When sewing with metallic thread, use a topstitching needle in size 90/14 and lingerie thread in the bobbin. This will help alleviate thread breakage.

Libby Lehman

Try Twisted Metallics

If metallic threads tend to fray as you sew with them, try a heavier weight. When you shop for metallic threads, look for the twisted types, which are less apt to fray than the wrapped metallic threads that have a filler core of a different fiber content.

Sharee Dawn Roberts

A Frayless Finish

Here's a quick-and-easy decorative method to finish off fabrics that have a tendency to fray. It works wonders along the edges of lingerie, lightweight knit fabrics, ribbon trim, and areas where you have made tucks in the fabric.

Step 1: Attach a zigzag or embroidery foot to your machine. Select the shell stitch or blind hem stitch, a wide stitch width, and a short stitch length.

Step 2: If your garment isn't already finished, turn under a ½-inch hem along the raw edge. With the right side facing up, place your garment under the needle so that the folded edge is to the left of the needle. Stitch, letting the left swing of the needle sew off the edge of your fabric to create a curved edge.

Karen Kunkel

SMART SHOPPER

I'm a real fan of Sulky products. I've found that Solvy water-soluble stabilizer makes my sewing easier and gives me better results when I monogram, make lace, or do cutwork. Totally Stable iron-on or tear-away stabilizers helps me tame even the most flimsy of fabrics. Sulky transfer pens save hours of my time in fabric painting, appliqué work, and quilting. And Sulky rayon and metallic threads have been the boost that many fabric artists, like me, have longed for to make their creativity shine on long and strong.

Joyce Drexler

Decorative Machine Stitching

A Narrow Finish

For added flourish, I like to finish the edges of collars, cuffs, tucks, and hems with narrow trim or several strands of embroidery floss. I even use it to finish home decorating projects.

Step 1: Thread your machine and bobbin with monofilament thread for invisible stitching. Set the machine for a blind hem stitch and attach a zigzag foot.

Step 2: Lay the trim, yarn, or multiple strands of embroidery floss along the finished edge of the fabric, as shown in **Diagram 1.**

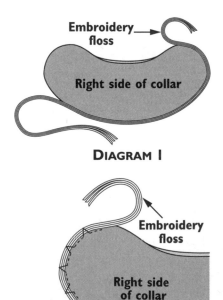

Embroidery floss

Right side of collar

DIAGRAM 1

Embroidery floss

Right side of collar

DIAGRAM 2

Step 3: Sew along the edge of the fabric so that the zigzag swing of the needle catches the trim, as shown in **Diagram 2.** You may need to adjust the width of the stitch to accommodate the thickness of the trim.

Verna Erickson
Singer Sewing
Company

Machine Embroidery Basics

The sewing machine is your most creative, timesaving tool. Use its built-in embroidery capabilities and rayon thread to create works of art that will outlast and outshine the fabric. Here are some pointers.

- Always use a new needle for decorative stitches. Try size 90/14 because its large eye reduces friction.

- For heavily filled-in satin stitch patterns, thread your machine with durable #30 or #40 rayon thread. Use matching thread or cotton-covered polyester thread in the bobbin.

- Use an embroidery or satin stitch foot with wide-set toes so you can see where you're stitching.

- Reduce the top tension and lower the presser foot pressure slightly.

- Test your satin stitch on a fabric scrap first to regulate stitch length and tension.

- To prevent puckers and skipped stitches, use light- to heavy-weight fusible stabilizers.

- Stabilize your fabric with a lightweight fleece to add a soft touch to your decorative stitching.

Sulky of America

Handle with Care

The less special threads are handled, the better. I purchase the thinnest-weight clear vinyl I can find and cut it into 2-inch-wide strips with a rotary cutter. Then I cut these strips into suitable lengths to wrap around each spool. Adding slight pressure as I wrap the vinyl holds it in place on the spool. This protects the thread from dust. When the spools are empty, I recycle the strips by using them on my next set of specialty threads.

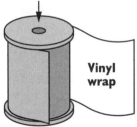

Spool of metallic thread

Vinyl wrap

Sharee Dawn Roberts

Ribbons of Fun

To give your garment or home decorating project a raised effect with a brilliant band of color, try using ribbon floss thread in the bobbin. Use the floss to add tone-on-tone color to a flared dress hem. Or run a ribbon rainbow down the sleeves of a dress. Whatever form of decoration you choose, you are sure to have ribbons of fun!

Step 1: Wind a bobbin with ribbon floss. Insert the bobbin into the bobbin case, but don't thread the floss through the tension spring. (Elna owners should use the bypass tension hole in the bobbin case.) Thread the upper part of your machine with a matching color thread and set the machine for a long stitch length. Tighten the upper tension to between 7 and 9.

Step 2: With the wrong side of the garment facing up, sew along the area you want to decorate. Remove your garment from the machine, leaving 4-inch tails of thread and floss.

Step 3: Use a needle threader to pull the floss on the right side of your garment through to the wrong side. To do this, insert the needle threader into your garment from the wrong side, thread the eye, and pull the tail of floss to the wrong side.

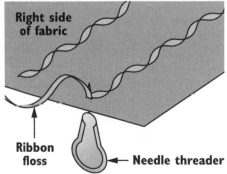

Right side of fabric

Ribbon floss

Needle threader

Step 4: Tie a knot in the ends of the thread and floss, and secure it in place with a drop of liquid seam sealant.

Jane M. Burbach
Elna Inc.

Decorative Machine Stitching

A Rose by Any Other Name

There's no need to purchase an expensive ribbon rose for a wedding gown, prom dress, or other formal garment when you can make your own. It's fast and easy.

Supplies

- ¾ yard of 2½-inch-wide white eyelet without binding
- ¾ yard of 1½-inch-wide white ribbon
- ¼ yard of ¼-inch-wide green ribbon
- Hand-sewing needle
- Sewing thread to match the eyelet and ribbons
- Pin back (available at craft-supply stores)
- Fabric glue

Step 1: Set your machine for a long stitch length and increase the thread tension. Attach a gathering foot.

Step 2: Sew along the raw edge of the eyelet, leaving a 20-inch tail of thread at the beginning and the end. Repeat for the white ribbon.

Step 3: Pull up the bobbin threads on the ribbon and the eyelet, forming a tight circle, as shown in **Diagram 1.**

Step 4: Turn under ¼ inch along one short end of the ribbon and whipstitch in place. Thread the needle with one of the 20-inch tails of thread. Begin

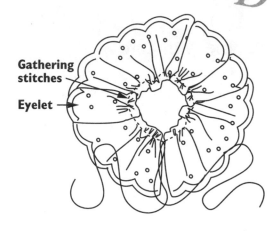

Gathering stitches

Eyelet

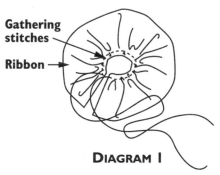

Gathering stitches

Ribbon

DIAGRAM 1

wrapping the ribbon around itself, tacking as you go, to form a rose, as shown in **Diagram 2.** Turn under ¼ inch along the remaining short end of the ribbon and whipstitch in place.

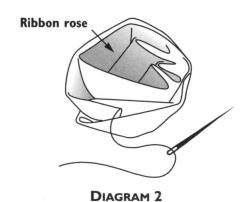

Ribbon rose

DIAGRAM 2

Step 5: Fold the green ribbon in half crosswise, and tack the fold of the ribbon to the center back of the rose so that the ribbon tails hang down. Cut the tails at an angle, as shown in **Diagram 3.**

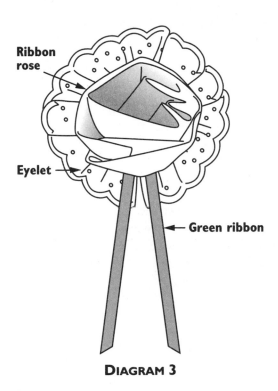

Ribbon rose

Eyelet

Green ribbon

DIAGRAM 3

Step 6: Place the circle of eyelet behind the ribbon rose. Thread the needle with the remaining 20-inch tail of thread and tack the eyelet to the ribbon rose. Center the pin back on the wrong side of the rosette and glue it in place.

Dorothy R. Martin

A Thread of Difference

Using one of the many specialty threads available can add instant sparkle and shine to your favorite machine-art technique. But many beginners are frustrated by what they consider to be low performance of decorative threads. For example, metallic thread can snap, rayon thread tends to fray, and tinsel threads can form tight twists that eventually cause the thread to break. But don't despair! Knowing what kind of thread to use can make all the difference in your sewing. Here are some helpful suggestions.

Use good-quality, lightweight thread in your bobbin. My favorite is Bobbin-fil by Madeira. This #70 weight polyester thread is available in black and white only. For machine-art techniques, the bobbin thread will not show on the surface of the fabric, so the color is not important.

When using Bobbin-fil, I sometimes need to tighten the bobbin tension slightly. I do this if the thread pulls from my bobbin case too freely. Once the bobbin tension has been adjusted, my work slides more smoothly beneath the presser foot, and the specialty thread sews better.

Other bobbin threads I recommend are YLI's lingerie and bobbin thread and Sew-Art's Sew-Bob.

Sharee Dawn Roberts

Decorative Machine Stitching

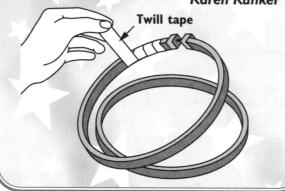

★ Bright Idea ★

TO HOLD A PIECE OF FABRIC TAUT IN YOUR PLASTIC EMBROIDERY HOOP, TRY THIS TRICK. **Wrap the outer hoop ring with a piece of cotton twill tape. This will add some friction and grip your fabric better when the hoop is closed.**

Karen Kunkel

Twill tape

Corded Entredeux Beading

Here's a technique that makes heirloom sewing fast and easy. The addition of cording in the entredeux stitch produces a raised-edge effect. You may want to practice several times before actually making a length long enough for embellishing a garment.

Supplies (for a 6-inch square)

- Two 6-inch lengths of insertion lace
- 2 × 14-inch piece of water-soluble stabilizer

- 14-inch length of pearl cotton
- 6-inch square of batiste
- Buttonhole foot
- Wing needle
- Spray starch
- Lightweight cotton sewing thread to match the lace
- Tapestry needle, size 11/18
- Ribbon floss

Step 1: Attach a buttonhole foot to your machine and insert the wing needle. Select an entredeux stitch or any stitch with left-to-right motion.

Step 2: Spray the lace with starch to stiffen it.

Step 3: Center the stabilizer under the needle and lower the needle into it. Place one piece of spray-starched lace on either side of the needle, as shown in **Diagram 1**.

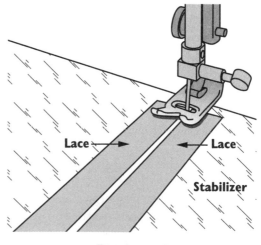

Lace → ← Lace

Stabilizer

DIAGRAM I

Step 4: Raise the buttonhole foot. Fold the pearl cotton in half, wrap the loop end behind the needle, and hold the thread ends in front of the needle, as shown in **Diagram 2.** If your buttonhole foot has a groove in the center, wrap the thread around it.

Lower the presser foot and begin stitching. You will be incorporating the pearl cotton into the entredeux stitch while joining the lace pieces together. This gives the lace its corded effect.

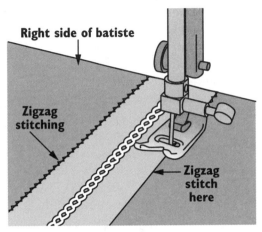

Right side of batiste

Zigzag stitching

Zigzag stitch here

DIAGRAM 3

Step 7: To finish, thread the tapestry needle with the ribbon floss, and weave the floss through the holes down the center of the entredeux stitching, as shown in **Diagram 4.**

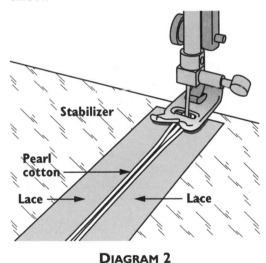

Stabilizer

Pearl cotton

Lace   **Lace**

DIAGRAM 2

Step 5: Trim away any excess stabilizer.

Step 6: Spray the bastiste with starch, then pin the lace to it. Using a very narrow zigzag stitch, sew the lace to the batiste very close to the edge of both pieces of the lace, as shown in **Diagram 3.**

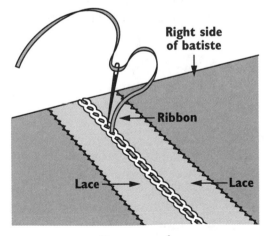

Right side of batiste

Ribbon

Lace   **Lace**

DIAGRAM 4

Jane M. Burbach
Elna Inc.

Free-Motion Monogramming

Personalize your family's wardrobe, your home decorating projects, and crafts with free-motion machine monogramming.

Supplies

- Garment to be monogrammed
- Size 90/14 sewing machine needle
- #40 thread
- Alphabet monogramming book
- Water-soluble or fusible tear-away stabilizer
- Machine embroidery hoop

Step 1: Make sure the area of your garment and two layers of stabilizer are big enough to extend at least 2 inches beyond your embroidery hoop. Trace your letter design onto one piece of water-soluble or fusible tear-away stabilizer.

Step 2: Sandwich your fabric between a piece of unmarked stabilizer and the stabilizer marked with your design. Fuse the stabilizer to the fabric if necessary, following the stabilizer manufacturer's instructions. Place all three layers in an embroidery hoop.

Step 3: Remove the presser foot from your machine and lower or cover the feed dogs. Set your machine for a medium-width zigzag stitch. Lower the presser foot lever.

Step 4: Monogram by satin stitching over the letters, moving the hoop slowly to allow the thread to create a smooth, closely stitched letter. Follow the letters with the needle in the same manner as if you were writing with a pencil. Do not turn or twist the hoop, and keep the letters facing you.

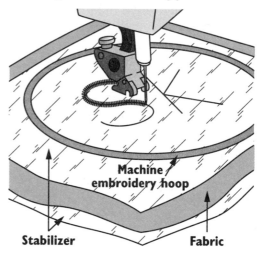

Sulky of America

Trapunto by Machine

Trapunto is a form of quilting that features a stuffed and raised design. A similar technique can be accomplished quickly and easily on your sewing machine.

Step 1: Trace your design onto the right side of your fabric with a water-soluble marking pen or chalk pencil.

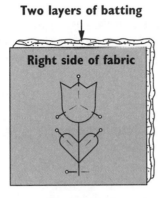

Two layers of batting

Right side of fabric

DIAGRAM 1

Step 2: With the right side of your fabric facing up, pin two or three layers of poly-ester quilt bat-ting to the wrong side of your fabric, as shown in **Diagram 1.** You only need to pin the batting to the area that will be stuffed.

Step 3: Thread the needle and bobbin of your sewing machine with water-soluble basting thread and decrease the tension to almost zero. Don't worry about a balanced tension because the stitches will be washed away.

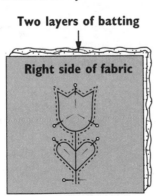

Two layers of batting

Right side of fabric

DIAGRAM 2

Step 4: With machine stitching, out-line the larger areas of your design that you want to stuff, as shown in **Diagram 2.** Don't outline any design de-tails, such as leaf veins, at this time.

Step 5: With appliqué scissors, trim the batting outside the stitching to within ⅛ inch of your stitching.

Step 6: Pin together your backing fabric (with the wrong side facing up), a layer of cotton or polyester batting, and your design (with the right side facing up). Pin generously in the areas where you have already sewn the batting.

Step 7: Change the thread in the top of your machine to invisible nylon monofilament, cotton, or any other thread of your choice. Change the bobbin thread to match the color of your backing fabric. Readjust the sewing machine tension to accommo-date the fabric.

Step 8: Quilt your entire design, making sure to sew over your previous stitching, and any additional design de-tails you now want to add.

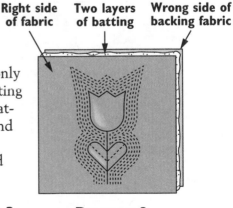

Right side of fabric **Two layers of batting** **Wrong side of backing fabric**

DIAGRAM 3

Step 9: Closely quilt the areas that are not stuffed. This not only provides a contrasting texture but also flat-tens the background of your design, making the stuffed areas stand out in greater relief, as shown in **Diagram 3.**

Step 10: Wash the project to remove any markings and fluff it.

Annie T. Tuley

Decorative Machine Stitching

GUIDE TO STABILIZERS

Stabilizers are vital to star-quality decorative stitching. But with so many kinds available, it's hard to know which one to choose. I suggest experimenting with them all! However, remember always to consider your fabric and the technique you will be using. No stabilizer is perfect for every project.

Sharee Dawn Roberts

STABILIZER	BRANDS AVAILABLE	IDEAL FOR	ADVANTAGES	DISADVANTAGES
Wooden machine embroidery hoops		Heavy decorative machine stitching	Nothing to tear, rinse, or burn away	Takes time and care to stretch fabric; limits stitching area
Plastic spring craft hoops		Lightweight decorative machine stitching that does not put stress on background fabric; straight stitch machine embroidery; quilting	Easy to use with background fabric	Cannot stretch fabric tight; not suitable for heavy decorative machine stitching
Cotton or polyester batting	Hobbs; Fairfield; Mountain Mist; Morning Glory; Warm and Natural	Machine appliqué; couching; quilting	Built-in stabilizing effect	
Bond paper; deli paper; freezer paper	Reynolds freezer paper	Machine appliqué	Inexpensive	Can tear stitches when removed
Tear away	Pellon Stitch-N-Tear; No Whiskers Tear Away; Easy Stitch; Sulky's Tear-Easy	Lightweight decorative machine stitching	Easily removed with little stress to stitching	Not suitable for heavy decorative machine stitching or techniques that require maximum stability

Decorative Machine Stitching

Stabilizer	Brands Available	Ideal For	Advantages	Disadvantages
Fusible tear away	Sulky Totally Stable	Lightweight decorative machine stitching; machine appliqué; charted needlework	Temporarily bonds to fabric; can use for pattern designs	
Liquid stiffeners	Palmer/Pletsch's Perfect Sew; Helmar's Liquid Fabric Stiffener	Heavy decorative machine stitching	Provides maximum stability; washes away	Not suitable for fabrics that can't be washed
Spray	Helmar's Lite Fabric Stiffener	Machine appliqué; lightweight decorative machine stitching	Leaves no residue; suitable for lightweight fabrics, such as silk and rayon	Not suitable for fabrics that can't be washed
Water soluble	Wash-A-Way; Madeira Melt-Away; Sulky's Solvy	Cutwork; three-dimensional appliqué; Battenberg lace; stitching without fabric	Rinses away with water; easy to remove; Wash-Away is ideal for monogramming on knit fabric	Not suitable for fabrics that can't be washed
Burn away	Vanish-Away; Sulky's Heat-Away; Aardvark Hot Stuff	Cutwork; Battenberg lace; stitching without fabric	Disintegrates with a hot iron; easy to remove; can use Aardvark Hot Stuff without a hoop	Can't use Sulky Heat-Away without a hoop, which limits stitching area

Elastic

Working with elastic is quick-and-easy sewing at its best. Elastic can give a garment shape or a sporty look and make it more comfortable to wear as well. Here are some tried-and-true tips plus new sewing techniques that are sure to become part of your repertoire of favorite sewing shortcuts.

No-Roll Elastic

To prevent elastic from rolling within a casing, topstitch the elastic in place ⅛ inch from the upper folded edge of the casing.

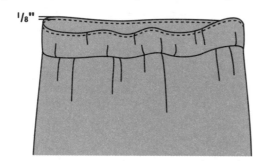

Janis Bullis

Under Stress

Use clear elastic to stabilize areas of stress on your garment, such as necklines and shoulder seams. Make sure the elastic is slightly narrower than the width of the seam allowance.

Step 1: Measure the area on your pattern to be stabilized. Don't measure your garment because it may have been stretched during cutting.

Step 2: Sew the elastic into your seam, making sure the elastic is flush against the inside edge of the presser foot. If you are using a serger, be sure to position the elastic to the inside edge of your seam so it does not get trimmed by the serger's blade.

Laurie Baker

Keep It Long

Here's a simple trick to prevent the end of your elastic from disappearing into the casing as you insert it. Measure and mark the correct length on your elastic but don't cut it. Insert a safety pin into one short end of the elastic, and pull the entire piece of elastic through the casing. Now cut off the elastic at the mark.

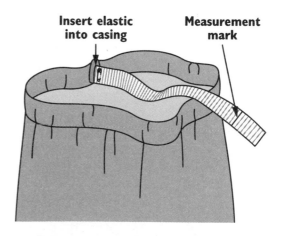

Insert elastic into casing   Measurement mark

Claire Shaeffer

Clear Choices

Clear elastic is lightweight and stretchy and will give you more mileage per inch. It is available in ¼- to ¾-inch widths. The first few times you stretch it, it will elongate up to 10 percent of its original length. So before you measure and cut the elastic, stretch it a few times, then release it. After this warm-up, it will have 100 percent recovery.

Cindy Kacynski

Be Kind to Your Waist

My favorite waistband elastic is Ban-Rol because it does not roll. I use it for all types of fabric, including knits, wovens, Ultrasuede, and Ultraleather. Ban-Rol is kind to your waist because it gives when you do. You can eat dessert even when you shouldn't!

Clotilde

A Short Fuse

When you insert elastic into a casing, does it ever get caught in the seam allowance? If so, try this simple trick. After you sew and press open the seam allowance of your casing, cut two lengths of fusible web the length and width of each side of the seam allowance. Place each length of web underneath the seam allowance and fuse it in place. Then finish your casing according to the pattern directions. When you insert the elastic into the casing, you'll be surprised at how smoothly it will glide through.

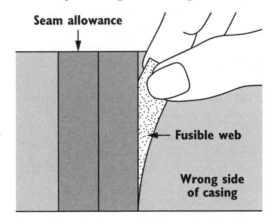

Glorian Friedel

★ Bright Idea ★

USE ELASTIC INSTEAD OF CORDING ON GARMENTS THAT CALL FOR A DRAWSTRING WAIST. Just cut a length of elastic to fit your waist measurement. Then construct two ties from fabric that matches your garment, and attach one tie to each end of the elastic. Insert the elastic through the casing. You will have a snug-fitting waist with the look of a drawstring waistband.

Karen Kunkel

Elastic

Recovery Test

Before you sew a length of elastic into your garment, calculate its recovery, or how much it will return to its original shape, once it is stretched and released. Here is a simple test you can try.

Step 1: Cut a 2-inch length of elastic.

Step 2: Measure and mark a 3-inch length on your fabric.

Step 3: Pin the elastic to the fabric, making sure to line up the ends of the elastic with the 3-inch marks, as shown in **Diagram 1**.

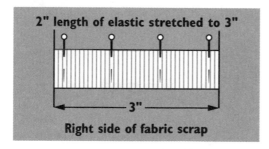

DIAGRAM 1

Step 4: Sew your elastic to the fabric in the same way you would sew it to your garment.

Step 5: Measure the length of the elastic, as shown in **Diagram 2**. Has it grown ⅛ inch? ¼ inch? Now that you know the recovery, you can cut the elastic for your garment accordingly. For example, if the wrist on the sleeve

of your garment requires a 5½-inch length of elastic, but your recovery test shows that the elastic stretches ¼ inch, you should only cut a 5¼-inch length.

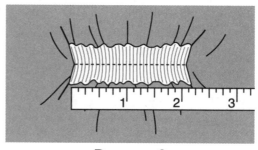

DIAGRAM 2

Claire Shaeffer

A Custom-Fit Waist

One in four elastics stretches differently. So when pattern directions say to cut your elastic 2 inches less than the measurement of your waist, don't do it! To determine the correct length of elastic to cut, safety pin a piece around your waist. Wear it for about a half hour to know if it's a comfortable measurement or not.

Clotilde

Elastic Thread

Looking for a quick way to gather a length of fabric? Use elastic thread and a cording foot on your machine. It is a great way to gather

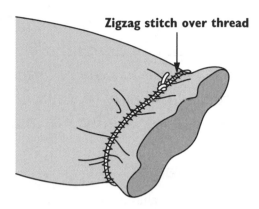

Zigzag stitch over thread

DIAGRAM 2

ruffles, make cuffs on dresses, or sew a waistband. Here's what to do.

Step 1: Insert the desired length of elastic thread through the center slot of the cording foot, keeping it between the foot and the wrong side of the fabric.

Step 2: Knot the thread behind the foot to secure it, as shown in **Diagram 1**.

Make sure the width of the zigzag stitch is enough to clear the thread on either side so the needle doesn't pierce it.

Karen Kunkel

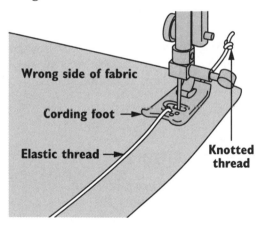

Wrong side of fabric

Cording foot

Elastic thread

Knotted thread

DIAGRAM 1

Step 3: Sew the thread to your garment with a zigzag stitch, stretching it as you sew, as shown in **Diagram 2**.

SMART SHOPPER

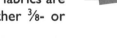

When sewing a swimsuit, look for elastic labeled safe for swimwear. This special elastic is resistant to deterioration from sun, oil, chlorine, and salt water. It will not shrink or lose its stretch when wet. You can usually find this elastic where swimwear fabrics are sold. Most suits require either ⅜- or ½-inch-wide elastic.

Karen Kunkel

Fabric

What sewer doesn't have a stockpile of fabric stashed away waiting to be transformed into the wardrobe of her dreams? Are you partial to wools and silks? Have you tried the fabulous fakes? Do you like the luxurious look of lamé? Whatever your personal taste may be, from Ultrasuede to ultrasheer, you should know how to cut it, sew it, and take care of it.

Get It Straight

When purchasing print fabric, make sure the grain line and the printed pattern are straight. Fabric that is off-grain or off-pattern may cause cutting and matching problems. Ask the fabric-store clerk to cut you a swatch. Then check your fabric by tearing it along the straight of grain. If the grain isn't straight, you won't be able to tear the fabric, and you shouldn't buy it.

Tear fabric to test grain

Charlotte Biro

Don't Go against the Grain

If you're tempted to save fabric by cutting on the crosswise grain when the pattern calls for the lengthwise grain, think twice before doing so for the following reasons.

⊞ Your garment will lose its strength since there are fewer threads per inch in the crosswise direction.

⊞ Pattern pieces will be out of proportion since the lengthwise threads are stretched more tightly than crosswise ones during manufacturing. After you cut your fabric, there is more potential for shrinkage as the threads return to their prestretched length.

⊞ Your garment will hang incorrectly since there is usually more stretch and give in the crosswise grain.

Judi Abbott

Design Matters

To get ultra results from Ultrasuede, follow these professional pointers.

⊞ Opt for patterns that have few pieces and simple lines.

⊞ Choose patterns suitable for woven fabrics and not knits. Those designed for knits don't usually offer enough wearing ease for Ultrasuede.

⊞ Avoid designs with curved seaming because it's difficult to join concave and convex curves smoothly with Ultrasuede. Instead, choose designs with straight lines, then call attention to your seams with decorative machine topstitching.

- Look for simple sleeve designs, especially if you've never worked with this fabric before. Kimono, raglan, and other dropped-shoulder designs work better than set-in sleeves.

- Eliminate designs with darts, and choose a pattern with yokes instead.
  Springs Industries

Bring Back Body

If your fabric loses its body during the prewash cycle, just use a little spray starch when you press it, and the crispness will be restored.
Richard M. Braun

Sharp As a Needle

For best results when sewing with a pile fabric, always sew with a sharp new needle in your machine.

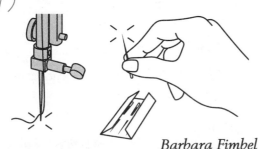

Barbara Fimbel

Do Not Fold, Spindle, or Mutilate

To prevent permanent creases in pile fabrics such as velvet or corduroy, loosely fan-fold the fabric from selvage to selvage. Then insert large safety pins through the layers along the selvage, and hang the fabric on a hanger until you plan to use it.

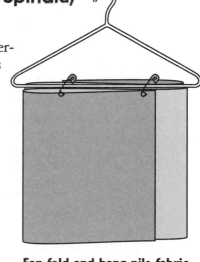

Fan-fold and hang pile fabric

Elizabeth M. Barry

A Direct Cut

Lay out and cut all of your pattern pieces in the same direction, unless directed otherwise by the pattern. If you don't, the fabric's sheen will reflect the light differently on different parts of your garment when complete. Take precautions by lightly marking the selvage with directional arrows to ensure that you work in one direction. If you have any doubt, use the "with nap" cutting layout on your pattern instructions.

Barbara Fimbel

Seams Perfect

You can easily avoid bulky seam allowances when sewing with heavyweight Ultrasuede by creating a lapped seam. With right sides facing up, overlap two of your garment pieces along the seam line. Trim away the seam allowance on the top layer but not on the bottom layer. Align the edge of the top layer along the seam line of the bottom layer and sew two rows of stitching along the seam, with the right sides of the fabric facing up.

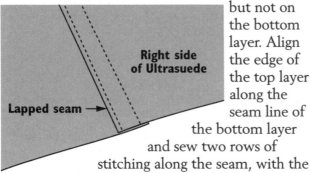

Right side of Ultrasuede

Lapped seam →

Springs Industries

● Always use a press cloth and very little pressure when pressing the right side of the fabric. Use steam sparingly, as satin will water spot.

● Stop seam edges from unraveling by overlocking them with a serger or applying a very thin line of liquid seam sealant before you sew.

Gay Quinn

Ultrasuede for Ultra Contrast

Use leftover pieces of Ultrasuede to accent or contrast woven or knit fabrics. Collars, cuffs, yokes, and band trims look great when made from this opulent fabric.

Springs Industries

No-Stress Seams

In a satin garment, seams can be trouble spots, both when sewing and later as points of wear, because the fabric is so delicate. But you can troubleshoot those seams in the following ways.

● Line or underline fitted bodices and skirts to remove stress from seams so they don't spread and shred.

● Control puckering while stitching by holding the fabric taut behind and in front of the presser foot.

Choose a Fusible

Fuse lightweight tricot interfacing to the wrong side of lamé fabric before you cut. The extra body will help prevent the edges from unraveling.

Marinda Stewart

Be Kind to Your Skin

Fabrics with metallic threads can irritate skin, so line garments or finish seams with a sheer tricot binding.

Elizabeth M. Barry

Get the Rumples Out

Linen is infamous for wrinkling. But if you line a linen garment, the fabric will wrinkle much less when you wear it. You'll also find that wrinkles "hang out" better when the garment is lined.

Richard M. Braun

No Grain, Your Gain

Since faux leather does not have a nap or grain, you can cut pattern pieces off-grain. This will save you money because you'll probably need considerably less fabric than the pattern calls for.

Donna Salyers

Starch, but Hold the Shine

If you use spray starch when you press your linen garments, use a press cloth. This will help to avoid creating a shine on the right side of your garment.

Jane F. Cornell

Lessons for Lamé

When sewing with lamé, use a fine needle and change it often to prevent damage to the fabric from dull or chipped needle surfaces. And because it is difficult to ease lamé fabric when sewing, choose a pattern with few design lines and an unconstructed fit.

Barbara Fimbel

Under the Iron

Wool fabrics tend to stretch when they are ironed, so always steam press them instead.

American Wool Council

The Proper Pin

To ensure that no marks will remain in your Ultrasuede fabric, use long, fine 0.05 mm pins. If you don't want to take a chance with pins, use pattern weights instead.

Springs Industries

 Bright Idea

TO AVOID MARRING SATIN'S LOVELY SURFACE, mark fabric on the wrong side with an air-soluble marking pen or tailor's chalk. When pinning, place the pins in the seam and hem allowances and never on the right side of the fabric.

Robin Rose

Tame Your Faux Fur

You need not be afraid to sew with faux fur. Just follow these simple tips to avoid the most common trouble spots.

- Always use a razor knife and cut with the knitted backing facing up, making sure to work with one thickness at a time, as shown in **Diagram 1.** Gently pull the thicknesses apart to separate them.

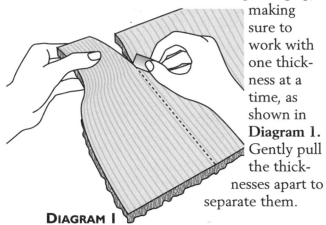

DIAGRAM 1

- Hold the pattern with pattern weights while you trace around it with a chalk pencil or fine-point, felt-tip pen, as shown in **Diagram 2.**

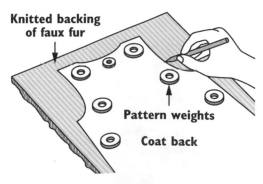

Knitted backing of faux fur

Pattern weights

Coat back

DIAGRAM 2

- Use hair canvas or medium- to heavy-weight nonwoven interfacing when interfacing is necessary.

- Always stitch in the direction of the nap.

- Release any faux fur caught in the stitching of a seam with a T-pin, as shown in **Diagram 3.** Pick out two or three strands of faux fur at a time.

Use a T-pin to release faux fur caught in seam

DIAGRAM 3

- Press the seams open with your fingers and not an iron, which can ruin the nap.

Sonja Dagress

Listen to Your Fabric

To find the grain line on a remnant of fabric with no selvage, grasp the fabric between both hands and tug. Lengthwise grain will produce a loud "snap," and crosswise grain will produce a lower-pitched "thud."

Gay Quinn

Pressing vs. Ironing

Do you know the difference between pressing and ironing your fabric? Pressing involves lifting and lowering the iron lightly on the garment, while ironing involves pushing the iron from side to side along the fabric. If you are working with a fabric that has a tendency to stretch, press, don't iron!

Julia Bernstein

Wear and Care

You'll prolong the life of your wool garments if you follow these simple rules.

- Always hang your garments for 24 hours to give them a rest between wearings.

- Hang your garments on shaped, and preferably padded, hangers.

- Don't hang wool knits. Fold them and store them flat.

- Refresh wools by hanging them in a steamy bathroom.

- If wools get wet, dry them at room temperature away from a heat source.

- Always brush wool garments in the direction of their nap.

American Wool Council

Pinless Pinning

Use paper clips or flat hair clips to hold layers together on hard-to-pin fabrics like fake fur and leather. Both types of clips are easy to attach and leave no permanent marks.

Knitted backing of faux fur

Hair clip

Paper clip

Barbara Fimbel

Machine Wash Your Wool

If the care label on your wool fabric says you can machine wash it, go ahead. Follow the directions to the letter, and use the recommended cleaning product. The wash and rinse cycles should use water of the same temperature because marked changes in temperature can mat wet wool.

American Wool Council

Out, Out Darn Spot!

If you prick your finger and stain your work with blood, dab the spot with a drop of your own saliva before trying any other remedy. The enzymes in your saliva will make the bloodstain easier to remove.

Barbara Fimbel

The Proper Layout and Cut

When laying out your pattern on knit fabric, use the "with nap" layout and cut with straight, not pinking, shears. Pinking shears will cause the edges of your fabric to curl.

Sonja Dagress

Get Over That Seam

Flat-fell seams in denim jeans can be the dickens to sew over by machine. But here's how to get over the problem, literally.

Step 1: To make a hem along the bottom of your pants, sew right up to the flat-fell seam, as shown in **Diagram 1.**

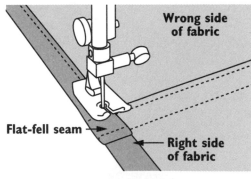

DIAGRAM 1

Step 2: Take one more stitch, placing the needle down into the beginning of the seam, and then lift the presser foot.

Step 3: Place a piece of folded fabric or cardboard that is the same height as the seam under the back of the presser

foot, then lower the foot, as shown in **Diagram 2.** The folded fabric will create a surface even with the seam, so the machine needle can continue smoothly.

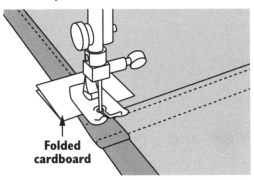

DIAGRAM 2

Barbara Fimbel

Can't Take the Heat

Lamé is great for a steamy look on you, but it requires a cool, dry iron when pressing. Steam will dull the fabric, and heat could melt its surface.

Richard M. Braun

Burn Test

If you don't know the fiber content of a piece of fabric, hold a lighted match to a small swatch. A natural fiber such as silk will burn into ashes, while a synthetic such as polyester will melt and shrivel.

Karen Costello Soltys

Be Pushy with Knits

Knits have a tendency to stretch when sewn because the feed dogs hold onto them more than they do other fabrics. This slows down the movement under the needle. To avoid this problem, gently push your fabric toward the presser foot as you sew.

Barbara Fimbel

Pinning Pile

When working with pile fabric, pin only in the seam allowance to avoid permanent marks on the fabric.

Judi Abbott

New Life for Matted Pile

Renew crushed or matted cotton pile fabric, such as velveteen or corduroy, by tumbling it with a damp towel in your dryer set on low heat. When the towel is dry, the fabric will have new life.

Barbara Fimbel

A Pile of Color

Did you know that the color of pile fabrics is adjustable? Velvet, velveteen, corduroy, and other pile fabrics appear deeper and richer in color when the pile runs upward.

When the pile runs downward, the color appears lighter and slightly silvered. Garments that are constructed with the pile running downward collect less dust and are easier to clean.

Charlotte Biro

Buttons Should Be Smooth as Satin

Finish satin garments with smooth-surfaced buttons. Textured and metal buttons will cause snags or pulls to the delicate satin surface.

Use smooth buttons   **Don't use textured buttons**

Julia Bernstein

A Test of Tension

To see if you need to make any adjustments in your tension when sewing with a pile fabric, test a double layer of scrap fabric first. If the seam looks puckered, try loosening the upper tension. If slippage is a problem, pin or thread basting your garment will help. If all else fails, use an even feed, or walking, foot to further reduce the problem.

Sonja Dagress

Bright Idea

IF YOU DIDN'T PURCHASE ENOUGH ULTRASUEDE FABRIC FOR YOUR PROJECT or if you accidentally cut the fabric in the wrong place, you can cheat a little with your pattern layout and get away with it. Though it's important to cut as many Ultrasuede pieces of your pattern in the same direction as possible, you can cut up to 45 degrees from your chosen direction without causing any apparent difference in the grain line.

Springs Industries

Watch Out, Creep!

When you sew two layers of pile fabric together, the lower layer moves more slowly than the upper layer as you sew. Therefore, it is important to sew *with* the nap rather than *against* it. This will lessen the fabric's tendency to creep and ensure that both layers remain together.

Robin Rose

On a Roll

Although man-made furs are nearly indestructible, they are prone to crushing and creasing. Careful storage will keep your faux fur fresh.

Roll your fabric on a cardboard tube in the direction of the nap, with the pile on the outside. If you don't have a tube, simply roll the fabric into a tube shape, with the cut edge on top. Store it on a shelf by placing a book or brick underneath each end of the tube.

Donna Salyers

Design Basics for Fabulous Fakes

When working with faux fur, the less cutting, stitching, and piecing the better. Fake fur isn't an easy fabric to sew because the pile can be thick and difficult to maneuver under the machine needle, so choose a simple pattern with few seams. Once you've sewn a seam, pick out any threads that have been caught in the stitching, as shown in **Diagram 3** on page 120.

Claudia Larrabure

Keep That Machine Squeaky Clean

If stitches skip when you're sewing on pile fabrics, check your machine. Loose pile fibers can accumulate and interfere with smooth sewing. It's a good idea to clean your machine, particularly the bobbin area, once or twice during your project as you sew with a pile fabric.

Gay Quinn

KNIT-PICKIN'

Do you know how to tell the difference between knit fabrics? This quick lesson will help you tell them apart and facilitate fabric selection the next time you shop.

Barbara Fimbel

KIND OF KNIT	DESCRIPTION	APPEARANCE
Single	These knits are similar in structure to those made by hand knitters. They have a definite front and back. The front is identified by wales, or vertical rows of stitches that look like Vs.	
	The back is recognizable by its courses, or horizontal rows, of loops. Single-knit fabrics curl at the edges when stretched.	
Ribbed	These knits are used when a high degree of stretch is desired. They look the same on the front and back and do not curl. When relaxed, they return to their pre-stretched width.	

Freezer Paper

Freezer paper has made a great leap from the kitchen to the sewing room to become a staple for sewers and quilters alike. If you haven't already discovered the marvelous ways to use freezer paper as a stabilizer, then you're in for a surprise.

Quick-Fold Artist

When repeatedly tracing a symmetrical template for freezer paper appliqué, fold the paper into quarters, as shown in **Diagram 1.** Then trace and cut out your shapes. If, however, you're cutting an equal number of right side and reverse pieces, accordion-fold the paper, with the matte side facing you, as shown in **Diagram 2,** to produce the same number of each.

Freezer paper folded in quarters

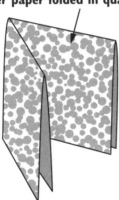

DIAGRAM 1

Freezer paper accordion folded

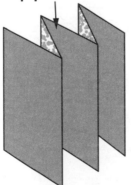

DIAGRAM 2

Robin Rose

A Little Dab'll Do Ya'

When appliquéing with freezer paper, use a liquid glue stick to control fraying as you shape your fabric around the edges of the freezer paper pieces. Follow the heart-shaped example here, then try other shapes.

Step 1: Clip several V-shaped notches into the curves of the fabric heart to make the fabric lie flat when you fold it over the freezer paper. Apply glue around the curved edges of the freezer paper heart. Then fold the fabric tight against the edge of the paper and finger press firmly in place, as shown in **Diagram 1.**

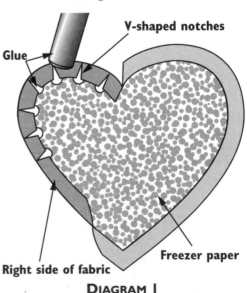

Glue

V-shaped notches

Right side of fabric

Freezer paper

DIAGRAM 1

Step 2: Continue gluing the straight sides of the heart, but do not make any notches before applying the glue. Stop before you reach the point at the bottom of the heart. Turn up the point of the fabric heart onto the freezer paper and note where the point touches the freezer paper. Apply glue to this spot on the freezer paper heart. Then fold up the point of the fabric and finger press it firmly in place, as shown in **Diagram 2.**

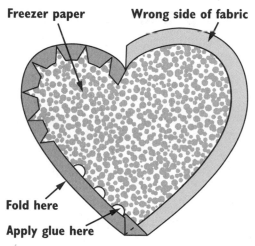

Freezer paper | Wrong side of fabric

Fold here

Apply glue here

DIAGRAM 3

manner as on the left side, as shown in **Diagram 4.** Then follow Steps 5 through 8 in "Easy Appliqué Stabilizer" on page 128 to complete the appliqué process.

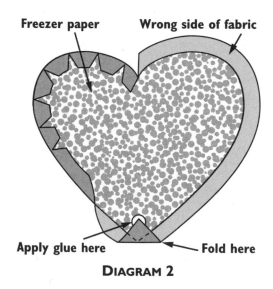

Freezer paper | Wrong side of fabric

Apply glue here | Fold here

DIAGRAM 2

Step 3: Apply glue to the remainder of the left side of the freezer paper heart. It is not necessary to notch the fabric to make it lie flat. Then fold the fabric up over the edge, as shown in **Diagram 3.**

Step 4: Fold up, notch, and glue the fabric on the right side in the same

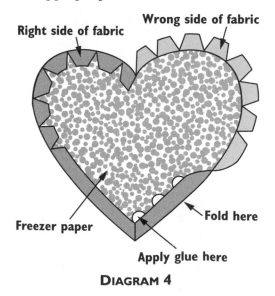

Right side of fabric | Wrong side of fabric

Freezer paper

Fold here

Apply glue here

DIAGRAM 4

Gay Quinn

Freezer Paper

Easy Appliqué Stabilizer

If you like to hand appliqué, freezer paper can save you lots of time. Because it adheres lightly to fabric when ironed, it helps to stabilize shapes during the appliqué process. By folding and pressing the fabric over the edge of the freezer paper, the outline of the appliqué shape will be crisp.

Step 1: Cut out your appliqué shape from freezer paper. Be sure to cut one freezer paper piece for each fabric piece.

Step 2: Pin the nonshiny side of the freezer paper shape to the wrong side of your fabric, as shown in **Diagram 1.**

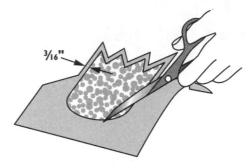

DIAGRAM 2

Step 4: With the freezer paper facing up, clip several V-shaped notches into the edge of the fabric shape so that the fabric will lie flat when folded. Fold the fabric over the edge of the freezer paper, and press the shape lightly with a warm iron, as shown in **Diagram 3.**

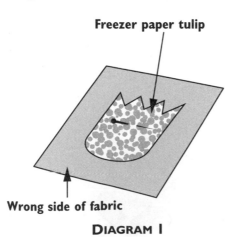

Freezer paper tulip

Wrong side of fabric

DIAGRAM 1

Step 3: Cut out the fabric shape ³⁄₁₆ inch beyond the edge of the freezer paper, as shown in **Diagram 2.**

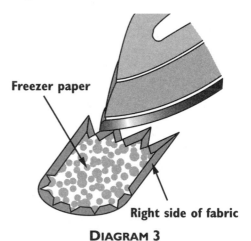

Freezer paper

Right side of fabric

DIAGRAM 3

Step 5: Iron the shape onto the background fabric, then appliqué it in place. When you've finished appliquéing, follow either Step 6 or Steps 7 and 8 to remove the freezer paper.

Step 6: With the wrong side of the background fabric facing up, trim away the fabric behind your shape to within ³⁄₁₆ inch of the edge of the shape, as shown in **Diagram 4.** Then dampen the entire area slightly and gently remove the freezer paper through the opening, as shown in **Diagram 5.**

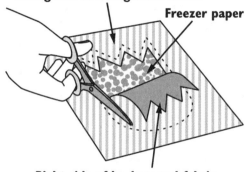

Wrong side of background fabric

Freezer paper

Right side of background fabric

DIAGRAM 4

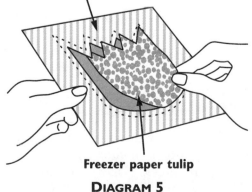

Wrong side of background fabric

Freezer paper tulip

DIAGRAM 5

Step 7: With the wrong side of the background fabric facing up, carefully cut a small slit only in the fabric behind the shape, as shown in **Diagram 6.**

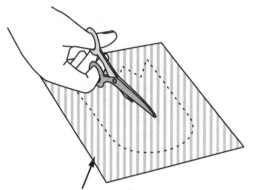

Wrong side of background fabric

DIAGRAM 6

Step 8: Dampen the fabric slightly and gently pull the freezer paper through the slit, as shown in **Diagram 7,** and press the area dry.

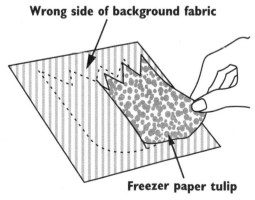

Wrong side of background fabric

Freezer paper tulip

DIAGRAM 7

Margit Echols

SMART SHOPPER

There's no need to purchase specialized stabilizers when you are doing a small amount of decorative machine stitching or embroidery. Freezer paper works just as well and is much less expensive. Lightly press the shiny side of the freezer paper to the wrong side of your fabric, causing the paper to adhere to the fabric. This will prevent your freezer paper stabilizer from shifting as you stitch. When you have finished stitching, gently pull out the freezer paper from the wrong side of your project.

Marya Kissinger Amig

Cut Out for the Job

Freezer paper makes a great stencil for fabric painting. It's thin enough to be folded into quarters for tracing symmetrical designs, such as snowflakes. Plus, freezer paper is more flexible than oak tag.

Step 1: Fold a square of freezer paper into quarters, as shown in **Diagram 1.**

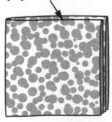

Freezer paper folded into quarters

DIAGRAM 1

Step 2: Draw your design on the freezer paper, as shown in **Diagram 2.** Then cut it out, making sure you don't cut on the folded edge.

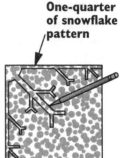

One-quarter of snowflake pattern

DIAGRAM 2

Step 3: Unfold the freezer paper, and your stencil is ready to use, as shown in **Diagram 3.** You'll find that it's sticky enough to use several times before having to replace it.

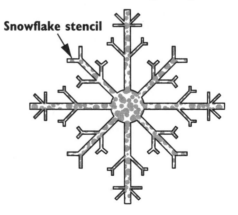

Snowflake stencil

DIAGRAM 3

Julia Bernstein

Pattern Preservation

Freezer paper can give new life to much-used and worn-out pattern pieces. Place your pattern piece, right side up, on top of the shiny side of the freezer paper. Press lightly with a warm iron, making sure you keep the iron on the pattern pieces only. Trim the excess freezer paper, and the pattern will look like new.

Elizabeth M. Barry

Easy-to-Read John Hancock

When making a label to personalize your quilt, you certainly want your signature to be readable. Cut a piece of freezer paper the same size as your label area. Then place the freezer paper, shiny side up, under the wrong side of the quilt where the new label will be. Press lightly with a warm iron. Your newly stablized fabric will be much easier to write on. After your signature has dried, simply peel off the paper.

Right side of fabric

MACHINE QUILTED FOR

_ _ _ _ _ _ _ _ _ _

BY

_ _ _ _ _ _ _ _ _ _

DATE _ _ _ _ _ _ _ _

Freezer paper

Barbara Fimbel

Hems

Although fashion dictates whether hems will be long or short each season, your own figure, height, leg length, and posture should not be ignored. When it comes to hems, there are numerous styles and techniques to choose from. The choice of a hem finish can mean the difference between a homemade and a ready-to-wear look.

The Perfect Blind Hem

Many sewing machines have a built-in blind hem stitch, but many sewers find it difficult to actually produce a blind hem. This is especially true with tightly woven fabrics. To obtain a perfect blind hem, decrease the top tension. This releases more thread into your stitch, allowing the fabric to lay flat. You'll know when the tension is correct because the stitches on the back of the hem will have an unbalanced appearance.

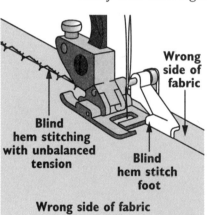

Blind hem stitching with unbalanced tension

Blind hem stitch foot

Wrong side of fabric

Wrong side of fabric

Verna Erickson
Singer Sewing Company

Handsome Hem

Do you love the look of lightweight or sheer fabrics but don't know how to make a nearly invisible hem? This technique produces a narrow finish with a delicate appearance to complement your fabric.

Step 1: On the wrong side of your fabric, mark the hemline of your garment ⅛ inch lower than the finished length you want. Trim the raw edge of your garment so that it is ½ inch from the marked hemline, as shown in **Diagram 1.** Follow the pattern directions to complete your garment, except for the hem.

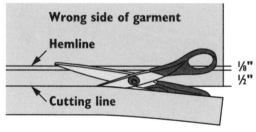

Wrong side of garment

Hemline

Cutting line

⅛"
½"

DIAGRAM 1

Step 2: With the wrong side of your garment facing up, turn up ½ inch along the bottom edge and press it.

Step 3: Edge stitch along the fold of the hem on the right side of your garment, as shown in **Diagram 2.**

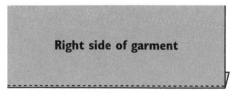

Right side of garment

DIAGRAM 2

Step 4: Turn your garment wrong side out and trim the excess fabric close to your stitching, as shown in **Diagram 3.**

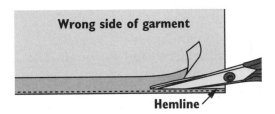

DIAGRAM 3

Step 5: Turn up the hem ⅛ inch and press it.

Step 6: Edge stitch the hem close to the fold, as shown in **Diagram 4.**

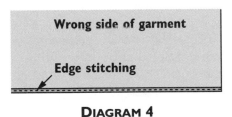

DIAGRAM 4

Janet Klaer

Better Hem Basting

 Purchase a spool of silk thread in an unusual color, like chartreuse, and use it strictly for hand basting hems. The unusual color will make your stitches very easy to spot, and the silk thread will make it easier to remove them.

Elizabeth M. Barry

Hemming Synthetic Suede

 For a soft appearance and a professional finish, synthetic suede should be hemmed by hand. To ensure an even hem, start by setting your machine for a long stitch length and sew ¼ inch from the lower edge of the garment. Then turn up the hem and slip stitch it in place by catching the needle in the machine stitching in the hem instead of sewing through the fabric. Synthetic suede is difficult to penetrate with a needle, so wear a thimble.

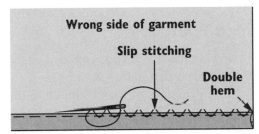

Ronda Chaney

★ Bright Idea ★

TO SEW A NEAT, EVENLY STITCHED HEM BY HAND, try this clever trick. Turn up your hem, press it, and pin it in place. Then pin the hem to a small pillow. Place the pillow in your lap and hem away, repinning as you go! The pillow will keep your hem from stretching and allow you to work on a flat surface.

Karen Kunkel

Hems

Hang That Hem!

Before making a rolled hem in a chiffon skirt or dress, allow the garment to hang for several days first. Because seams are usually sewn on bias edges, this fabric tends to stretch from its weight. By letting the fabric stretch before it's hemmed, you'll avoid a skirt length that grows each time you wear it.

Karen Costello Soltys

Face Your Hem

When fabric is too crisp or too bulky to turn under for a hem, it is more practical to make a faced hem. You can do this in one of two ways.

One method is to purchase a package of hem facing, which already has finished edges, and follow the manufacturer's directions to apply it and finish the hem of your garment.

The second method is to make bias binding. If you have a lightweight fabric in a color similar to your garment, cut a 2-inch-wide bias strip to fit around the lower edge of your garment plus 1¼ inches. Fold the bias strip in half crosswise, with wrong sides facing, and sew the short ends together with a ⅝-inch seam allowance. Press the seam open. With the wrong side facing up, turn up a ⅝-inch hem along one raw edge of the bias strip and press.

With right sides together, pin the remaining edge of the bias strip to the lower edge of your garment. Sew the strip to your garment using a ⅝-inch seam allowance. Trim the fabric close to the stitching. Turn up the hem of your garment and sew it in place.

You'll see how much easier it is to sew through the layer of facing and fabric instead of two layers of fabric.

House of Fabrics
So-Fro Fabrics

Hemming a Ruffle

Hemming circular ruffles can be challenging. Here are three options to ensure smooth sewing.

- Line the ruffle using self-fabric or fabric that is lighter in weight or a contrasting color. There is no hem to worry about.

- Machine stitch ¼ inch from the raw edge of your ruffle. With the wrong side of the ruffle facing up, turn up the stitched edge ¼ inch and press. Stitch close to the fold, using a short stitch length. Trim the fabric close to the stitching. Turn up another ¼ inch to enclose the raw edge of the fabric, and edge stitch the hem in place.

- Serge a narrow rolled hem.

House of Fabrics
So-Fro Fabrics

Hemming Along

For added stability in lightweight fabrics, use pinking shears and cut a strip of tricot interfacing slightly less than the width of the garment's hem. Fuse the interfacing to the wrong side of the hem area before turning up the hem and sewing it in place.

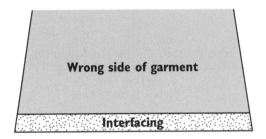

Linda Griepentrog

A Stitch in Time

To save time when hemming or basting by hand, I keep a separate pincushion handy with sewing needles threaded with long lengths of thread. This way I don't have to stop and rethread my needle while working on a garment.

Elizabeth M. Barry

Fast Fuse It!

If hemming is your least favorite sewing task, then try this no-sew approach. First, snip the lower edge of your garment with pinking shears.

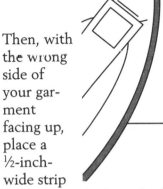

Then, with the wrong side of your garment facing up, place a ½-inch-wide strip of fusible web along the hemline. Fold up the hem and iron over a press cloth to fuse the web in place. This works best on sportswear and casual garments. Remember to test the web on a scrap of your fabric first.

Karen Kunkel

Serge to the Finish

My favorite hemming technique for knit fabrics is a serged finish. After serging the raw edge on my garment, I turn the hem to the wrong side. Then I use a regular or twin needle to topstitch the hem in place with a

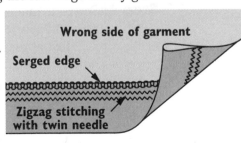

straight or zigzag stitch. The diagram shows the effect of topstitching with a twin needle. For an even speedier finish, try substituting fusible thread in the lower looper when serging and fuse the hem in place instead of topstitching it.

Lori Bottom

Hemming Round the Curve

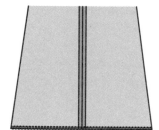

Try this technique for achieving a smooth curve when hemming a full skirt.

Step 1: Finish the lower edge of your garment with a serger or by turning under ¼ inch and machine or hand sewing it in place, as shown in **Diagram 1**.

Step 3: Turn up the hem and pin it in place. Pull up the gathering stitches where the hem requires easing to lie flat, then repin the hem in place, as shown in **Diagram 3**.

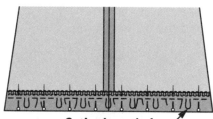

Gathering stitches
pulled to ease hem

DIAGRAM 3

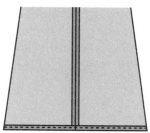

Finished with a serger

Finished with a sewing machine

DIAGRAM 1

Step 4: Blindstitch the hem in place by hand, catching the needle in the serged stitching instead of through the fabric, as shown in **Diagram 4**.

Step 2: Set your machine for a long stitch length, and sew a row of gathering stitches just above the finished edge, as shown in **Diagram 2**.

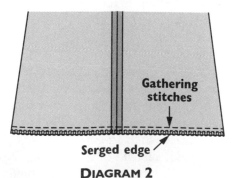

Gathering
stitches

Serged edge

DIAGRAM 2

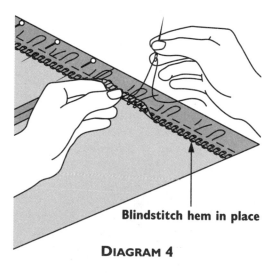

Blindstitch hem in place

DIAGRAM 4

Glynda Black

Sheer Elegance by Hand

Elegant hems for full-skirted garments in chiffon, georgette, and voile are best achieved with a hand-rolled edge finish.

Step 1: Turn up ⅛ inch along the raw edge of your garment.

Step 2: Thread a hand-sewing needle and anchor the thread inside the fold, as shown in **Diagram 1**. Take a tiny stitch in the garment just above the raw edge.

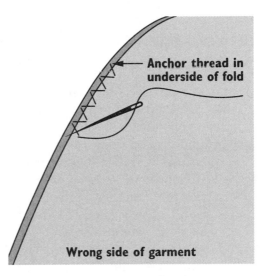

Anchor thread in underside of fold

Wrong side of garment

DIAGRAM 2

Step 4: After sewing five or six stitches, pull on the thread so the stitches automatically draw the hem into a roll, as shown in **Diagram 3**.

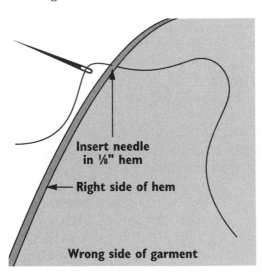

Insert needle in ⅛" hem

Right side of hem

Wrong side of garment

DIAGRAM 1

Step 3: Now take a tiny stitch at the fold. Continue stitching in this manner for five or six stitches, making sure to space each stitch about ¼ inch apart, as shown in **Diagram 2**.

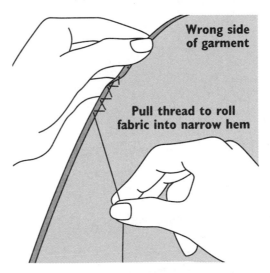

Wrong side of garment

Pull thread to roll fabric into narrow hem

DIAGRAM 3

House of Fabrics
So-Fro Fabrics

Hems

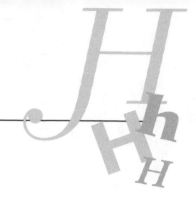

Let Your Friend Do All the Work

For the best possible hemming results, have a friend mark the hemline on your garment while you're wearing it. Try on the garment with the shoes you plan to wear with it. Then stand in one spot with your feet together. Let your friend move around you, measuring to establish an even hemline and pin marking. The pins should be placed parallel to the floor about 2 to 3 inches apart.

Simplicity Pattern Company

Easy Iron Basting

Why waste time basting or even stitching your hems in place? To save time, just follow these simple steps.

Step 1: Finish the edge of your hem by either of the following methods. If you finish the edge of your hem on a serger, replace the thread in your lower looper with fusible thread, and serge along the edge of your hem. If you finish the edge of your hem on a sewing machine, fill a bobbin with fusible thread, place it in your machine, and fold over and edge stitch your hem on the right side.

Step 2: Fold up your fabric along the hemline, and pin it in place.

Step 3: Place a nonstick pressing sheet over your hem. Using the tip of your iron, lightly press the edge of your hem to your garment. The fusible thread will melt and hold your hem in place. If desired, you can stitch your hem by hand or machine. A good-quality fusible thread will maintain its bond through washing and dry cleaning.

Marya Kissinger Amig

HEMMING DO'S AND DON'TS

Here are a few do's and don'ts to remember when sewing a hem by hand.

Karen Kunkel

Do	Don't
Ask for assistance when marking your hem	Forget to wear the same shoes you'll wear with your garment when the hem is being marked
Work on a flat surface	Thread a needle with more than a 20-inch length of thread
Secure the first stitch in place with a backstitch	Secure the first stitch with a bulky knot
Secure the last stitch in place with several backstitches	Secure the last stitch with a bulky knot

Interfacing

Every beautifully tailored garment owes its good looks and longevity to a carefully hidden secret—interfacing. It adds shape, strength, and body to garments. You can use interfacing to create a structured or soft tailored look. With the tremendous variety of fusible and sew-in interfacings on the market today, it takes time to become familiar with them all. Here's what you need to know.

Turning Up the Heat

If your iron doesn't provide enough heat and steam for a good bond between the interfacing and fabric, use a piece of aluminum foil as a reflective surface, intensifying the heat and steam of your iron.

Simply place a sheet of aluminum foil on your ironing board underneath the layers to be fused. Then iron for the full amount of time recommended by the interfacing manufacturer. Never slide the iron to fuse the interfacing to your fabric. Lift it, then lower it, overlapping the same areas throughout the surface, as shown. Go through the fusing process twice, first on the wrong side of your pattern pieces, then on the right side. This will ensure a strong bond and no missed spots. Remember to use the recommended press cloth when pressing on the right side of your fabric pieces.

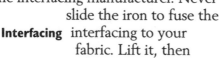

Interfacing

Press cloth

Butterick Company

Interface with Care

When selecting interfacing, make sure you read the information on the package carefully. Your choice of interfacing must have the same care instructions as your fabric. A permanent press interfacing doesn't belong in a silk blouse, and a dry clean–only interfacing is a poor choice for a machine-wash-and-dry fabric. The directions that come with the interfacing tell you everything you need to know about its performance, care requirements, and application. When you have finished interfacing your garment, store the directions with your leftover interfacing so you'll have them the next time you use the interfacing.

Marya Kissinger Amig

A Weighty Matter

When selecting interfacing for your garment, you should choose one that is slightly lighter in weight than your fabric. If you opt for a fusible interfacing rather than a sew-in type, your garment will feel crisper. This is the result of the reaction between the bonding agent in the interfacing and the heat of your iron.

Butterick Company

Applying Sew-Ins

If you aren't sure how to apply sew-in interfacing to garments, here are some pointers to help you achieve a professional look.

◉ Use a glue stick or pins to baste the interfacing in place on the wrong side of your fabric. Be sure to match seam lines and markings. Hand or machine baste the interfacing in place ½ inch from the raw edges. Trim the interfacing close to the stitching and clip the corners, as shown in **Diagram 1**. This will reduce bulk when turning the piece right side out.

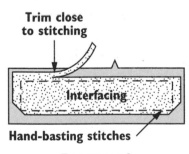

Trim close to stitching

Interfacing

Hand-basting stitches

DIAGRAM 1

◉ For garments that have a self-facing area on the pattern piece, such as a jacket or blouse front, cut the interfacing from this area of the pattern piece. Then hand baste the interfacing to your jacket or blouse front along the fold line. Baste the interfacing in place along the seam lines by hand or machine, and then trim the interfacing close to the basting stitches, as shown in **Diagram 2**.

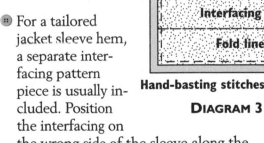

Fold line → ← **Interfacing**

Hand-basting stitches

DIAGRAM 2

◉ For fully inter-faced pattern pieces, such as waist-bands and cuffs, first baste the interfacing to the wrong side of your garment piece along the outer edges. Then hand baste it in place along the fold line, as shown in **Diagram 3**.

Trim close to stitching

Interfacing

Fold line

Hand-basting stitches

DIAGRAM 3

◉ For a tailored jacket sleeve hem, a separate inter-facing pattern piece is usually in-cluded. Position the interfacing on the wrong side of the sleeve along the hemline. Referring to **Diagram 4**, hand baste the interfacing in place along the vent fold line and the sleeve hem-line. Hand baste the upper edge, catching only one thread of fabric so that the stitches don't show on the right side.

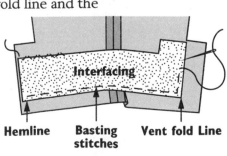

Interfacing

Hemline   **Basting stitches**   **Vent fold Line**

DIAGRAM 4

Butterick Company

Interfacing

Coordinate Colors

Interfacings don't come in a wide range of colors, so choose one that matches the color of your fabric as closely as possible. Use a light interfacing with light-color fabrics and a dark interfacing with dark ones. Little threads or edges of the interfacing can show around buttonholes or other cut edges, so the interfacing should be as inconspicuous as possible.

Butterick Company

Preshrinking Fusibles

To preshrink fusible interfacing, cover it with hot water and let it stand until the water cools. Then hang the interfacing to dry.

Marya Kissinger Amig

Applying Fusibles

Fusible interfacings are easy to apply but take a little patience and practice. Here are a few surefire tips to help you get started.

Step 1: Cut out the interfacing pieces. To reduce bulk, trim ½ inch from all seam allowances before fusing.

Step 2: Pin the interfacing, sticky side down, to the wrong side of the fabric, matching seam lines and markings. Steam baste the interfacing in po-

sition with the tip of your iron, pressing lightly at a few points around the edges, as shown in **Diagram 1.**

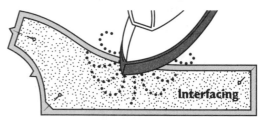

DIAGRAM 1

Step 3: Remove the pins, then fuse the interfacing into position permanently, following the interfacing manufacturer's directions, as shown in **Diagram 2.** If your iron is lightweight, you may have to add some pressure to ensure a tight bond. Try lowering your ironing board so you can lean harder on the iron and help the fusing process.

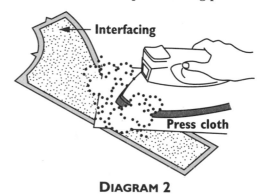

DIAGRAM 2

Step 4: Let the fabric cool thoroughly, then check the bond. If you missed any spots, repeat the fusing procedure in those areas.

Butterick Company

Getting out of a Sticky Situation

If you accidentally get fusible interfacing on the sole plate of your iron, don't panic. Remove it while the iron is still warm by gently rubbing the area with a small piece of steel wool until the spot is completely gone. The interfacing won't harm your iron, and you can continue ironing immediately.

This method should not be used on an iron with a Teflon sole plate. If you have a Teflon sole plate, use a plastic scrubber instead.

Karen Costello Soltys

Don't Come Unglued

A good bond between your fabric and the fusible interfacing is the key to success. Heat, pressure, and moisture are all required. Since techniques vary slightly from interfacing manufacturer to manufacturer, it is important to follow the fusing directions that come with your interfacing to the letter. Some directions tell you to use a dry iron and a damp press cloth, while others instruct you to use a steam iron and a dry press cloth. These little variations matter, so follow directions, and your interfacing won't come unglued from the fabric.

Butterick Company

 Bright Idea

I KEEP AN INTERFACING REFERENCE LIBRARY to help me become more familiar with different types of interfacing. I save a small square of fabric and a piece of the interfacing I used with it from each sewing project. I label the samples and place them in large plastic sleeves. Then I file the plastic sleeves in a three-ring notebook. I keep a separate notebook for fusible interfacings and sew-in interfacings. After a while, choosing the proper interfacing for future projects becomes a breeze.

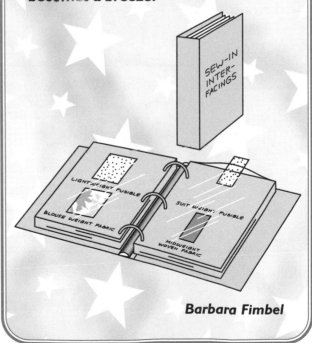

Barbara Fimbel

Interfacing

THE READY REFERENCE GUIDE TO FUSIBLE INTERFACINGS

Today's choice of interfacings can be mind-boggling if you don't know where to begin. Should you choose a sew-in or a fusible? Do you need a lightweight cotton or a heavyweight? Can you throw it in the washer, or should it be dry-cleaned? The more you understand about interfacings, the better your garments will look. So take a few minutes to become better acquainted with the interfacings listed here. You may even want to take this with you on your next trip to the fabric store!

Barbara Fimbel

	PRODUCT NAME	IDEAL FOR	COLOR CHOICES	TYPE OF WEAVE	DIRECTION OF STRETCH	CARE INSTRUCTIONS
LIGHTWEIGHT FABRICS	Pellon Fusible 906F	Sheer to light-weight fabrics	White, beige, and charcoal	Nonwoven	Crosswise	Machine wash and dry
	HTC Sheer D'light Featherweight and Sheer D'Light Lightweight	Lightweight knits and wovens	White and charcoal	Nonwoven	Crosswise	Machine wash and tumble dry
	HTC So-Sheer	Wovens; laces; lightweight knits. It can also be used as an under-lining.	White, ivory, and black	Knit	Crosswise	Machine wash and tumble dry
SOFT MIDWEIGHT FABRICS	Dritz Knit Fuze	Tricot knit	White, beige, and black	Knit	Crosswise	Machine wash and dry
	Dritz Soft 'N Silky	Knit	White and black	Warp insertion knit	All directions	Machine wash and dry

	Product Name	Ideal For	Color Choices	Type of Weave	Direction of Stretch	Care Instructions
SOFT MIDWEIGHT FABRICS	HTC Fusi-Knit	Lightweight and mid-weight knits and wovens. It can also be used as an underlining.	White, black, ivory, and gray	Knit	Crosswise	Machine wash and dry
	HTC Sofbrush	Silks	White, black, and ivory	Warp insertion knit	All directions	Dry-clean
	Stacy Easy-Knit	Lightweight to heavyweight fabrics	White, black, and natural	Knit	All directions	Machine wash and tumble dry or dry-clean
	Pellon Fusible 911	Dress-weight fabrics	White and gray	Nonwoven	All directions	Machine wash and dry
CRISP MIDWEIGHT FABRICS	Dritz Shape Maker All-Purpose	Crisp shaping in wovens	White and black	Woven	Doesn't stretch	Machine wash and dry
	Stacy Shape-Flex All-Purpose Pellon	Crisp support in detail areas in 100% cotton	White	Woven	Doesn't stretch	Machine wash and tumble dry
	HTC Form-Flex All Purpose	Firm support in 100% cotton	White and black	Woven	Doesn't stretch	Delicate machine wash and tumble dry

(continued)

Interfacing

THE READY REFERENCE GUIDE TO FUSIBLE INTERFACINGS—Continued

PRODUCT NAME	IDEAL FOR	COLOR CHOICES	TYPE OF WEAVE	DIRECTION OF STRETCH	CARE INSTRUCTIONS
HTC Armo Form-Flex, Nonwoven	Firm support and stability	White	Nonwoven	Doesn't stretch	Machine wash and dry
HTC Armo Fusi-Form Suitweight	Firm support in knits and wovens	White and charcoal	Nonwoven	Crosswise	Machine wash and dry
HTC Armo Weft	Soft tailoring in knits and wovens	White, black, gray, and beige	Weft insertion knit	Doesn't stretch	Machine wash and tumble dry
Pellon Fusible 931TD	Wovens or knits	White	Nonwoven	Crosswise	Machine wash and dry
Pellon Sof-Shape 880F	Soft shaping in dresses, suits, and sportswear	White and gray	Nonwoven	All directions	Machine wash and dry
Dritz Shape-Up Suitweight	Midweight knits and wovens; suits; coats; tailored dresses	White and charcoal	Nonwoven	Crosswise	Dry-clean
Dritz Suit Maker	Tailoring wovens and knits; simulates hair canvas	Natural	Weft insertion knit	Doesn't stretch	Machine wash and dry
Pellon Pel-Aire 881F	Midweight suit fabric	Natural and gray	Nonwoven	Doesn't stretch	Machine wash and dry

MIDWEIGHT TO HEAVYWEIGHT FABRICS

THE READY REFERENCE GUIDE TO SEW-IN INTERFACINGS

	Product Name	Ideal For	Color Choices	Type of Weave	Direction of Stretch	Care Instructions
LIGHTWEIGHT FABRICS	Pellon Sew-In 905	Blouse-weight fabrics; knits; wovens; silks; laces	White and beige	Nonwoven	Crosswise	Machine wash and dry
	HTC Armo Intra-Face Bias Featherweight	Lightweight stretch wovens and knits	White	Nonwoven	All directions	Machine wash and dry
	Dritz Sew-In Durapress	Gentle support in knits and wovens	White and black	Woven	Crosswise	Machine wash and dry
	HTC Armo Press Soft	Wovens	White and black	Woven	Doesn't stretch	Machine wash and tumble dry
MIDWEIGHT FABRICS	HTC Armo Intra-face Mediumweight	Soft shaping in wovens	White	Woven	Doesn't stretch	Machine wash and dry
	HTC Armo Press Firm	Detail areas in wovens	White and black	Woven	Doesn't stretch	Machine wash and tumble dry
	HTC Form Flex Woven	Soft shaping in wovens	White	100% cotton woven	Doesn't stretch	Machine wash and dry
	Pellon Sew-In 910	Soft shaping in dress-weight fabrics	White and gray	Nonwoven	All directions	Machine wash and dry

Linings

Linings not only prolong the life of your garments but they also make them more comfortable to wear. Many of us never seem to find the time to line our garments, but believe it or not, it is faster to line them than not to! If your garment feels complete, you'll feel good about yourself and your sewing accomplishments.

Give It Some Shape

An underlining helps to add shape to a garment. Underlining can be made from fabric or interfacing, and it is sewn or fused to the garment fabric, and the two pieces are treated as one. When underlining large sections of a garment, use a woven or weft insertion interfacing. Cut it on the bias for maximum drapability, or use the straight grain for optimum stability.

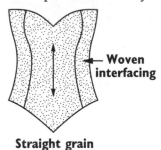

— Woven interfacing

Straight grain

Lisa Shepard
Handler Textile Corporation

Collar and Cuff Camouflage

Hide the seam allowance of a collar and cuffs made from lace or crocheted fabrics by lining them with organdy or organza fabric. The pieces will take on a lovely opaque cast and still retain their lacy look.

House of Fabrics
So-Fro Fabrics

Lining to the Edge

Did you know that a lined-to-the-edge vest can be sewn almost entirely by machine? This method is great because it's simple, quick, and encases all of the raw edges so there isn't a need to turn under and sew the raw edges of the seam allowances. After you try it once, you'll want to line all of your vests this way.

Step 1: Cut out your vest pieces from your fabric, then cut identical vest pieces from your lining.

Step 2: With right sides together, sew the shoulder seams of the vest together with a ⅝-inch seam allowance. Repeat for the lining. Press all seams open.

Step 3: With right sides together, pin the lining to the vest, making sure raw edges are even. Using a ⅝-inch seam allowance, sew the layers together along the neckline, front, armhole, and lower edges, making sure to leave the side seams open, as shown in **Diagram 1.** Clip the corners and trim the seam allowances. Turn the vest right side out through the side seams, as shown in **Diagram 2,** and press.

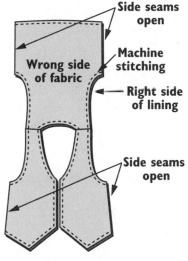

DIAGRAM 1

Step 5: Turn under and press a ⅝-inch seam allowance along the open side seams of the lining. Slip stitch the side seams closed, as shown in Diagram 3.

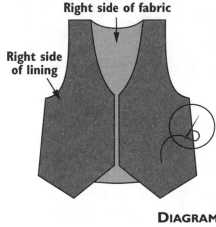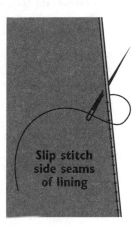

DIAGRAM 3

Nancy Nix-Rice

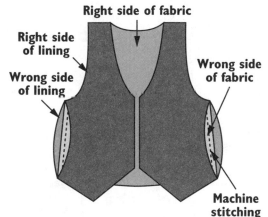

DIAGRAM 2

Step 4: With right sides facing, pin the sides of the vest together, and pin 1 to 2 inches of the lining together at the underarms and bottom edges. With a ⅝-inch seam allowance, start sewing the lining together at the point you pinned near the armhole, and continue sewing the vest sides and into the lining at the bottom edge. Press the seams open.

★ Bright Idea ★

THE BEST WAY TO LINE A VELVET GARMENT IS TO UNDERLINE IT FIRST WITH FLANNEL. Because the underlining will never be seen, I sometimes have fun and use a flannel fabric with a juvenile print. One time I made a cape for a customer and used a baby print flannel for the underlining!

Kenneth D. King

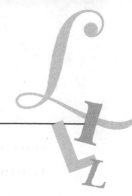

Bright Idea

RECYCLED TERRY CLOTH TOWELS MAKE GREAT LININGS FOR GARMENTS and other items that constantly need to be washed, such as children's bibs, hats, and bathrobes.

Karen Kunkel

Lining an Unlined Jacket

Here's an easy-to-follow technique for lining an unlined jacket.

Step 1: Place the center back of your jacket pattern piece 1½ inches from the fold of the lining fabric, as shown in **Diagram 1**. Mark the center back with a chalk pencil, and extend the pattern lines to the fold line. Cut out your pattern. You will now have a lining back that is 3 inches wider than your jacket back.

Fold

Jacket back pattern

1½"

Selvage

DIAGRAM 1

Step 2: Make a 5-inch slash in the jacket front pattern piece from the center of the shoulder to the bust point, as shown in **Diagram 2**.

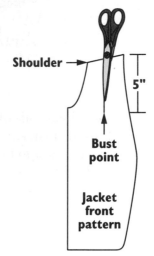

Shoulder →

5"

Bust point

Jacket front pattern

DIAGRAM 2

Step 3: Spread the slashed area of the pattern 2 inches apart at the shoulder, as shown in **Diagram 3**. Pin the jacket front pattern piece to your lining fabric and cut two pieces, making sure you transfer the slash lines to the lining pieces. They will be used to make darts.

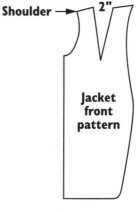

Shoulder →

2"

Jacket front pattern

DIAGRAM 3

Step 4: Assemble the jacket lining following the pattern directions, with two exceptions. Fold a pleat in the extra 3 inches in the center back of your jacket lining. Sew the pleat to the lining. Then, to ensure that the pleat lies flat, hand tack it in place at

the neck, waist, and hem, as shown in **Diagram 4.**

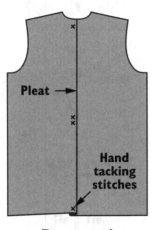

DIAGRAM 4

Step 5: Fold and sew an open-ended dart on each lining front piece, following the slash lines, as shown in **Diagram 5.** Assemble and sew the lining into your jacket.

DIAGRAM 5

Janis Bullis

Underarm Comfort

If you've ever had a jacket lining pull and bunch up at the underarm, then follow my all-time favorite tip to solve this problem. A simple pattern adjustment is all it takes to add just the right amount of ease under the arm.

Before cutting the lining, draw a new cutting line on the front, back, and sleeve pattern pieces as follows. Beginning at the armhole on the front pattern piece, add ⅝ inch to the pattern. Taper to nothing as you approach the arm-

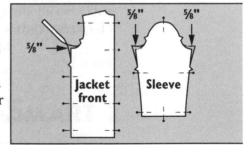

hole notch in one direction and the side seam notch in the other direction, as shown. Do the same for the back and sleeve pieces. Then sew your jacket together according to the pattern directions.

Claire Shaeffer

Don't Skirt the Issue

If you want your skirts to look professionally made, line them. A lining helps the skirt hold its shape, wrinkle less, and stay fresh longer.

Claire Shaeffer

Pink It

When only a partial underlining is called for, trim the edges of the interfacing with pinking shears. This will create a smooth line and make the interfacing line almost invisible on the right side of your garment.

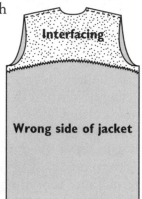

Interfacing

Wrong side of jacket

Lisa Shepard
Handler Textile Corporation

No-Show Lining

When lining a garment with a white background, be sure to select a solid white lining fabric. Test your lining choice by holding it up to the light. If you can see through it, don't use it.

Clotilde

Save Time and Underline

Instead of lining a jacket, which is time-consuming, I underline it. This method works well with any unlined jacket pattern. Simply cut the front, back, and sleeve pieces from your fashion lining and fabrics.

Pin together the fabric and lining, with wrong sides facing and raw edges even. Serge or sew along the outer edges to create one underlined piece. Then construct your jacket from these lined pieces according to the pattern directions. Try this technique on skirts and pants, too, but remember, it doesn't replace the interfacing.

Sue Hausmann
Viking/White
Sewing Machine Companies

Serge a Strong Seam

The fastest way to sew the strongest lining for your garment is to serge it using the widest 3-, 4-, or 5-thread stitch. The extra threads will make it nearly impossible for your seams to tear.

Gail Brown

Interface to Underline

I always use a second layer of fusible interfacing as an underlining on jacket fronts. It allows the garment to skim the body, and the garment hold its shape splendidly.

Cut one layer of interfacing from the front pattern. Then cut another layer for the area above your bust. Fuse the first layer to the second and insert it into your jacket front so that the longer layer is against the fabric.

For a more subtle look, cut the front interfacing on the bias.

Claire Shaeffer

Lengthen That Stitch

Do front facings seem to shrink after you sew them to your jacket front? If so, then increase your stitch length when sewing. This will reduce puckers and pulls as you sew through multiple layers of fabric. And if you're planning to use piping, increase your stitch length even more.

Sandra Betzina

If They Could See through You Now

To test if a light-color fabric needs a lining, wrap the yardage around your body while standing in your undergarments in the sunlight or a well-lit room. If you can see through the fabric, your garment needs to be lined.

Laurel Hoffmann

Line on the Cross Grain

Cut the lining or underlining of a slim skirt on the cross grain of your fabric, making sure to align the lower edge along the selvage. Not only will the extra strength of the grain protect the seat of the skirt fabric from wearing out but you also won't have to hem the lining!

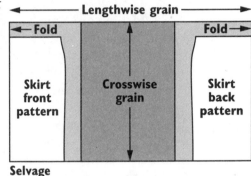

Nancy Nix-Rice

SMART SHOPPER

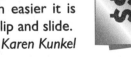

When shopping for lining material, avoid acetate. Instead, choose a firmly woven, stable fabric, such as crepe or blouse-weight polyester. You'll be surprised at how much easier it is to sew because it doesn't slip and slide.

Karen Kunkel

Machine Quilting

Quilting by machine is speedier than quilting by hand, but it takes just as much patience and skill to master. It gives you the freedom to work over large areas with few starts and stops. Decorative threads and intricate machine stitching allow you to embellish your garments and quilts with intriguing contrasts of color and texture.

Take a Break

Machine quilting can be a pain in your neck, shoulders, back, and hands. As you work with your head bent and your hands and arms strained to push and pull the fabric, you become tense, and your muscles tighten up. So remember to stop at regular intervals, such as after a certain number of rows of quilting or after completing a motif or two. Stand up and stretch and flex your muscles. Slowly bend your neck from side to side. Relax it backward and then forward. Move your shoulders up and down. Wiggle your fingers. A bit of exercise is good for you, and what's good for you is good for your quilt!

Jan Burns

For Less Stretch

When joining long strips, alternate the direction of your sewing to eliminate excess stretching. Sew your first seam from top to bottom. Then turn your work around, and sew the second seam from bottom to top. Keep alternating your sewing in this manner until you've sewn all of your strips together.

Barbara Fimbel

Keep Layers from Wandering

Do you have a problem keeping your backing fabric in place as you put your quilt layers together? If so, try this simple solution. With the wrong side of your backing fabric facing up, tape all edges to a flat surface, making sure the fabric is taut and smooth. Then place a layer of batting on top of your backing fabric, and place your quilt top right side up on the batting. Finally, pin the layers together.

Jill Abeloe Mead

Play It Safe with Safety Pins

When doing any type of free-motion quilting, I never take a chance with straight pins. Instead, I pin baste my fabric, batting, and backing together with rustproof safety pins. This is a surefire way to guarantee the pins will stay put as I sew. Beginning at the center of my work, I place the pins at 3- to 4-inch intervals over the surface of my fabric. I pin evenly out toward all edges, smoothing the fabric as I go. Then I can concentrate on my quilting, and I don't have to worry about losing any pins.

Jill Abeloe Mead

Is Your Batting Relaxed?

To get the maximum use from your batting, let it relax first. Unfold it and let it stand overnight to remove any creases or folds. This will make pinning, basting, and stitching easier.

Julia Bernstein

Quick Patchwork

Use the stripe in your fabric to reduce the amount of piecing in your project and still retain the patchwork effect.

Step 1: Cut your fabric into strips, making sure you add a ¼-inch seam allowance on either side of the strip. Cut the strips against the stripe. For example, if your fabric has horizontal stripes, cut it vertically. If your fabric has vertical stripes, cut it horizontally, as shown in **Diagram 1.**

Cut striped fabric into strips

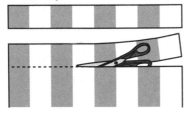

DIAGRAM I

Step 2: Sew the strips together using a variety of combinations to give you different patchwork looks. Try alter-

nating the colors, as shown in **Diagram 2A.** Or rejoin the strips but stagger the placement of the color, as shown in **2B.** Or cut different-width strips and create the variation shown in **2C.**

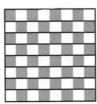 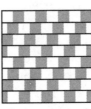 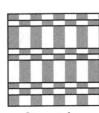

Sew strips together to create a patchwork look	Sew staggered strips together	Sew strips of different widths together
A	B	C

DIAGRAM 2

Jacquelyn Smyth

SMART SHOPPER

Add a little pizzazz to your machine quilting with metallic thread. Replace monofilament nylon thread with metallic thread, and change the needle to a special machine embroidery or Metalfil needle. Both needles have a larger eye, which makes them easier to thread and produces less stress as you sew. For best results, sew at an even-paced, medium speed. Sewing fast and then slowing down will only result in a tangled knot of threads.

Jill Abeloe Mead

Nine Patch in a Hurry

This quick-and-easy method for making a Nine Patch block uses only two different-color fabrics. But once you've mastered the technique, try several different colors at once.

Step 1: Begin with equal amounts of fabric in two different solids or prints. Designate one fabric as A and the other one as B.

Step 2: To figure out how wide to cut each strip of fabric, determine the finished size you want for your Nine Patch block and divide it by three. For example, if your finished block size is 9 inches square, and you divide that by 3, then each of the nine squares making up the design will have a finished size of 3 inches. Then add ¼ inch to each side of the strip for seam allowances, and the final measurement for the width of your strips is 3½ inches.

Step 3: Cut your fabric into the correct-width strips.

Step 4: Position two strips of fabric A and one strip of fabric B, with the B strip between the two A strips. Sew the strips together using a ¼-inch seam allowance, as shown in **Diagram 1.** Press the seam allowance to one side.

Step 5: Repeat Step 4 with one strip of fabric A and two strips of fabric B, as shown in **Diagram 2.**

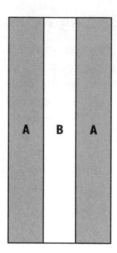

DIAGRAM 1

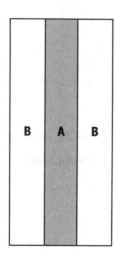

DIAGRAM 2

Step 6: Place your pieced strips horizontally on a flat surface, and cut them into 3½-inch-wide strips using scissors or a cutting mat and rotary cutter, as shown in **Diagram 3.**

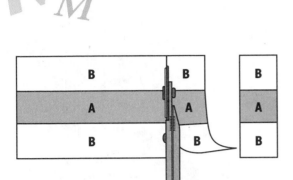

DIAGRAM 3

Step 7: Align two different 3½-inch strips, as shown in **Diagram 4.** Then with right sides facing, sew the strips together with a ¼-inch seam allowance.

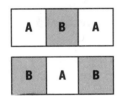

DIAGRAM 4

Step 8: Complete one Nine-Patch block by sewing a third strip to the first two, making sure it matches the second, as shown in **Diagram 5.** Make as many blocks as you need to complete your project.

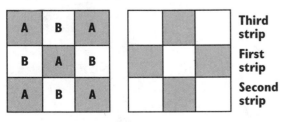

DIAGRAM 5

Charlotte Biro

 Bright Idea

WHEN SEWING QUILTED GARMENTS, YOU CAN AVOID THE STUFFY AND STIFF LOOK that sometimes results when fleece or low-loft batting is used. Simply purchase a baby-weight or light-weight flannel for your batting. Your vests and jackets will be less bulky and will drape much better.

Karen Bolesta

Cut It with Care

When I plan to machine quilt a garment, I cut my pattern pieces at least 2 inches larger on all sides. Because the fabric is pulled toward the center as I quilt, I don't want to run the risk of making my garment too small. When I'm finished quilting, I simply repin my pattern to the fabric and recut the pieces if necessary.

Jill Abeloe Mead

North, South, East, West

To prevent your fabric layers from shifting as you machine quilt, first do some quilting in different areas of your project, for example, in the center and in each of the corners. Then quilt the rest of your project.

Karen Costello Soltys

Free-Motion Warm-Up

Free-motion machine quilting is a technique that will give you hours of sewing pleasure. It is a key part of stipple and echo quilting, as well as quilting around curved patterns. The secret to success is practice, practice, practice. This exercise will get you started.

Step 1: Thread your machine with a dark all-purpose thread in the top and a contrasting thread in the bobbin. Lower or cover the feed dogs and insert a machine quilting or top-stitching needle. Attach a darning foot and set the presser foot lifter in the darning position.

Step 2: Sandwich an 18-inch square of lightweight batting between two 18-inch muslin squares, and hold the layers together by inserting a safety pin into each corner. With a pencil, draw a 3-inch-diameter circle in the center of the top square. Then write the word "bottom" along one edge.

Step 3: Place the sandwich under the darning foot so the needle is at the top of the circle and the bottom edge of the square is closest to you, as shown in **Diagram 1.** Turn the flywheel by hand and take one stitch. Bring the bobbin thread to the right side of your work, then take two stitches in place to secure the threads. Cut the thread ends close to the fabric.

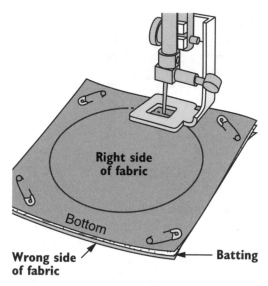

DIAGRAM 1

Step 4: Using your hands as an embroidery hoop, stretch the fabric taut. Working in a clockwise motion, move the fabric as you sew around the circle. Make sure the word "bottom" faces you at all times, as shown in **Diagrams 2** and **3.**

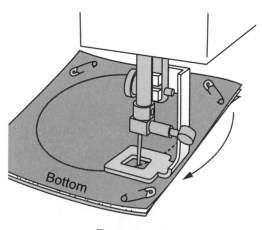

DIAGRAM 2

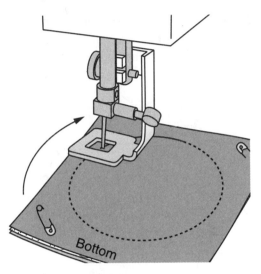

DIAGRAM 3

Step 5: To remove the fabric from the machine, take two stitches in place, then hold the threads as you pull your square away from the machine. Clip the threads.

Jan Burns

Follow the Leader

Before actually working on a free-motion project, try several test runs first. After trying the technique described in "Free-Motion Warm-Up," try outlining several selected lines on a preprinted fabric scrap to practice outlining design motifs. When you're pleased with the results on your fabric scraps, you're ready to move on to your project.

Jill Abeloe Mead

Bobbin Solution

If you have trouble stitching with monofilament thread in your bobbin, replace it with regular thread and quilt with monofilament only in your needle.

Karen Bolesta

A Frayless Start

Before starting to machine quilt with metallic thread, which can fray and breaks easily, loosen the thread coming off the spool by turning the spool one-half turn. Or lower the needle into your fabric by hand and then start stitching.

Karen Costello Soltys

★ Bright Idea ★

FUSIBLE THREAD IS A GREAT TIME-SAVER WHEN FINISHING QUILT TOPS. Simply fill your bobbin with fusible thread, and sew bias strips around the edge of your quilt. Then turn the strips to the back of the quilt and iron them to baste them in place. Your quilt binding is then ready for hand or machine stitching.

Jacquelyn Smyth

A Perfect Bias-Bound Edge

Here's a technique to beautifully create an invisible finish on quilt binding.

Step 1: When finishing a quilt with bias tape, start the tape at one corner. Sew around your quilt, mitering the first three corners as usual, as shown in **Diagram 1.** Stop stitching the fourth side about halfway down.

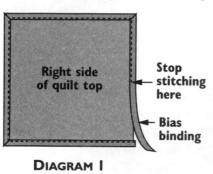

DIAGRAM 1

Step 2: To miter the fourth corner, trim the bias tape to the miter angle, making sure to add a ½-inch seam allowance, as shown in **Diagram 2.**

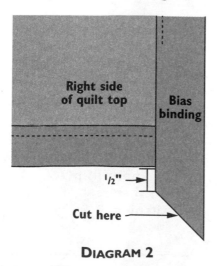

DIAGRAM 2

Step 3: Now open the tape completely and clip the point, as shown in **Diagram 3,** to create less bulk when refolded.

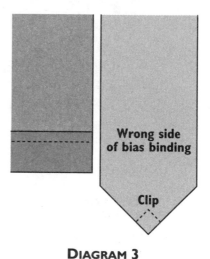

DIAGRAM 3

Step 4: Press the seam allowance to the wrong side, as shown in Diagram 4.

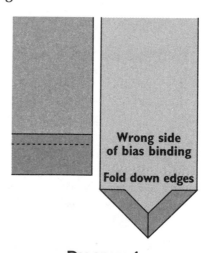

DIAGRAM 4

Step 5: Fold the tape into its original shape with the seam allowance at the point still turned under, as shown in **Diagram 5**.

Step 6: Sew the bias tape in place to form the last mitered corner, as shown in **Diagram 6**.

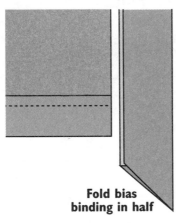

Fold bias binding in half

DIAGRAM 5

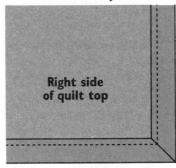

Place binding on quilt and sew in place

Right side of quilt top

DIAGRAM 6

Patricia De Santis

Matching Plaids and Stripes

Perfectly matched plaid and striped garments are the mark of a true professional. Although matching plaids and stripes is not hard to do, it does take a thorough knowledge and understanding of pattern layout and proper cutting. So if you want to go beyond the basics, this chapter is truly worth your while.

Mad for Plaid

Add a novel twist to plaid garments by unmatching! Simply cut garment design details, such as collars, cuffs, sleeves, and yokes, on the bias. Or go totally mad and mix different-size plaids and different plaid fabrics together on one garment, or use plaid details on a solid-color garment.

Bias cut pockets and collar   **Bias cut collar and cuffs**   **Mixed solids and plaids**

House of Fabrics
So-Fro Fabrics

Take a Walk on the Plaid Side

If you have a walking, or even-feed, foot, use it when sewing plaids. The foot's dual-feed system will keep your matched plaids, stripes, or printed fabric together for perfect results.
Karen Costello Soltys

Game, Set, Match

If you love to solve puzzles, then matching plaids is the game for you. When you lay out your pattern, be sure to match the following items so the plaid lines of your garment will flow evenly from one piece to the next:

● crosswise bars at all vertical seams;

● lengthwise bars wherever possible;

● pockets, flaps, and other design details to the plaid where they will be placed on the garment;

● set-in sleeves to the bodice front at the armhole notches;

● two-piece garments, such as skirts and tops, at the point where they overlap for a continuous plaid design.
House of Fabrics
So-Fro Fabrics

Plaid Pointer

I never leave matching to chance. When cutting plaids, I fold my fabric so that the plaids on the bottom layer match as closely as possible to the ones on the top. After laying out my pattern, I cut only the top layer of fabric. Then I carefully peel back the cut layer to make sure the bottom layer matches exactly. If it doesn't, I simply remove the pins, re-match the plaids, and repin my fabric before cutting out the bottom layer.

Margaret Islander

Made to Match

To match plaids, stripes, and even printed patterns easily, trace the fabric motifs onto the pattern tissue for a quick matching guide. Always match the motifs from one pattern piece to another on the seam line, not the cutting line.

Elizabeth M. Barry

A Different Stripe

Stripes don't have to run in the same direction within a garment. You can create a unique design ef-fect by placing the tissue pattern for pockets, flaps, waistbands, collars, hem borders, and yokes on the bias of the fabric and then cutting out the pieces. With some planning in the layout stage, you can also cut these same pieces so that they run perpen-dicular to the main pattern pieces of your garment. For example, cut the main pattern pieces so that the stripe of the fabric runs vertically, then cut

the detail pattern pieces so that the stripes run horizontally. Use your imagination and try some ideas of your own.

Karen Kunkel

Strike a Match

Though it takes a little more time, I recommend cutting out all of your pattern pieces from a single layer of plaid or striped fabric. It's well worth the extra effort, and the plaids and stripes will be accurately matched.

Karen Costello Soltys

SMART SHOPPER

USE a striped fabric to create a flattering optical illusion. Stripes running vertically will generally make you look taller and thinner. A very wide stripe or stripes that are far apart will have the opposite effect on your appearance.

Karen Kunkel

Matching Plaids and Stripes

Match Maker

Fold your plaid fabric according to your pattern layout. Place the centerline of the garment's front pattern piece along the most prominent plaid block of your fabric, making sure the horizontal lines don't fall on the bust area. Cut out the front piece. Then match the other pattern pieces to the front by laying the cut pieces next to the uncut ones. Move the uncut pieces around until the plaid aligns with your cut pieces. Remember to match your pieces on the seam line, not the cutting line.

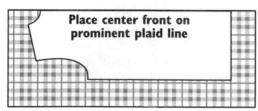

Place center front on prominent plaid line

Linda Griepentrog

Perfect Match

Instead of hand basting the pattern pieces of your garment together to make sure they match, use double-faced basting tape.

Step 1: Turn under and press the seam allowance along the edge of one of the two pieces of your garment that need to be basted together. Cut a length of ¼-inch-wide double-faced basting tape the length of the seam allowance of the

piece you just pressed. Apply the tape to the right side of the seam allowance, as shown in **Diagram 1**.

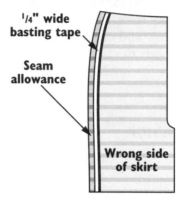

¼" wide basting tape

Seam allowance

Wrong side of skirt

DIAGRAM 1

Step 2: With the right side of the matching piece of your garment facing up, finger press the basting tape of the first piece to the seam allowance of the second, making sure the plaid or stripe of the fabric aligns across both pieces, as shown in **Diagram 2**.

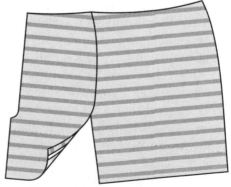

Align stripes and finger press seam allowances together

DIAGRAM 2

Matching Plaids and Stripes

Step 3: Turn back the top piece of fabric so that the wrong side is facing up. The raw edges of the seam allowances should align where the basting tape is holding them together. Sew the pieces together along the seam line. Remove the basting tape and press the seam open. Turn your piece to the right side to see the perfectly matched stripes or plaid!

House of Fabrics
So-Fro Fabrics

Stripe Down the Middle

Position the centerline of a front or back pattern piece in the middle of a stripe rather than at an edge. A bobble in the stitching line will be less evident than if you sew off the edge of the stripe.

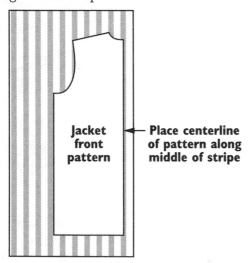

Jacket front pattern ← **Place centerline of pattern along middle of stripe**

Elizabeth M. Barry

Meet Your Match

You can easily view the entire fabric pattern for plaid and stripe placement by laying out your fabric and pattern pieces on your carpet. Pin a single layer of fabric to the carpet, making sure the pins are inserted perpendicularly.

Lay out the pattern pieces next to your fabric so they form as much of the shape of your garment as possible. Consider where you want the pattern of your fabric to fall on the garment. Then place your pattern pieces, one by one, on the fabric. Pin the pieces straight into the carpet to hold them temporarily while you make sure the pattern of the fabric will align along the seam lines of all of the pieces that will be sewn together. Remember to leave space along the same pattern of your fabric for pieces that need to be cut twice, such as sleeves.

Once all of the pieces are laid out properly, pin your pattern pieces securely to your fabric. Carefully cut out your pattern pieces, making sure you don't cut through the carpet.

Carpet — **Dress front**
← **Sleeve**
Selvage
Fold — **Dress back**

Linda Griepentrog

Mitering

Mitering is often the most professional way to finish the corners of many projects, including table linens, quilts, and garments. You can turn mitering into a decorative form of embellishment by applying ribbons and other decorative trims to your projects.

One-Step Mitering

If your trim is not too thick, try mitering it without trimming or seaming the corners. You'll save time, and it will look like it was applied by a professional.

Step 1: Mark the placement lines for your trim onto the right side of your fabric with a chalk marker or an air-erasable marking pen.

Step 2: Pin the trim to the placement lines along one side of the right side of the fabric, stopping at the corner. Fold the trim back onto itself so that the right sides are facing, as shown in **Diagram 1.**

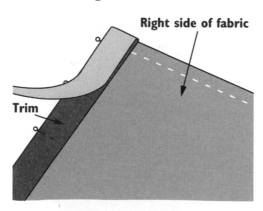

DIAGRAM 1

Step 3: Now turn the trim to create a diagonal second fold, as shown in **Diagram 2.** Adjust the trim so that the

diagonal fold lies exactly in the corner of the fabric and the rest of the trim lies flush with the edge of the fabric.

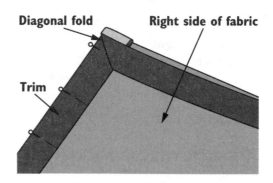

DIAGRAM 2

Step 4: Lightly press and pin the trim in place, as shown in **Diagram 3.**

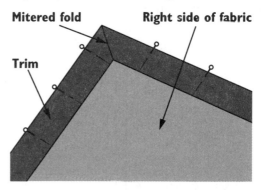

DIAGRAM 3

Step 5: To distribute the thickness of the trim more evenly beneath the miter, fold up and turn the trim to the wrong side. Open the folded dart you made, refold it, as shown in **Diagram 4,** and press it in place and pin.

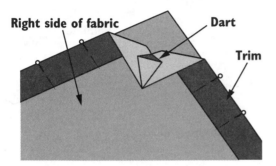

DIAGRAM 4

Step 6: Repeat Steps 2 through 5 to miter the remaining corners. Turn under ¼ inch at the end of the trim and overlap it onto the beginning of the trim already pinned in place, as shown in **Diagram 5.**

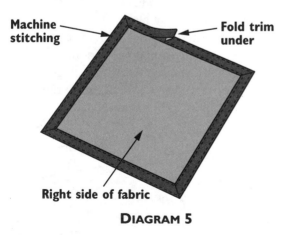

DIAGRAM 5

Step 7: Edge stitch along the outer edge and then the inner edge.

C. M. Offray & Son

 Bright Idea

TAKE EXTRA CARE WHEN ADDING MITERED TRIM TO A KNIT FABRIC. Keep the shape of your garment by laying it against the edge of the tissue pattern as you pin the trim in place. Periodically smooth out the knit fabric against the pattern once the trim has been pinned in place to make sure your garment hasn't stretched.

Karen Kunkel

Take Time to Save Time

To miter striped or patterned fabric, match the stripes or pattern along the seam line, not the cutting line. After adjusting the seam to match the pattern, baste the seam and check to see if the pattern matches. Then sew the seam. If you check your work this way, you will save time later.

Gay Quinn

Stripes for Borders

A striped fabric makes an attractive mitered border. Cut the striped fabric into strips the width you desire, plus the seam allowance. Sew the strips to the edge of your project, matching the stripes as you miter the corners.

Marya Kissinger Amig

Mitering a Hemmed Corner

Here's the way to a perfect finish for tablecloths and other hemmed items with right-angle corners.

Step 1: Mark the hemline on the wrong side of your fabric. Then turn up the edge ¼ inch to the wrong side of the fabric on all sides and press.

Step 2: Turn up the hem on one side of the fabric and press. Unfold the hem. Turn up the hem along one adjacent side and press well. Unfold the hem. There will be a square creased into your fabric at the corner, as shown in **Diagram 1**.

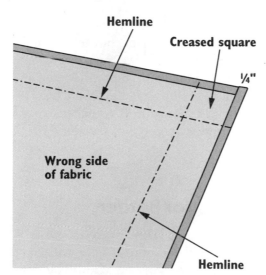

DIAGRAM 1

Step 3: Fold the corner of the square diagonally to meet the opposite corner and press it, as shown in **Diagram 2**.

Unfold the corner. You will now have a diagonal crease that divides the square in half.

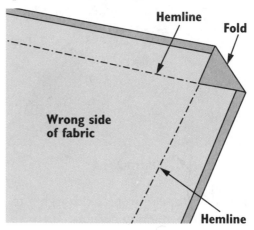

DIAGRAM 2

Step 4: With right sides together, fold the entire piece of fabric diagonally, creating a second fold in the creased square. Sew along the crease that was formed in Step 3. Trim the corner seam allowance to ¼ inch. Then clip off the corner at the diagonal fold line along the remaining raw edge, as shown in **Diagram 3**.

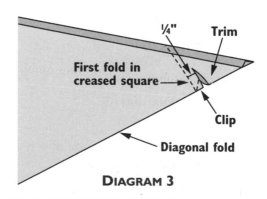

DIAGRAM 3

Step 5: Open out the fabric, making sure the right side is facing up. Press the hem in place to regain the shape of the corner. Then press the seam open and trim any excess fabric, as shown in **Diagram 4.**

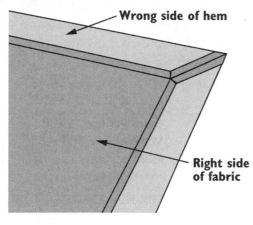

DIAGRAM 4

Wrong side of hem

Right side of fabric

Step 6: Turn the corner to the wrong side of your fabric and press the hem in place, as shown in **Diagram 5.**

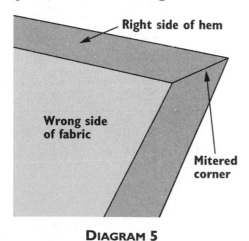

Right side of hem

Wrong side of fabric

Mitered corner

DIAGRAM 5

Step 7: Repeat Steps 2 through 6 for the remaining sides of your fabric. The corners will be perfectly mitered, leaving the hem ready to be sewn in place.

Barbara Fimbel

No-Sew Mitering

This easy, no-sew mitering method works well with ribbons and trims that don't fray.

Step 1: With right sides facing up, place one strip of ribbon on top of another to form a right angle, leaving ¼ inch extended beyond the overlap. Pin the ribbons together and draw a diagonal line along the top ribbon to create the mitering angle, as shown in **Diagram 1.** Cut along the diagonal line through both strips of ribbon, and discard the excess pieces.

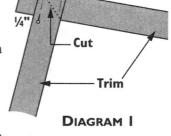

¼"

¼"

Cut

Trim

DIAGRAM 1

Step 2: Glue the strips of ribbon in place on your project, making sure the cut corners are positioned to form a miter, as shown in Diagram 2.

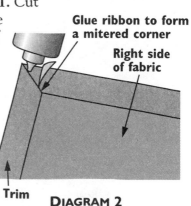

Glue ribbon to form a mitered corner

Right side of fabric

Trim

DIAGRAM 2

C. M. Offray & Son

Mitering

Easy Mitered Pillow

Here is a way to lay out pillow pattern pieces so the pattern of the fabric matches along the mitered corners. This technique will turn a plain pillow into an eye-catching graphic if you use bold striped, plaid, or check fabric.

Step 1: To make a 14-inch-square pillow, begin by cutting a 15-inch-square pattern piece from a sheet of tissue paper. Draw two diagonal lines on your pattern to divide the square into four triangles, as shown in **Diagram 1.** Cut out the triangles.

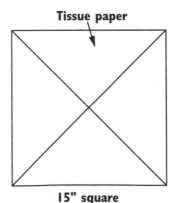

Tissue paper

15" square

DIAGRAM 1

Step 2: If you're using a fabric with an uneven stripe, place and pin the triangles next to one another along the length of your fabric, as shown in **Diagram 2.** This will keep the pattern lines of the fabric running in the same direction when you sew the pillow together. Cut out the pillow pieces.

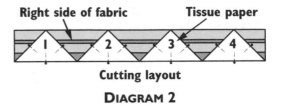

Right side of fabric   **Tissue paper**

Cutting layout

DIAGRAM 2

Step 3: If you're using a fabric with an even stripe, place the triangles as shown in **Diagram 3.** Cut out the pillow pieces.

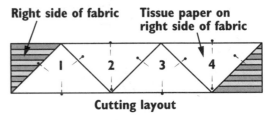

Right side of fabric   **Tissue paper on right side of fabric**

Cutting layout

DIAGRAM 3

Step 4: To sew the pillow top together, place two triangles with right sides together and sew along a short side using a ¼-inch seam allowance. Press the seam open and turn the triangles to the right side. The lines of your pattern will match, as shown in **Diagram 4.**

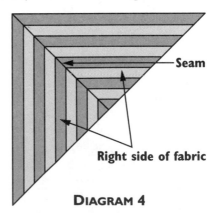

Seam

Right side of fabric

DIAGRAM 4

Step 5: Repeat Step 4 to sew the remaining triangles together. Your finished pillow top will look like **Diagram 5.**

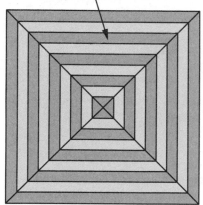

Right side of fabric

Complete pillow top
DIAGRAM 5

Step 6: Sew your pillow front to the pillow back with right sides together, using a ¼-inch seam allowance. Leave a 6-inch opening along one side for turning. Turn the pillow right side out. Stuff the pillow with polyester fiberfill or a pillow form. Turn under the seam allowance along the opening and slip stitch it closed.

Barbara Fimbel

Square Off with Lace

Mitering lace on an outside edge is quick and easy. You can use this technique to add lace or trim to a square collar or neckline.

Step 1: Lay your lace on a flat surface with the right side facing up. Fold the lace back onto itself and then fold it to form a diagonal corner where desired and press, as shown in **Diagram 1.**

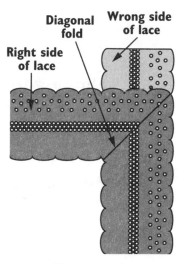

Diagonal fold Wrong side of lace

Right side of lace

DIAGRAM 1

Step 2: Set your machine for a medium stitch length and a narrow stitch width. Sew a row of zigzag stitches along the diagonal to join the lace together along the fold, as shown in **Diagram 2.**

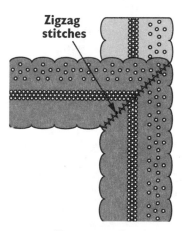

Zigzag stitches

DIAGRAM 2

Step 3: Turn the lace to the wrong side and cut the excess at the corner, as shown in **Diagram 3.** Press the seam open.

Step 4: Sew the lace to the edge of the right side of your project.
Karen Kunkel

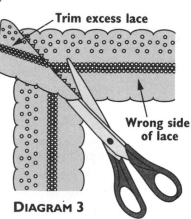

Trim excess lace

Wrong side of lace

DIAGRAM 3

Mitering the Simple Way

It's easy to miter ribbon, braid, and other trims when you follow these steps.

Step 1: Mark the placement lines for your trim on the right side of your fabric with a chalk marker or an air-erasable marking pen.

Step 2: Hold the fabric so you are working in a vertical position, from top to bottom. With right sides together, pin the trim to the fabric at one corner of the placement lines. Turn the trim back onto itself to create a diagonal fold, as shown in **Diagram 1.** This will hide the raw edge of the trim.

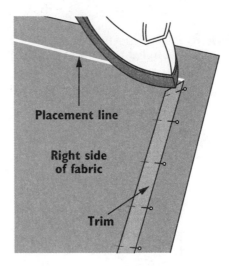

DIAGRAM 2

Step 4: When you reach the second corner, turn the ribbon under to create a diagonal fold, as shown in **Diagram 3.** Lightly press the fold in place and trim excess ribbon. Pin the corner of the trim along the placement line.

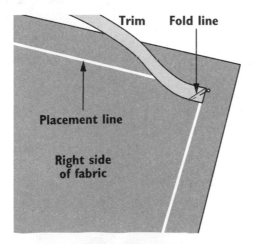

DIAGRAM 1

Step 3: Pin your trim to the fabric along the placement line. Lightly press the fold in place, as shown in Diagram 2.

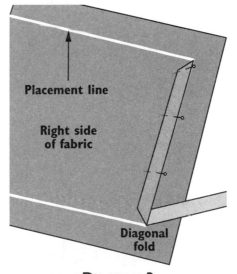

DIAGRAM 3

Step 5: Repeat Steps 2 through 4 until you have pinned trim to all placement lines, have completely mitered all of the corners, and have returned to the beginning, as shown in **Diagram 4.**

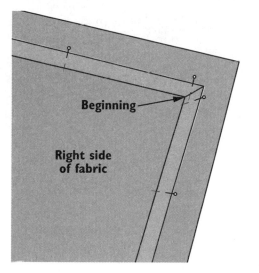

DIAGRAM 4

Step 6: Edge stitch the trim along the outer and inner edges. Then slip stitch the mitered corners in place, as shown in **Diagram 5.**

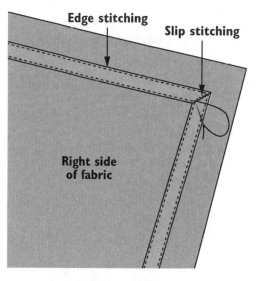

DIAGRAM 5

C. M. Offray & Son

Necklines

A neckline should complement your garment and flatter your figure. It can be the focal point of your ensemble or disguise a figure flaw. In this chapter, the sewing professionals reveal the secrets to selecting the most desirable neckline for your figure. You'll also learn some invaluable sewing tips, smart scarf tricks, and a host of handy hints to help you hone your sewing skills.

Facing Facts

Many ready-to-wear garments have an extra-wide back facing along the neckline so the garment will appeal to you while on a hanger. But wide facings are a bother when the garment is being worn because they always seem to flip out. To solve this problem, I trim the facing to 2½ inches and finish the raw edges.

Facing — **Wrong side of dress**

Clotilde

Sheer Sense

Facings tend to show and look sloppy in garments made from sheer fabrics. So instead of using a facing, I either cover my seams with a bias binding made from the same fabric as the garment, or I turn under the seam allowances twice and stitch them.

Karen Kunkel

Dress Up Your Neckline

Dress up your neckline with a dickey scarf. Use it in place of a scarf or blouse. Here's how to make one.

Supplies

- ⅜ yard of 60-inch-wide fabric or 1⅝ yards of 45-inch-wide fabric. (If your fabric has a definite right and wrong side, the scarf should be double layered, so purchase twice the amount of yardage.)
- Sewing thread to match your fabric

Step 1: For a single scarf, cut your fabric according to the measurements in the diagram. For a double-layer scarf, cut two pieces of fabric according to the measurements, then follow the directions in Step 3.

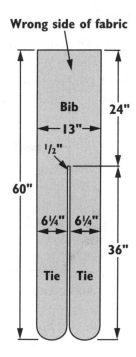

Wrong side of fabric

Bib

24"

13"

½"

60"

6¼" 6¼"

36"

Tie | Tie

Let's Face It

Keep the facing of your garment from hanging out by stitching in the ditch at the shoulder seams. Not only does it look better than hand tacking but it's also faster and more secure.

Karen Kunkel

Fuse It Fast

To save time when cutting neckline facings, I press a piece of fusible interfacing to a piece of fabric large enough to accommodate all of my facing pieces. Then I lay out the pieces on the interfaced fabric and cut them out.

Laurel Hoffmann

Step 2: Hem the edges of the single-layer scarf by machine, by hand, or with a serger.

Step 3: For a double-layer scarf, sew the two pieces of fabric together with right sides facing and raw edges aligned, leaving a 4-inch opening on one side of the bib for turning. Turn the scarf right side out and slip stitch the opening closed.

Step 4: For either scarf, position the bib in front, wrap the ties around your neck, and knot the ends over the bib. Tuck the bottom portion of the bib into the waistband of your skirt or slacks.

Ronda Chaney

SMART SHOPPER

When shopping for accessories to complement your garment's neckline, look for those that don't mimic your face shape. For example, if you have a round face, don't choose round beads with a round neckline because they will only emphasize the shape of your face. Instead, choose a longer, angular necklace for a slimmer look. Conversely, if you have a thin, angular face, choose rounded accessories to enhance your face and make it look fuller.

Jan Larkey

Necklines

Stressed Out

When a neckline has a stress point, such as the point of a V-neck or the corners of a square neck, I reinforce it with a small patch of lightweight fusible interfacing. Then to prevent stretching, I stay stitch the neck edge before applying the facing.

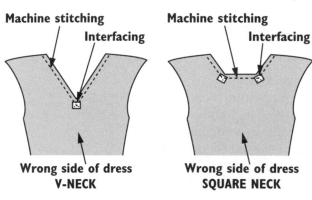

Machine stitching   **Interfacing**

Machine stitching   **Interfacing**

Wrong side of dress
V-NECK

Wrong side of dress
SQUARE NECK

Marian Mongelli

No-Gap Neckline

To get a nicely rolled neckline, use fusible tape or ½-inch-wide fusible interfacing to reinforce your neckline seams. At the ironing board, pin the tape to the wrong side of the garment so that it extends ⅛ inch over the seam line into the garment. Pull the tape slightly taut as you fuse it to the neckline. The facing will lie flat, and the neckline won't gap. This technique is especially helpful for women with a large bust.

Susan Huxley

The Z-Scarf

One of my favorite scarves is the Z-shaped scarf because it eliminates bulk at the neckline. Here's how to make a single or double-layer scarf.

Supplies

⊞ ⅝ yard of 45-inch-wide fabric (enough for a double-layer scarf)

Step 1: For a single scarf, cut your fabric according to the measurements in **Diagram 1,** then follow the directions in Step 2. For a double-layer scarf, cut two pieces of fabric according to the measurements, then follow the directions in Step 3.

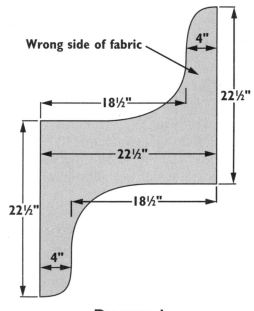

Wrong side of fabric

4"

18½"   22½"

22½"

22½"   18½"

4"

DIAGRAM 1

Step 2: Hem the edges of the single-layer scarf by machine, by hand, or with a serger.

Step 3: For a double-layer scarf, sew the scarves together with right sides facing and raw edges aligned, leaving a 4-inch opening on a straight edge for turning. Turn the scarf right side out and slip stitch the opening closed.

Step 4: Hold the rounded ends of the scarf, letting the two square corners drop in the center. Tie the ends around your neck, positioning the ties either at the side or the back, as shown in **Diagram 2.**

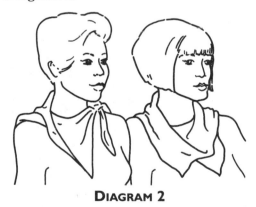

DIAGRAM 2

Ronda Chaney

Treat Your Necklines Right

This method will tell you how to construct the neckline of your garment properly so it will retain its shape.

Step 1: Stay stitch your neckline ½ inch from the raw edge with a very small stitch length. Always sew from the back of the neckline to the front.

Step 2: Sew the facing in place and trim the seam allowance to ¼ inch. Finish the seam allowance with an overcast or zigzag stitch or by serging it.

Step 3: Understitch the facing by edge stitching ⅛ inch from the edge of the seam allowance through the facing and the seam allowance.

Glynda Black

The Finish Line

When sewing blouses and un-lined jackets, try this fast and easy finishing technique for neckline facings. Cut out one piece of fusible interfacing to match each neckline facing piece. With the right side of the facing and the nonadhesive side of the interfacing together, sew each piece of fusible interfacing to each facing piece along the outer edges, not along the seam lines. Trim the seam allowances and turn each piece right side out. Then press your pieces to fuse the interfacing to the facing. Finish sewing your garment according to the pattern directions.

Elizabeth M. Barry

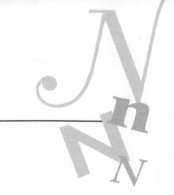

★ Bright Idea ★

OFF-THE-SHOULDER NECKLINES, no matter how elegant and sexy, are not flattering if they slip off your shoulder and slide down your arm! To remedy this, follow this simple technique. Using a double thickness of thread, hand sew a thread casing along the shoulder area from the front to the back using a cross-stitch wide enough to cover a piece of narrow elastic. Use a safety pin to insert the piece of elastic through the casing, making sure to adjust it for a snug fit. Hand sew each end of the elastic to the inside of the garment. You can move freely about, knowing your neckline will now stay in place.

Karen Kunkel

by shaping the cording. As soon as you find the best style, trace it onto your bodice with a water-soluble marker. Remove the bodice, even out the lines, and you have the perfect neckline template for your next garment!

Ronda Chaney and Lori Bottom

Choose the Perfect Neckline

Do you know which neckline shape flatters your figure the most? Finding out is simple. First make a muslin bodice with a high neckline for your template. Then put it on and stand in front of a full-length mirror. Drape a length of decorative cording around your neck like a necklace. Experiment with different necklines

Lovely Lace

If you're sewing a lace blouse or dress with a lace bodice and want to keep your garment sheer, eliminate facings and interfacings

in the neck area if possible. Cut a bias strip from your lace fabric and bind it to the edge of the neckline, or stitch a lace trim to the neckline area.

House of Fabrics
So-Fro Fabrics

Understanding Understitching

I like to understitch the facings on all of my garments because it's the best way to keep the seams from rolling to the outside. Fold the facing to the outside of the garment. With the right side up, sew through

the facing and the seam allowance underneath as close to the seam as possible. If you have already clipped the curved area on your facing, make sure you catch all of the edges as you sew.

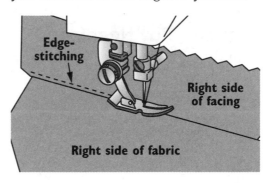

Karen Kunkel

Needles and Pins

Your fabric deserves the very best treatment as you sew, so take the time to select the correct needles and pins. Knowing how and when to use the proper tools of the trade can save you time and make your sewing more efficient. The wide range of needles and pins can be confusing, even if you are an advanced sewer, so photocopy the handy reference charts on pages 182–185 and hang them in your work area.

Neat and Tidy Needles

Here's a clever trick to keep all of your sewing machine needles sorted so that you know exactly where to locate the one you want—when you want it.

Step 1: Buy a tomato-style pin cushion that is divided into six sections. With a permanent marker, draw a dashed line midway between each of the sections to create 12 equal sections, as shown in **Diagram 1**.

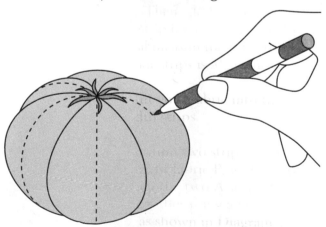

DIAGRAM 1

Step 2: Mark each section near the top of the pin cushion with one of the needle sizes you use. Along the side,

write the type of fabric for which the needle is best suited, as shown in the examples in **Diagram 2**.

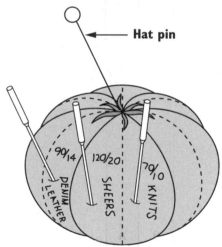

Hat pin

90/14 · 120/20 · 70/10 · DENIM · LEATHER · SHEERS · KNITS

DIAGRAM 2

Step 3: Place your needles in the appropriate sections. Stick a small hat pin or quilt pin at the top of the pin cushion. When you remove a needle, replace it with the hat or quilt pin. This way you will always know which needle is presently in your machine and where to store it when it's not in use. And you won't have to get out a magnifying glass to read those tiny numbers on the needle!

Lee Wiegand

The 8-Hour Rule

A sewing machine needle is only good for about eight hours of sewing. To find out when yours is ready to retire, listen for a thumping noise as it penetrates your fabric and look for skipped stitches.

Coats & Clark

Plan Ahead

Before you begin a hand sewing or quilting project, thread a group of similar needles with the thread you're planning to use. You'll sew faster and save time because you won't have to stop and rethread once you've finished with one needle.

Claudia Larrabure

Keep Needles Clean

Fabric finishes can produce residue buildup on a sewing machine needle, resulting in skipped stitches. If you think the needle still owes you more use, clean it with a cotton ball and oil, detergent, or a cleaning solvent, then try it again.

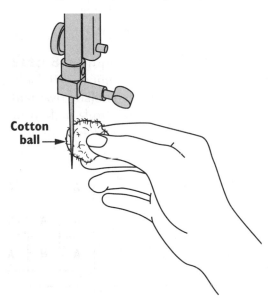

Cotton ball

Coats & Clark

Know When to Throw Them

Don't be penny-wise and pound-foolish. Discard any less than perfect pins or needles. You don't want them to snag and catch your expensive fabric, turning something beautiful into a disaster.

Sonja Dagress

Needles and Pins

PRIMER ON NEEDLES AND PINS

Here are three handy charts for quick reference if you are ever in doubt as to what pin, hand-sewing needle, or machine-sewing needle to use on your fabric.

Barbara Fimbel

HAND-SEWING NEEDLES	DESCRIPTION
Sharp	Available in sizes 1 through 12; medium length with a small rounded eye
Between	Available in sizes 1 through 12; similar to a sharp but shorter
Ballpoint	Available in sizes 1 through 10; has a special tip that lets the needle slide between knit threads
Milliner's	Available in sizes 1 through 10 and 15 through 18; long and fine with a small rounded eye
Tapestry	Available in sizes 13 through 26; short needle with a blunt tip and long eye for use with several strands of thread

MACHINE-SEWING NEEDLES	DESCRIPTION
Sharp	Available in sizes 60/8 through 120/20; has a sharp point for piercing fabric
Universal	Available in sizes 60/8 through 120/20; has a somewhat rounded tip for piercing fabric
Ballpoint	Available in sizes 60/8 through 100/16; has a rounded tip for piercing fabric
Twin (also called double needle)	Available in sizes 80/12 through 90/14 with the distance between the needles ranging from 1.6 to 6 mm; two needles attached to one shank

Use	Appearance (enlarged for detail)
Good for all-purpose sewing	
Good for all-purpose sewing; also suitable for detailed handwork and quilting	
Suitable for all-purpose sewing on knit fabrics	
Suitable for basting and gathering	
Suitable for embroidery on loosely woven fabrics	

Use	Appearance (enlarged for detail)
Suitable for heavyweight and dense-weave fabrics; also good for decorative topstitching	
Suitable for all-purpose sewing; larger sizes are good for decorative topstitching	
Suitable for sewing on knit fabrics	
Suitable for a variety of decorative machine stitches	

(continued)

Needles and Pins

PRIMER ON NEEDLES AND PINS—Continued

MACHINE-SEWING NEEDLES	DESCRIPTION
Wing	Available in sizes 100/16 through 120/20; two winglike extensions on either side of the needle pierce the fabric to create holes
Topstitching	Available in sizes 80/12 through 110/18; has a large eye for use with heavy thread
Jeans (also called denim needle)	Available in sizes 90/14 through 110/18; has an acutely rounded point and slender eye

PINS	DESCRIPTION
Dressmaker	Available in several sizes ranging from 1 to 2 inches with flat, glass, or plastic heads; no. 16 is 1 inch long; no. 17 is $1\frac{1}{16}$ inches long and is the standard length for dressmaking; no. 20 is $1\frac{1}{4}$ inches long
Silk	Available in several sizes; no. 17 is $1\frac{1}{16}$ inches long, and no. 20 is $1\frac{1}{4}$ inches long; easy to grip and see; holes made in fabric are small and disappear fast
Ballpoint	Available in size 17, which is $1\frac{1}{16}$ inches long
Quilting	Available in size 28, which is $1\frac{3}{4}$ inches long
Pleating	Available in size 16, which is 1 inch long; fine pin with a ballpoint

Use	Appearance (enlarged for detail)
Suitable for decorative hemstitching, decorative entredeux, and a variety of other decorative machine stitching where an open-hole effect is desired	
Suitable for topstitching and for decorative machine stitching with metallic thread	
Suitable for use with tightly woven fabrics, such as denim, and fabrics with a heavy finish	

Use	Appearance (enlarged for detail)
No. 16 is a good all-purpose pin; no. 17 is suitable for light- to medium-weight fabrics; no. 20 is suitable for heavyweight fabrics	
Both sizes are suitable for fine silk and synthetic fabrics	
Specially designed for knit fabrics	
Suitable for several layers of fabric, loose weaves, synthetic furs, and thick or bulky fabrics	
Suitable for light- to medium-weight woven and knit fabrics	

Patterns

Professional-looking garments begin with proper fit and planning. Before you begin purchasing patterns, consider pattern design, design ease, skill level, and size, so you get the best fit. A little preliminary planning will save you time and money. Our experts offer their best tips, from figure flattery to wardrobe planning, pin fitting to pattern alteration. The information on these pages may forever change the way you select patterns!

Flatter Your Figure

Before you rush to the register with a pattern for a garment that looks like it will be fun to wear, consider how it will look on *you*. Fashion is only flattering if the style makes you look fantastic. Anything short of that simply isn't worth your time or investment.

To select flattering patterns, make a list of your figure attributes, both negative and positive. Use this list to determine which styles will emphasize your positive attributes and de-emphasize the negative ones.

Diana L. Carswell

Figure Wise Means Fashion Wise

If you're like many women, you may be struggling with trying to camouflage a figure problem, such as being bottom- or top-heavy. You can use design principles to create fashionable illusions that overcome these common figure problems.

Here are several ways to flatter your figure if you're bottom-heavy.

- Purchase patterns with centered, vertical lines and simple shapes.

- Balance the width of your hips by wearing blouses with extended or padded shoulders, gathered sleeves, or shoulder yokes.

- Draw attention to the upper part of your body with design details, such as wide collars, shaped necklines, soft bows, and scarves.

- Choose loose-fitting jackets that end above or below the hip, but not right at the hip.

- Use bold accessories at the neckline to attract the eye.

- Avoid patterns with gathered waists, hip yokes, bias cuts, and side-seam pockets.

If you're top-heavy, try these camouflage ideas.

- Purchase patterns that emphasize fullness and/or horizontal lines in the hip area or the hemline to balance out your figure.

- Accent vertical pattern lines in the upper garment area only.

- Choose styles with hipline details, such as pockets, dropped waists, or long jackets with peplums.

- Keep your necklines simple and uncluttered.

- Let hemlines go to short or long extremes, with bands of pattern, color, or special treatments below your waist.

- Avoid bodice details like pockets, ruffles, wide lapels, empire waistlines, and boxy, unbelted shapes.

Butterick Company

Alterations Can Seam So Easy

Figure variations are universal—everybody has a few! That "ideal" figure doesn't really exist. So before you sew, it is important to realize that you will likely have to make some pattern adjustments. The closer an alteration is to the seam line, the more accurate the alteration will be. Fit as you sew, and make adjustments along the way. Achieving a good fit takes time and practice.

Judith Rasband

 ★ **Bright Idea** ★

YOU DON'T NEED TO PURCHASE A TON OF PATTERNS TO SEW A TERRIFIC WARDROBE! I practice the cluster concept of wardrobe building. A cluster is simply a small group of coordinated garments. A beginning cluster of five to eight garments will get you started. They can be combined to create more than 12 different outfits. Eight garments may include one jacket, two skirts and/or pants, three blouses, one cardigan sweater or vest, and one pullover sweater.

No two pieces in a cluster should be styled exactly alike. A matched suit is a practical item to start with. Ideally, one jacket should go with a day dress and a variety of skirt lengths.

Coordination is the key to making a small cluster of clothes work together. Purchase patterns so your garments coordinate in line and shape. Then purchase your fabric so that your garments coordinate in color. As you expand beyond your initial cluster, feel free to include an "ego" item—something that you absolutely love! With the cluster wardrobe plan, you can update or add to what you already own to create a truly versatile, workable wardrobe.

Judith Rasband

SMART SHOPPER

Monster in Swedish means pattern. Monster Pattern Paper is fabulous because it is so versatile. You can use it to create patterns or to read patterns placed under it. You can even sew through it to make a sample garment for fitting purposes. A pencil or marking pen works well on this paper and doesn't tear it, so the paper is great to use to trace multisize patterns. It even sticks to fabric for easy marking. To order, write to The Fabric Carr, P.O. Box 32120, San Jose, CA 95152-2120.

Roberta C. Carr

More Style, Less Time

It isn't always necessary to spend lots of time to get lots of style. Sometimes it pays to eliminate the time-consuming details. For example, I always roll up my sleeves, so I tend to omit cuffs on my blouses. Instead, I make a simple faced sleeve and save sewing time.

Marcy Tilton

Quick Shortening Lesson

If you have a flared skirt pattern with a hem that needs to be altered, follow this quick-and-easy method.

Step 1: With a ruler and pencil, measure and mark your pattern for the correct hem, as shown in **Diagram 1**.

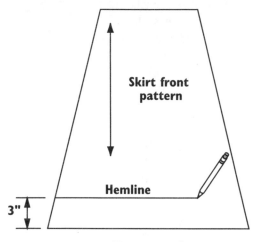

Skirt front pattern

Hemline

3"

DIAGRAM 1

Step 2: Cut along the marked line, one-quarter of the way into each side of the skirt pattern, as shown in **Diagram 2**.

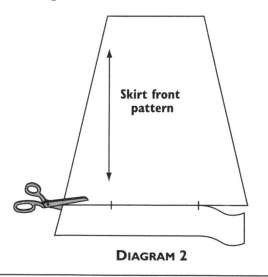

Skirt front pattern

DIAGRAM 2

Step 3: Fold the bottom cut edges toward the center of the pattern, as shown in **Diagram 3.** The edges may overlap.

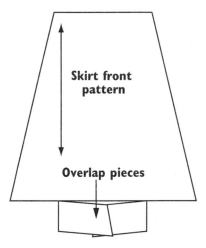

DIAGRAM 3

Step 4: Fold the bottom edge up so that it lies flat on the pattern, and use masking tape to hold it in place so it doesn't unfold, as shown in **Diagram 4.**

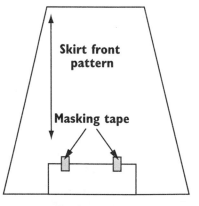

DIAGRAM 4

Karen Kunkel

Beware of Built-in Ease

If you want a pattern to flatter your figure, be sure to consider pattern and design ease. Every pattern has basic wearing ease built into its style so that you can move and breathe in the garment. Minimum wearing ease is 2½ inches at the bust, ½ to 1 inch at the waist, and 2 to 3 inches at the hips. In addition to wearing ease, patterns have differing amounts of design ease added to the finished garment measurements in order to create a specific style. A loose-fitting style may have a design ease that will add as much as 12 inches to the finished garment measurements. So before you buy, carefully consider how much ease will look right on you.

McCall Pattern Company

What's Your Size?

If you have a full bust, you should take two measurements to determine how to select the appropriate pattern size. Take your bust measurement over the fullest part of your bust, under your arms, and straight across your back. Then take your high bust measurement above your bust, under your arms, and straight across your back. If there is more than a 2-inch difference between these two measurements, select your pattern size according to your high bust measurement.

McCall Pattern Company

Patterns

The Long and Short of Fit

Follow these basic pattern alteration essentials to shorten or lengthen your pattern pieces.

When You Need to Shorten

Step 1: Measure up from the lengthen/shorten line the necessary amount and draw a line parallel to it, as shown in **Diagram 1**.

Step 2: Accordion-fold the lengthen/shorten line to meet the line you drew, as shown in **Diagram 2**. Finger press in place.

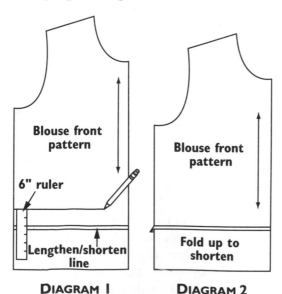

Step 3: To hold the fold in place, use pins or sewer's repair tape, which will not stiffen your pattern piece. Then correct the cutting lines.

When You Need to Lengthen

Step 1: Cut the pattern apart on the lengthen/shorten line, and spread the pattern pieces evenly to accommodate the increase in measurement, as shown in **Diagram 3**.

Step 2: Place and pin a piece of paper under the cut edges of your pattern pieces, then redraw the cutting lines along the side edges, as shown in **Diagram 4**. Trim the edges of the paper.

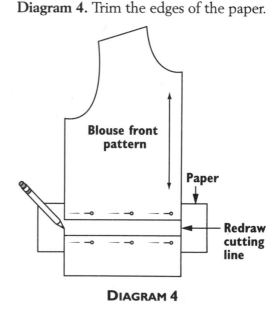

Simplicity Pattern Company

Patterns Know Best

Don't use a fabric that is not rec- ommended on the pattern envelope because your garment will not fit the way it is intended. Substituting a thick, heavy fabric for a thin, light- weight fabric will reduce the required amount of ease. If your pattern calls for a stretch knit, then less ease was built into the design, so do not substitute a woven fabric for the knit.

Similarly, your choice of notions can also influence the fit of your garment. For example, if you choose thicker shoulder pads than those suggested, you'll use up the necessary ease in the armhole and shoulder areas.

McCall Pattern Company

Long on Fit

If you need to lengthen the crotch depth of your garment, you can do it in the same manner as described in "The Long and Short of Fit."

Begin by subtracting your crotch depth body measurement from the standard pattern body measurement. Then adjust your pattern along the lengthen/shorten line. For example, if your measurement is 1 inch longer than your selected pattern size, cut along the lengthen/shorten line on both the front and back pattern pieces and spread your pattern 1 inch, as shown. Tape the pattern pieces to a piece of paper, making sure you main-

tain the proper spacing, and then trim the edges of the paper.

After you've made all of the necessary adjust- ments, be sure to correct any other pattern pieces that will be sewn to the pieces you've adjusted. For ex- ample, if you've made a change to the front, you'll need to do the same to the back.

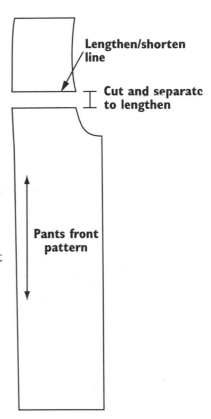

Simplicity Pattern Company

Lace Layout

Planning and layout are the most important steps of sewing a lace garment. It is important to fit the garment before planning the place- ment of lace motifs or starting to sew. Cut your lace over a dark surface so that the motif pattern will be ob- vious. Inspect the lace closely to de- termine if there is a one-way design. When cutting out your pattern pieces, only cut through a single layer of lace at one time.

House of Fabrics
So-Fro Fabrics

Patterns

Easy-Fit Checkpoints

If you need to alter your patterns as you sew, but aren't sure when to do it, follow these fitting steps.

Garments with a Waistband

Step 1: If your garment wrinkles below the waist in the back, it's too long for you between the waist and hips. This means you might be sway-backed. To adjust for this, correct the garment itself, rather than the tissue pattern, before the waistband is sewn to the garment.

Step 2: After basting the waistband to your garment, try on the garment and have a friend pinch the excess fabric to see how much needs to be adjusted, as shown in **Diagram 1**.

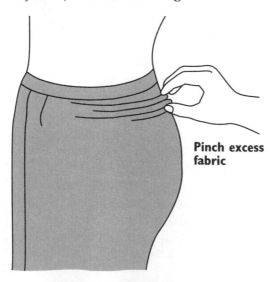

Pinch excess fabric

DIAGRAM 1

Step 3: Release the entire waistband seam in the back of the garment. With a water-soluble marking pen, mark a new, lower waistline seam that gets rid of the excess fabric. Taper the seam to nothing at the side seams, as shown in **Diagram 2**.

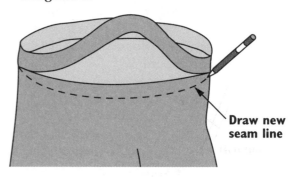

Draw new seam line

DIAGRAM 2

Step 4: Sew the waistband to your garment along the newly marked seam line. The result of your alteration will be a slightly larger circumference around your waist. To restore the original waistline size, you may need to sew slightly deeper side seams.

Pants

Step 1: After you sew the inner seams and crotch of your pants, fit the pants to your waist and hips. Try on the pants, right side out, over the undergarments you plan to wear with them. Pin the front to the back, wrong sides together, along the outer side seams, making sure the pins are parallel to the raw edges, as shown in **Diagram 3**.

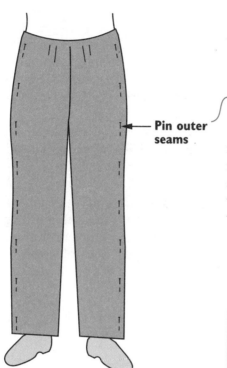

 Pin outer seams ◀

DIAGRAM 3

Marking Napped Fabrics

If you're working with a napped fabric, transfer only essential markings from your pattern using an air-erasable marking pen or pins and a chalk pencil, so that you leave as few marks as possible on the fabric. Do not mark notches by snipping into the seam allowance, and never use a tracing wheel on pile fabrics because it will ruin the nap.

House of Fabrics
So-Fro Fabrics

Step 2: If your pants are too loose, then pin deeper seams. If they are too snug, then pin narrower seams. Just make sure you have at least a ⅜-inch seam allowance remaining after the adjustment. Take off the pants, but don't disturb the pins. Mark the new seam lines on the wrong side of the fabric with a chalk pencil or sliver of soap. Transfer any other pattern markings to the new seam lines. Remove the pins and sew along your newly marked seam lines. Be sure to adjust any other pattern pieces that will be sewn to the adjusted areas.

Simplicity Pattern Company

 ★ **Bright Idea** ★

IF YOU'RE WORKING WITH A MULTISIZE PATTERN, cut out the pattern pieces along the appropriate size cutting line. Then mark the seam lines on the pieces. Do this by placing a clear acrylic quilter's ruler ⅝ inch from the cutting line and mark the seam line with a pencil. For curved seam lines, use a double tracing wheel—it works great and doesn't require tracing paper. Place your pieces on a padded work surface, such as an ironing board. Set the wheels ⅝ inch apart, then place the outer wheel on the cutting line. The seam line will be traced simultaneously. The imprint is all you need.

Fred Bloebaum

The Ins and Outs of Pin Fitting

You might think that pin fitting is a waste of time. But unless you are positive about the proportion, style, and fit of your pattern, pin fitting can actually save you time and money in the long run. When I pin fit a pattern, I stand in front of a full-length mirror. The process works best when I wear a camisole or undergarment I can pin my pattern pieces to, but I've also taped the pieces to my skin. If you've never pin fitted before, you might want to enlist the aid of a friend to ensure accuracy.

Step 1: Cut out only the basic pattern pieces that you'll need, such as the front, back, sleeve, and undercollar. Also cut out any details that you want to check the placement of, such as patch pockets or flaps.

Step 2: Mark the shoulder and side seams, then pin the pattern together. When pinning the sleeve together, avoid pinning it at the armhole because it will tear. Instead, just pin the sleeve to the shoulder seam at the shoulder dot.

Step 3: If your garment has a collar, try to pin the undercollar or collar to the neckline carefully.

Step 4: Place a pin at the waistline mark on both the front and back pattern pieces. This is especially important if you are pin fitting alone because you can feel the pin and tell if the pattern is hitting your waistline.

Step 5: Pin on any details. If your pattern calls for shoulder pads, place them on your shoulders.

Step 6: Line up the center front of the pattern pieces along the center front of your body, as shown. Do the same for the back pieces along the center back of your body.

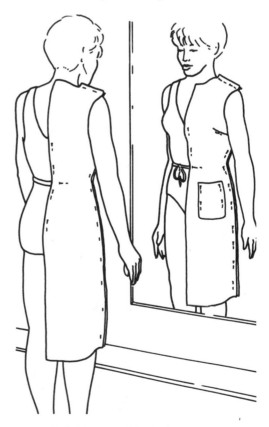

Step 7: Check the finished length of the pattern and the sleeves, the pocket placement, and any other details, as well as the proportion of the pattern to your body. Mark any changes you want to make right on the pattern so you won't forget. Carefully unpin the pattern and make the necessary changes to the pattern pieces before cutting out your garment.

Fred Bloebaum

Ease-y Rules of Thumb

The difference between your figure measurements and the finished garment you intend to sew must be at least 2½ inches at the bust and 2 to 3 inches at the hips for ease and a proper fit. Anything less will make your garment uncomfortable, unflattering, and unfashionable. So follow these rules to purchase the perfect size pattern for your figure.

- Measure yourself often to make the best judgments about ease. You may gain or lose a little weight, or your contours may change over time even if your weight remains the same.

- Don't try to sneak into a smaller pattern size by using up the built-in ease. Your garment will never fit properly. Use both the body measurement and the finished size measurement charts to select the appropriate size pattern you need.

- The fuller your figure, the more ease you'll require. A pattern with a design that has a slightly looser fit erases pounds and looks more elegant.

- Garments such as jackets and coats need extra ease to fit comfortably over garments worn underneath. A coat may have 5 inches of ease at the bust, but a blouse may have only 3 inches.

- If you're between pattern sizes, select the larger pattern size for a loose-fitting silhouette. Select the smaller pattern size for a more closely fitted look.

McCall Pattern Company

A True Time-Saver

You can get a lot of mileage out of your patterns by using them again and again. I often make as many as six shirts in six different fabrics from one basic pattern. I save time by sewing with a familiar pattern, and nobody realizes it's the same design.

Clotilde

Patterns

CUSTOMIZE YOUR FIT

Fitting begins with customizing your pattern. Not everyone fits the standard measurement size for all parts of her body. But multisize patterns provide you with the flexibility you need to select the cutting lines for your sizes. The chart here shows you where to take proper body measurements so you can determine your correct size.

Simplicity Pattern Company

AREA OF BODY: Bust

WHERE TO MEASURE: Over fullest part of bust

AREA OF BODY: Chest

WHERE TO MEASURE: Above fullest part of bust

AREA OF BODY: Waist

WHERE TO MEASURE: Around natural waistline

AREA OF BODY: Hips

WHERE TO MEASURE: Around the fullest part, approximately 9 inches below the waistline

AREA OF BODY:
Shoulder

WHERE TO MEASURE: Length from base of neck to the shoulder point

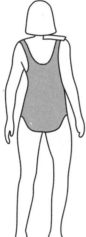

AREA OF BODY:
Back waist length

WHERE TO MEASURE: From prominent bone at back of neck to waist

AREA OF BODY:
Pants length

WHERE TO MEASURE: Length measurement from waist to desired length

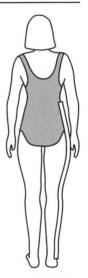

AREA OF BODY:
Crotch depth

WHERE TO MEASURE: From side waist to chair as you sit

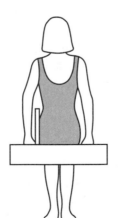

AREA OF BODY:
Crotch length

WHERE TO MEASURE: From center back waistline to center front waistline between the legs

Pillows

Successful decorating does not rely on color alone. Pillow shapes define the personality of a room, adding warmth, charm, and diversity. There are endless possibilities for creating your own designs with the variety of fabric patterns, textures, and accessories that are available. Whether you love the look of a cluster of pillows or just one or two for accent, you'll enjoy using this chapter's tips and techniques for planning and sewing plush-looking pillows to enhance any room in your home.

"Ear"-resistible

The appearance of "ears" on a knife-edge pillow results from the corner seams being so close together that the pillow can't hold enough stuffing to make them puff out. Here is a simple technique to help you avoid this problem on square or rectangular knife-edge pillows.

Step 1: With the right side of the fabric facing up, fold your square or rectangular pillow front into quarters. Make sure the raw edges and corners are aligned. Then follow Step 2 to create rounded corners or Step 3 to create tapered corners.

Step 2: For rounded corners, align an upside-down saucer with the raw edges of the fabric, as shown in **Diagram 1.** Mark the curve with a chalk pencil or a water-soluble marking pen. Cut along the marked line through all four layers of fabric.

DIAGRAM 1

Cutting line
Upside-down saucer
Wrong side of fabric
Fold Fold

Step 3: For tapered corners, measure ½ inch in from one corner and mark with a dot using a chalk pencil or water-soluble marking pen. Then place a pin 4 inches from and on either side of the corner. With a chalk pencil or water-soluble marking pen, draw a line from each pin to the dot, as shown in **Diagram 2.** Cut along the marked lines through all four layers of fabric.

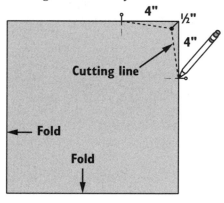

4"   ½"
4"
Cutting line
Fold
Fold

DIAGRAM 2

Step 4: Repeat Steps 1 and 2 or 1 and 3 for the pillow back.

Step 5: With right sides facing, sew the pillow front to the pillow back, leaving a 6-inch opening along one side for turning. Trim the seam allowances, turn the pillow right side out, and press. Stuff the pillow with polyester fiberfill. Turn under the seam allowance along the opening and slip stitch it closed.

Barbara Fimbel

Luxurious-Looking Pillows

If you fall in love with an extravagant remnant but it's not enough for an entire pillow, don't despair! Use the expensive fabric for the pillow front and a less expensive, complementary fabric for the pillow back. If your remnant isn't large enough for a pillow front, then center it on the less expensive fabric and stitch or fuse it in place. Cover the raw edges with a decorative braid or trim, and you'll have a one-of-a-kind pillow!

Donna Babylon

From Plain to Fancy

Turn a plain pillow into a posh one with the simple addition of two buttons. This technique, while not difficult, differs from sewing a button on a garment.

Supplies

- Two large buttons with shanks
- 6-inch doll needle
- 18-inch length of waxed heavyweight thread

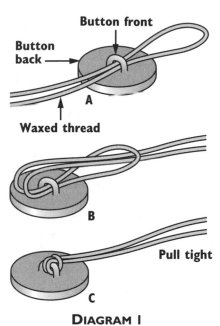

Step 1: Fold the thread in half, and insert the cut ends through the shank of one button, as shown in **Diagram 1A.** Then fold the cut ends back over the shank and through the loop, as shown in **1B.** Pull the thread tight, as shown in **1C.**

DIAGRAM 1

Step 2: Insert the cut ends of the thread through your needle. Push the needle through the pillow center from the front to the back. Pull the needle out of the back, and insert it into the shank of the second button.

Step 3: Remove the needle, and pull the threads slowly but tightly so that the button shanks become nestled into the pillow stuffing, as shown in Diagram 2.

DIAGRAM 2

Step 4: Wrap the threads several times around the buttton shank to maintain the tightness. Then knot the threads several times under the button on the pillow back to secure it in place. Trim the excess thread.

Victoria Waller

Variations on a Theme

Once you know the basic button technique for sewing a button to a pillow, as described in "From Plain to Fancy" on page 199, you can create an array of pleasing pillows with simple variations. Several buttons evenly spaced on the front of a pillow will produce a tufted effect, as shown below (top). Three or more colorful buttons in a row on a solid-color pillow will add an eye-catching accent, as shown below (right). A tassel looped around a button shank on a velvet pillow adds a luxurious look, as shown below (bottom).

Going with the Grain

Unless your design calls for ruffles cut from bias strips, cut the ruffles on the straight grain of your fabric. You'll save both fabric and sewing time. With this method, you can join strips on the diagonal for a nearly invisible, less bulky seam because the ends of each strip will fall in different places.

Step 1: To make a ruffle so that the right side of the fabric appears on both sides, cut strips of fabric twice as wide as the finished width and add 1 inch for a ½-inch seam allowance along the lengthwise edges. For example, to make a finished ruffle that is 2½ inches wide, cut a 6-inch-wide strip. Cut enough strips so that their combined length is 2½ times the perimeter of your pillow.

Step 2: With right sides facing, place two strips together at a 90-degree angle. Offset the ends slightly and draw a diagonal line, as shown in **Diagram 1A**.

Step 3: Sew the strips together along the marked line. Trim the seam and press it to one side, as shown in **1B**.

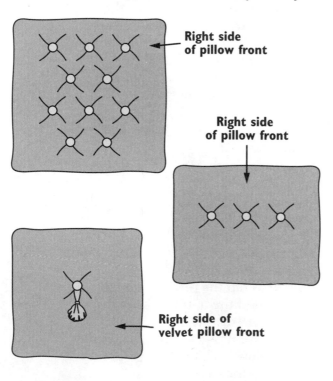

Right side
of pillow front

Right side
of pillow front

Right side of
velvet pillow front

Victoria Waller

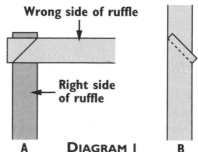

Wrong side of ruffle

Right side
of ruffle

A   **DIAGRAM 1**   B

Step 4: Repeat Steps 2 and 3 until all of the strips have been joined together. Then measure your strip to make sure it is 2½ times the perimeter of the pillow. If it isn't, cut more strips and add them to your pieced strip until you have the required length.

Step 5: Form a circle by sewing the last strip to the first, making sure the strips aren't twisted. With wrong sides together and keeping the circular shape, fold the strip in half lengthwise, as shown in **Diagram 2.** Press the strip.

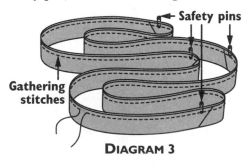

Circular strip folded lengthwise

DIAGRAM 2

Step 6: Sew a row of gathering stitches through both layers of fabric, inside the seam allowance.

Step 7: To evenly distribute the ruffle on the pillow front, divide the ruffle into quarters. Mark each quarter with a safety pin, as shown in **Diagram 3.**

← **Safety pins**

Gathering stitches

DIAGRAM 3

Step 8: Fold your pillow front into quarters and mark each quarter with a safety pin, as shown in **Diagram 4.**

Step 9: Gather the strip to fit the perimeter of your pillow, matching a safety pin on the strip to one pin on the pillow front, then pin, as shown in **Diagram 5.** Then sew the ruffle to the right side of the pillow front using a ½-inch seam allowance.

Step 10: Finish your pillow as you normally would.

Donna Babylon

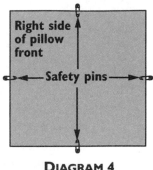

Right side of pillow front

←— **Safety pins** —→

DIAGRAM 4

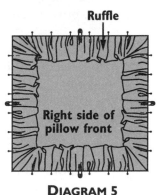

Ruffle

Right side of pillow front

DIAGRAM 5

Corner It

When the instructions for finishing a pillow say to sew three sides and leave the fourth side open for turning, that isn't all you should do. It is important that you sew three sides *and* four corners. It's easier to machine stitch a corner closed than it is to hand sew it. Slip stitch the fourth side closed only after you have tucked the pillow form snugly into each of the four corners.

Barbara Fimbel

Knot the Corners

Pillows with knotted corners not only look expensive but they also add a handsome touch of elegance to any sofa or chair. Your friends will be so impressed that they'll want to know where you purchased them!

Step 1: Attach a zipper foot to your machine. With the right side of your pillow front facing up, place ½-inch-wide welting along one side, leaving a 1-inch tail at the beginning and making sure the raw edges of the welting and fabric are even. Sew the welting to the pillow front on top of the row of stitches on the welting casing. Stop sewing 3 inches before the first corner, as shown in **Diagram 1**.

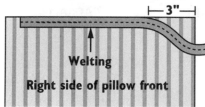

DIAGRAM 1

Step 2: Remove your work from the machine. Clip a V-shaped notch into the seam allowance of the welting casing 1½ inches from the corner of the pillow. Then measure 8 inches from this point and clip the casing again, as shown in **Diagram 2**.

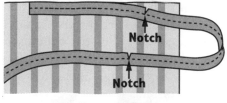

DIAGRAM 2

Step 3: Rip out the casing stitching between these two notches, as shown in **Diagram 3**. Open the casing to expose the cording. Fold the open edges of the casing to the wrong side so the raw edge is toward the cording, then press. Bring the folded edges together and slip stitch them closed, as shown. This is the finished section of the welting.

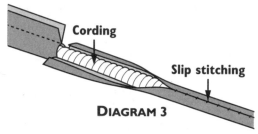

DIAGRAM 3

Step 4: Tie the finished section of the welting into an overhand knot, as shown in **Diagram 4**. Make the knot as tight as possible to keep it out of the way when you sew. The knot will be loosened later.

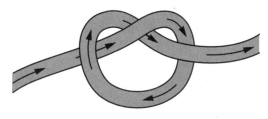

DIAGRAM 4

Step 5: Push the knot and the remaining finished section of welting out of the way of the pillow front 1½ inches before the corner, as shown in **Diagram 5**.

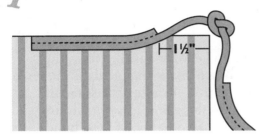

DIAGRAM 5

Step 6: Beginning where you stopped sewing, sew the welting to the pillow front to the 1½-inch mark; then sew only the pilow front to the corner and stop. With the needle in the fabric, lift the presser foot and pivot the pillow front. Position and pin the welting so that the second notch mark on the welting casing is 1½ inches from the corner. Lower the presser foot and sew along the pillow front for 1½ inches, then catch the welting in the seam line, as shown in **Diagram 6.** The knot and the finished section of welting will not be sewn to the pillow on either side of the corner.

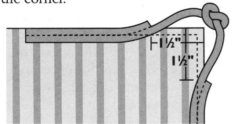

DIAGRAM 6

Step 7: Repeat Steps 1 through 6 to sew and knot the welting along the remaining sides of the pillow.

Step 8: To finish attaching the welting, stop sewing 3 inches before the starting point. Cut the welting so that it overlaps the beginning point by 1½ inches. Remove the casing stitching along the 1½ inches. Open the casing and cut the cording inside so that the two ends butt up to each other. Turn under ½ inch along one end of the casing. Wrap the casing around the beginning point, as shown in **Diagram 7,** and finish sewing the welting to the pillow front.

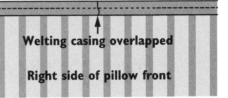

Welting casing overlapped

Right side of pillow front

DIAGRAM 7

Step 9: With right sides together, sew the pillow front to the pillow back, leaving one side open for turning. Trim the seam allowance and clip the corners. Turn the pillow right side out and press. Insert your pillow form and slip stitch the opening closed.

Step 10: Referring to **Diagram 8,** loosen each welting knot so it hugs the corner.

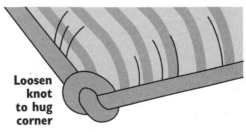

Loosen knot to hug corner

DIAGRAM 8

Victoria Waller

Bias on Ruffles

Ruffles cut on the bias require more fabric than if they were cut on the straight of grain, but they look fuller and won't wrinkle as easily. When working with plaids or stripes, the pattern on bias ruffles will lie on the diagonal and contrast nicely with your pillow.

Jacquelyn Smyth

Braid? Don't Be Afraid

If you love the look of braided trim but are daunted by the process of attaching it to a pillow, then try this stress-free approach.

Step 1: Cut a length of braided trim with heading tape 6 inches longer than the perimeter of your pillow front. With the right side of the fabric facing up, pin the braid to your pillow front, making sure the raw edges are even, as shown in **Diagram 1.** If your pillow is not round, begin pinning the braid along one side of the pillow, not at a corner.

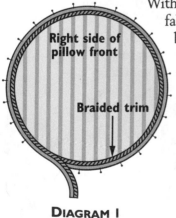

Right side of pillow front

Braided trim

DIAGRAM I

Step 2: Sew the braid to the pillow front inside the seam allowance, begin-

ning and ending 2 inches from the meeting point of the braid, as shown in **Diagram 2.** Trim the excess tail of braid so there is at least 1 inch to overlap the other end of the braid.

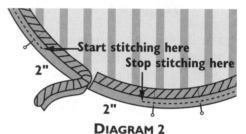

Start stitching here
Stop stitching here
2"
2"

DIAGRAM 2

Step 3: On either side of the meeting point, separate the braid from the heading tape by clipping the stitches that hold them together, stopping at the machine stitching. Separate the strands of the braid, and wrap each end with transparent tape to prevent it from unraveling.

Step 4: Secure the braid strands on the left side underneath the heading tape, retwisting them to look like the original braid. Overlap the 1-inch tail of heading tape onto the other end of the heading tape, and pin it in place, as shown in **Diagram 3.**

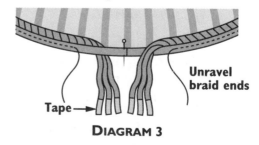

Unravel braid ends

Tape

DIAGRAM 3

Step 5: Twist and pull the strands on the right over the strands on the left until they appear to be one continuous braid. Use transparent tape to secure the strands from the right to the header tape, as shown in **Diagram 4.** Finish sewing the braid to the pillow front. Trim the ends and remove the tape.

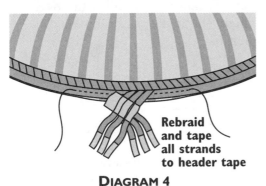

Rebraid and tape all strands to header tape

DIAGRAM 4

Step 6: Sew the pillow front to the pillow back as you normally would.

Charlotte Biro

Great Gathers

Unwaxed dental floss or buttonhole twist makes the perfect thread to gather ruffles for pillows. Both are strong and don't stretch when pulled. To create a pillow ruffle with floss or buttonhole twist, set your sewing machine for a wide zigzag stitch and a long stitch length. Place the buttonhole twist or dental floss ⅜ inch from the raw edge of your ruffle fabric. Zigzag over the length of twist or floss, making sure

not to catch it in the stitching. To gather the ruffle, simply pull on the floss or buttonhole twist.

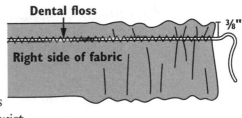

Dental floss
Right side of fabric
⅜"

Donna Babylon

A Measure of Success

Avoid unhappy endings by measuring your pillow form before you cut fabric or begin to sew. Forms do not always measure exactly what the package says.

Victoria Waller

Zipper Trick

If you can't find a zipper long enough to fit across a large pillow, use two short ones. Stitch them in place so that the zipper pulls meet at the center along one side.

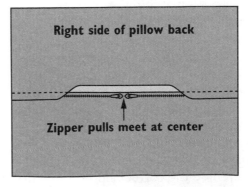

Right side of pillow back

Zipper pulls meet at center

Barbara Fimbel

A Pillow Sandwich

Do you find that pillows made from lightweight fabric look flimsy? If so, simply sandwich a layer of heavily needled fleece batting between the wrong side of your pillow front and the wrong side of a piece of muslin. Sew the three layers together inside the seam allowance, and treat it as the top layer of fabric.

Donna Babylon

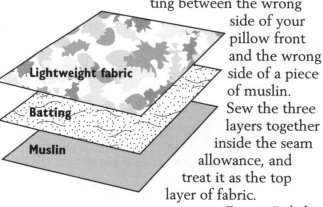

Lightweight fabric

Batting

Muslin

More Planning, Fewer Headaches

If you are making a pillow with decorative trim, thoroughly plan your design before you start sewing. Make a matching color paper pattern of the finished size of your pillow, then cut out scraps of colored paper to represent the various pieces of trim you want to use. Experiment with different designs by arranging the colored paper on your paper pattern. When you're pleased with the design, measure the different pieces of colored paper. Use these measurements to purchase the correct amount of trim.

Barbara Fimbel

A Tight Squeeze

For a compact, wrinkle-free pillow, omit the seam allowance when cutting your fabric. Simply cut your fabric the same size as your pillow form, then sew the seams with a ½-inch seam allowance. This will compress your pillow form slightly, causing it to fill your cover snugly and make your pillow look plump.

Victoria Waller

Just What the Doctor Ordered

What is the prescription for keeping fringe or tassels out of the way while sewing seams? Paper surgical tape, which is available at pharmacies. It is strong enough to hold the trim, and it has less sticky stuff than most other tapes. Therefore, it won't leave any residue behind, especially on napped fabrics.

Barbara Fimbel

Put a Little Extra in the Corners

To give square or rectangular pillows a lavish look, sew extra ruffled fabric into the corner areas.

Donna Babylon

Back It Up

To make a quick-and-easy pillow sham that requires no hemming along the edges of the back opening, try this method.

Step 1: Cut a 15-inch square of fabric for the pillow front and set it aside.

Step 2: Cut a 15 × 45-inch piece of fabric for the pillow back, then cut it in half crosswise, as shown in **Diagram 1**.

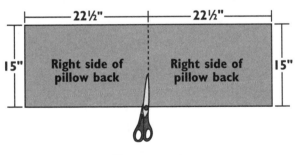

DIAGRAM 1

Step 3: With wrong sides facing, fold each pillow back piece in half crosswise and press, as shown in **Diagram 2**.

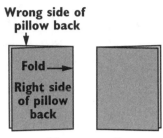

DIAGRAM 2

Step 4: With right sides facing, pin one pillow back piece to the pillow front along three sides, making sure the raw edges are even, as shown in **Diagram 3**.

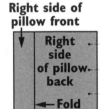

DIAGRAM 3

Step 5: With right sides facing, pin the second pillow back piece to the pillow front, as shown in **Diagram 4**. The folded edges of the pillow back pieces should overlap in the center.

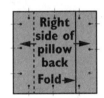

DIAGRAM 4

Step 6: Sew the pillow back pieces to the pillow front using a ½-inch seam allowance. Turn your pillow cover right side out and press.

Donna Babylon

Pleats

Pleats add eye-catching interest to the design of a garment or home decorating project. Pleats can be solid in color, plaid, or faced with a coordinating fabric for extra flair. In this chapter, our experts present the secrets of precision pleating, pressing, and stabilizing for professional-looking designs.

The Power of the Pleat

Add one hundred dollars to the look of your tailored blouses with the addition of a simple box pleat. Start with a blouse pattern that has a back yoke, then follow this easy technique.

Step 1: Position the center fold line of the blouse back pattern piece 1½ inches from the fold of the fabric, as shown in **Diagram 1,** and pin. This will add a 3-inch pleat below the yoke. Cut out the pattern piece.

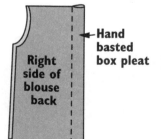

DIAGRAM 1

DIAGRAM 2

Step 2: With wrong sides facing, baste the blouse back along the original center fold line, as shown in **Diagram 2.**

Step 3: On the right side of the blouse back, press the pleat in place and baste ¼ inch from the upper edge, as shown

in **Diagram 3.** Then remove the basting stitches along the center back.

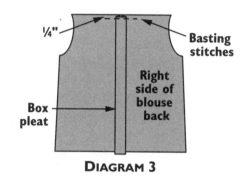

DIAGRAM 3

Step 4: Finish your blouse according to the pattern directions. The back of your blouse will have a fashionable pleat, as shown in **Diagram 4.**

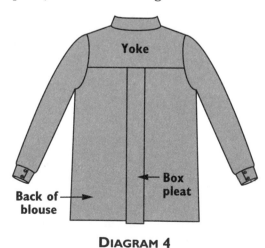

DIAGRAM 4

Clotilde

Perfect Pleating

Precision marking is the key to accurate pleating. A ⅛-inch mistake per pleat on a skirt with eight pleats means your skirt will be 1 inch too large or small. Here are some tried-and-true marking methods to ensure perfect pleats.

⊞ Use tailor's tacks to mark pleats on fragile fabrics, such as silk.

⊞ A tracing wheel and dressmaker's carbon provide the best results when marking on the wrong side of your fabric.

⊞ Fabric marking pens and pins work well when marking on the right side of your fabric.

⊞ If you don't want to mark or pin, try snipping your fabric along the pleat lines within the seam allowance.

Anne Marie Soto

Pleated Ruffles

If you have a ruffler attachment for your sewing machine, you can easily make ¼- to ½-inch-deep pleats. Your ruffler will form neat, narrow pleats and sew the pleated strip. If you'd rather, you can sew the pleats in place separately. As your ruffler forms each pleat, finger press it in place.

Karen Kunkel

No Impression Is a Good Impression

When setting pleats for the first time, place a strip of brown paper between the pleat you are setting and the next pleat before you press. The paper will prevent an impression of the pleat you are setting from appearing on the pleat to be set next. Press on the right side of the fabric, using a press cloth.

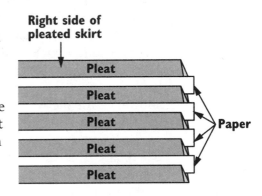

Barbara Fimbel

★ Bright Idea ★

CREATE AN INTERESTING EFFECT BY PLEATING A STRIPED FABRIC. Choose a fabric with at least 1-inch-wide stripes. The stripe will determine the width of your pleats. Using the stripes as your guide, fold and press the pleats. When you wear your completed garment, the stripe under the pleat will show as you move.

Karen Kunkel

Pleats

Knife-Pleated Skirt

It's easy to make a pleated skirt even if you don't have a pattern. The knife pleats on this skirt all face in the same direction.

Step 1: For the skirt, you need a piece of fabric that is three times as wide as your hip measurement plus a 1-inch center back seam allowance. To your desired skirt length, add a hem allowance and a ⅝-inch seam allowance for the waistband. Cut out the fabric for the skirt.

Step 2: Cut a waistband that has a width of 3 inches and a length equal to the measurement of your waist plus 2½ inches for the seam allowance and the facing. Cut a piece of interfacing to the same measurements.

Step 3: Turn up the hem that you added to the length of your skirt in Step 1 and blindstitch it in place, as shown in **Diagram 1.**

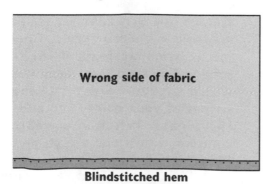

Wrong side of fabric

Blindstitched hem

DIAGRAM 1

Step 4: Pleat your fabric vertically, folding and pinning even pleats so that the finished result fits around your hips, as shown in **Diagram 2.** Baste the pleats in place inside the seam allowance along the upper edge and press.

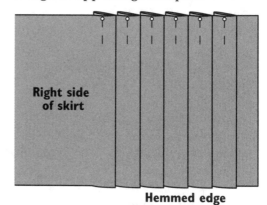

Right side of skirt

Hemmed edge

DIAGRAM 2

Step 5: Fold your skirt in half crosswise with right sides facing. Sew your skirt together along the short ends to form the center back seam, then insert a back zipper. Press the seam open.

Step 6: Adjust the pleats at the upper edge so that the skirt fits your waist, allowing an additional 1 inch for ease. Due to easing, the pleats may become deeper, as shown in **Diagram 3.**

Step 7: Sew the interfacing to the wrong side of your waistband along three sides. If you are using fusible interfacing, follow the manufacturer's directions. Then, with right sides to-

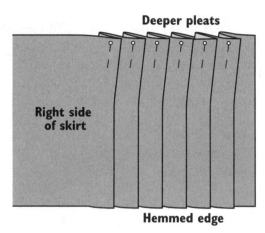

Deeper pleats

Right side of skirt

Hemmed edge

DIAGRAM 3

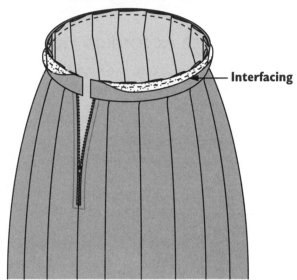

Waistband sewn to skirt

Interfacing

DIAGRAM 5

gether, sew each of the ends of the waistband together using a ⅝-inch seam allowance, as shown in **Diagram 4.** Trim the seam allowance, clip the corners, and turn the ends right side out.

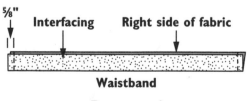

⅝"

Interfacing   **Right side of fabric**

Waistband

DIAGRAM 4

Step 8: With right sides facing, pin and sew the waistband to the upper edge of the skirt, as shown in **Diagram 5.** Turn under ⅝ inch along the unfinished edge of the waistband and press. Fold the waistband to the wrong side of the skirt, and blindstitch it in place. Finish the waistband by sewing a snap or a hook and eye to the ends of the waistband.

Step 9: On the right side of the skirt and beginning just below the waistband, edge stitch along the folded edge of each pleat for 7 inches. This will hold the pleats in place.

Marian Mongelli

Permanent Pleats

To make pleat creases permanent, use single strands of fusible thread. Cut the fusible thread into lengths that match the lengths of your pleats. Place one length of thread inside each pleat fold on the wrong side of the fabric. Using a press cloth, press each pleat. The thread will melt, fusing the creased edges together. Your pleats are now permanent!

Karen Kunkel

Stabilize Accordion Pleats

Here's how to use beautiful accordion-pleated fabric when making a classic-looking pleated skirt. You'll need 1½- or 2-inch clear packing tape without reinforcement strips to be used as follows.

Step 1: Lay out the pattern pieces on a single layer of fabric.

Step 2: To adhere the tape to the fabric under each pattern piece, lift the pattern as needed and lay the tape down so that it spans both the cutting line and the seam line along all pattern edges. All pleats should be taped in place, as shown in **Diagrams 1A** and **1B**. Pin the pattern to the accordion-pleated fabric, taking care to pin only inside the seam allowance. Cut out each pattern piece from the fabric.

Step 3: To stabilize the seams of your garment, place a strip of lightweight twill tape along the seam line on top of your fabric. Then sew each seam through the twill tape, the two pleated fabric layers, and the packing tape. The packing tape will make your needle sticky, so you will have to change it as needed.

Step 4: Before pressing the seams of your garment, carefully tear away the packing tape from your fabric along the perforations, as shown in **Diagram 2.** Be sure to pull the packing tape sideways and away from the stitching line rather than in an upward direction.

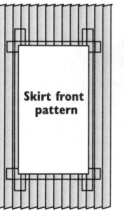

A

Transparent packing tape

Skirt front pattern

Skirt back pattern

B

Diagram 1

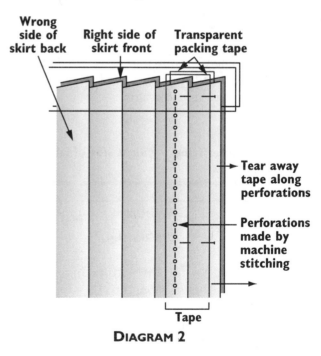

Wrong side of skirt back   Right side of skirt front   Transparent packing tape

Tear away tape along perforations

Perforations made by machine stitching

Tape

Diagram 2

If you have difficulty tearing the packing tape away from the seam, remove the thread from the needle and sew over the seam line again. This will

perforate the tape a second time, making it easier to tear.

Step 5: Finish your garment according to the pattern directions.

Barbara Fimbel

Pleat Preserver

To keep pleats crisp and to make pressing easy, try this tip. After hemming a pleated skirt, edge stitch the inner edge of each pleat through all thicknesses, including the hem, using a thread color that closely matches your fabric. There will be no more guessing where pleat fold lines are when it's time to press the skirt!

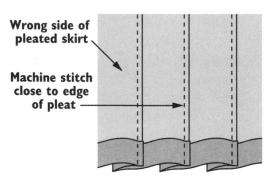

Wrong side of pleated skirt

Machine stitch close to edge of pleat

Barbara Fimbel

Up with Pleats

Do your pleats tend to ripple as you sew? Instead of sewing from the waistline toward the hem of your garment, sew from the hem toward the waistline. You'll be surprised at the difference.

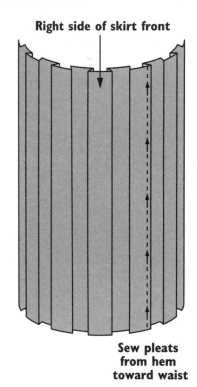

Right side of skirt front

Sew pleats from hem toward waist

Anne Marie Soto

Pockets

Whether you love pockets that make a design statement or those that remain invisible and are set into your garment, the more you know about pocket construction, the easier it will be to sew them. The pages that follow are filled with expert advice and techniques for marking, altering, and making perfect pockets.

The Easiest Matched Pockets

Here's a simple method for achieving rounded unlined patch pockets that match each other perfectly.

Step 1: Trace the pocket pattern piece onto a piece of cardboard to make a template, as shown in **Diagram 1**. Then trace the template onto the wrong side of your fabric and cut two pockets.

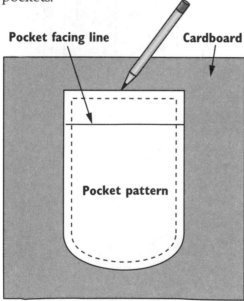

Pocket facing line   **Cardboard**

Pocket pattern

DIAGRAM 1

Step 2: Turn down the pocket facing along the facing line so that the right

sides of your fabric are together, as shown in **Diagram 2**. Sew the sides together. Clip the corners and grade the seam allowances. Turn the pocket facing right side out.

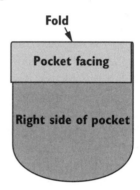

Fold

Pocket facing

Right side of pocket

DIAGRAM 2

Step 3: With the right side of your pocket facing up, topstitch the facing in place through both layers of fabric, as shown in **Diagram 3**.

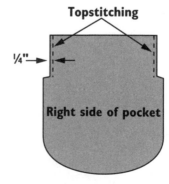

Topstitching

¼"

Right side of pocket

DIAGRAM 3

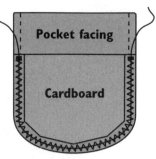

Step 4: On the right side of the pocket, place a length of topstitching thread inside the seam allowance ¼ inch from the unfinished edges, leaving a tail at the beginning and end. Set your machine for a narrow zigzag stitch and no stitch length. Sew a bar tack over the thread at the beginning of one unfinished edge. Then set your machine for a long stitch length and zigzag over the thread, ending with another bar tack at the opposite side, as shown in **Diagram 4.**

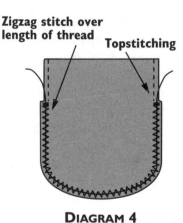

DIAGRAM 4

Step 5: Cut the cardboard template along the facing line and the seam lines. Slip the cardboard template into the pocket facing of your pocket. Use the topstitching thread on both ends of the pocket as a gathering thread to draw up the seam allowance around the template, as shown in **Diagram 5.** Press the pocket and let it cool.

Step 6: Remove the template and press the pocket again. Let it cool, then pull out the topstitching thread.

Step 7: Topstitch the pocket in place on your garment.

Ann Price Gosch

DIAGRAM 5

Lined for Stress

When stitching patch pockets for a jacket or coat, first sew the pocket and pocket lining together, with right sides facing, along the top edge. Turn the fabric right side out and press. Then, with right sides facing, pin only the lining to the jacket and sew along the seam line. Press the seam allowance of the lining toward the center of the pocket lining. Then fold under the seam allowance of the pocket fabric, and topstitch the pocket in place over the lining. With this method, the stress of putting your hands or objects in your pockets will be on the lining, which is stitched separately from the pocket.

Karen Costello Soltys

Pocket Flaps

Reduce the bulk from pocket flaps by cutting the top flap from fashion fabric and the underside from lining fabric.

Elizabeth M. Barry

No-Match Patch

Don't waste your time trying to match plaid patch pockets on a plaid garment. Instead, create an interesting pocket by cutting on the bias.

Step 1: Fold your pocket pattern piece so that the grain line forms a right angle. Crease it along the fold, as shown in **Diagram 1**.

Grain line forms right angle

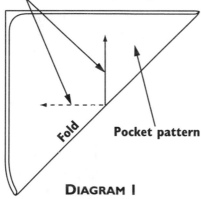

Fold

Pocket pattern

DIAGRAM 1

Step 2: Mark a new grain line along the crease, as shown in **Diagram 2**.

Pocket pattern

Fold

New grain line

DIAGRAM 2

Step 3: Open the pocket pattern and cut out as many pockets as required on the bias of the fabric, as shown in **Diagram 3**.

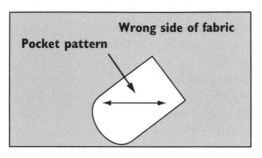

Wrong side of fabric

Pocket pattern

DIAGRAM 3

Step 4: To stabilize your bias pockets and keep them from stretching during wear, use the pocket pattern piece to cut a fusible interfacing piece for each pocket. Fuse a piece of interfacing to the wrong side of each fabric pocket before attaching it, then finish your garment according to the pattern instructions.

Nancy Nix-Rice

A New Angle

When I want to turn a curved patch pocket into an easy-to-handle angled pocket, I use this technique. I love the way it adds a designer flair to any garment I'm working on.

Step 1: Fold the pocket pattern piece in half lengthwise. Place the pattern on a large sheet of paper. Use a ruler and a pencil to extend and mark the

straight edges of the pocket so they intersect, as shown in **Diagram 1**.

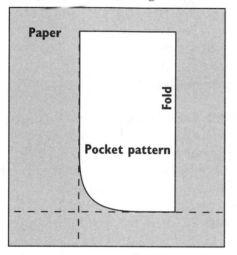

DIAGRAM 1

Step 2: Measure an equal distance from the intersection along both extended lines and draw a cutting line, as shown in **Diagram 2**.

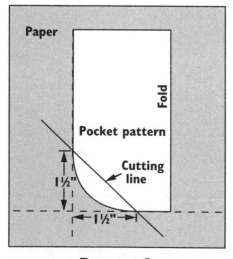

DIAGRAM 2

Step 3: Cut through both layers of the pattern piece along the new cutting line. Open up the pattern piece, as shown in **Diagram 3,** and use it to trace and cut out your pockets from fabric.

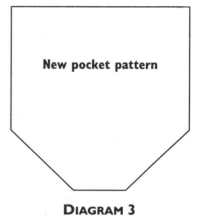

DIAGRAM 3

Step 4: With the wrong side of the pocket facing up, fold over ⅝ inch along the sides, bottom, and then the corners, as shown in **Diagram 4**. Sew the pocket to your garment, and finish your garment according to the pattern instructions.

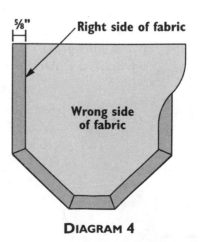

DIAGRAM 4

Nancy Nix-Rice

Pockets

Fuse It

Instead of using hand stitches to close the opening used for turning a lined pocket to the right side, fuse it with a strip of fusible web. No one will know the difference!

Patsy Shields

Drooping Pockets

To remedy drooping in-seam pockets on sewn or ready-to-wear garments, anchor them to the garment with twill tape. Turn the garment wrong side out and smooth the pockets over the garment front.

Place a pin in the waistband where each pocket starts to taper. Cut two pieces of twill tape long enough to reach from the pin in the waistband to each pocket plus 1 inch. Sew one piece of tape to each pocket, then to the lower edge of the waistband. Trim the tape as needed. This will keep your pockets from shifting.

Patsy Shields

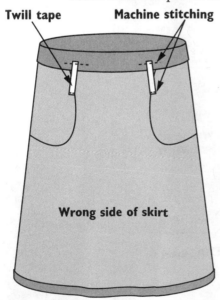

Twill tape **Machine stitching**

Wrong side of skirt

Pocket Pointers

Shaping and sewing patch pockets on a tailored garment isn't easy. But here is a technique that works every time. It involves lining the pockets, making them much easier to shape than unlined ones.

Step 1: Start with one rectangle of your garment fabric and one rectangle of your lining that is slightly larger than your pocket pattern, but do not cut the pocket from either fabric.

Step 2: Cut a piece of interfacing the size of the finished pocket. Fuse it to the wrong side of your fabric, making sure to align the grain lines, as shown in **Diagram 1.**

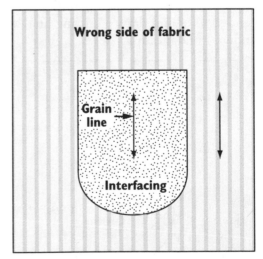

Wrong side of fabric

Grain line

Interfacing

DIAGRAM I

Step 3: With right sides together, pin the lining to the fabric. Sew

around the edge of the interfacing, leaving the upper edge open for turning, as shown in **Diagram 2.** Using pinking shears, cut out the pocket along the sides and curves, using a ¼-inch seam allowance. The pinking shears will notch the curves, so no seam grading is necessary.

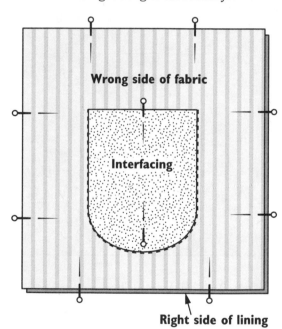

Wrong side of fabric

Interfacing

Right side of lining

DIAGRAM 2

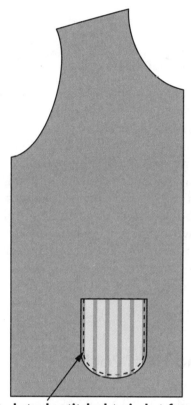

Pocket edgestitched to jacket front

DIAGRAM 3

Claire Shaeffer

Step 4: Turn the pocket right side out and press. Turn under the fabric and lining seam allowance along the opening and slip stitch the opening closed.

Step 5: As shown in **Diagram 3,** edge stitch your pocket to the garment using a zipper foot as your guide.

Pipe a Perfect Pocket

I've found that machine sewing piping to a patch pocket causes the pocket to bunch up and shrink as I sew. To remedy this, I hand baste the piping to the pocket. This lessens the chance of stretching the piping as I sew around the pocket curves. Then I use the hand basting line as my guide for sewing the pocket lining to the pocket.

Sandra Betzina

Easy Curves

To get a smooth curve around the edges of unlined patch pockets, first I stay stitch inside the seam allowance on the wrong side of the pocket. Then I use a pin to lift one stitch and pull it gently until the edges of the pocket start to gather and roll to the wrong side. This helps to shape the pocket by easing the fabric in place. Pressing and sewing are then a breeze.

Janis Bullis

Blind Hem Pocket

You can easily duplicate the look of hand-picked stitches with a blind hem stitch. This technique will create a perfectly flat pocket with the edges partially molded into the garment. And, best of all, the pocket lining will never show. Before trying this technique on your garment, practice by folding a piece of fabric in half and placing it on top of a sheet of white paper. The paper will serve as your background fabric and let you see your stitches clearly. As you sew, adjust the stitch width and length and record your machine's settings on the paper for future use.

Step 1: Set your machine for a blind hem stitch. Adjust the stitch so that it has a narrow width and a length shorter than the width.

Step 2: Attach the blind hem foot to your machine. Sew the pocket to your garment, guiding the pocket so that the straight stitch is hidden in the ditch where the pocket edge and garment meet. Let the zigzag swing of the needle catch the pocket edge to tack it in place.

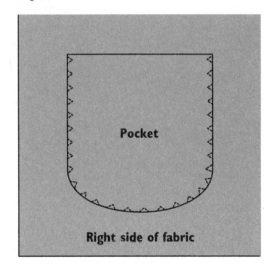

Pocket

Right side of fabric

Step 3: Now topstitch your pocket in place.

Nancy Erickson

Stabilizing Bias Pocket Edges

I'm a professional dressmaker, so techniques that save time translate into profit. This technique is a big time-saver, especially for pants and skirts with angled pockets. It requires changing the grain line of the inside

pocket of a skirt or pair of pants. Once you master this technique, don't hesitate to experiment and apply it to other areas of your sewing.

Step 1: Cut out your skirt or pants pieces from fabric, but don't cut out the pockets. Note that the pocket pattern and garment front pattern have the same angled edge and the same bias, as shown in **Diagram 1.**

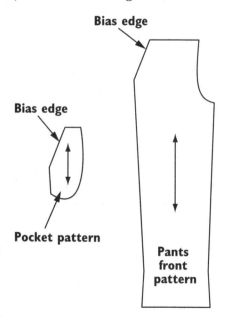

DIAGRAM 1

Step 2: Instead of using twill tape to stabilize the bias edge, let the grain do it for you. Cross out the grain line on the pocket pattern piece. Mark a new grain line that runs along the edge of the angled seam allowance of the pocket pattern, as shown in

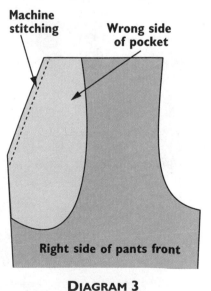

DIAGRAM 2

Diagram 2. This will work on a slightly curved pocket as well. Place the pocket pattern on your fabric, making sure you place the new grain line on the straight of the grain. Cut out the required number of pockets from your fabric.

Step 3: With right sides together, pin the pocket piece to the garment, matching the new straight of the grain to the garment's bias edge. Because the bias edge is slightly longer than the pocket edge, you will have to ease this edge in place along the pocket as you pin. Sew the pocket to the garment, as shown in **Diagram 3.** Your bias pocket edge is now stabilized, and the pocket pouch is still on the bias for a softer but stronger pocket.

DIAGRAM 3

Kathleen Spike

Presser Feet

Put your best foot forward, and learn how to maximize your sewing potential and increase the capabilities of your sewing machine. Knowing how to use the right foot will let you topstitch straighter, walk faster, and bind better. The pros put their heads together to give you the most up-to-date information about presser feet and how to make them an even more useful part of your sewing.

Get It Straight

Want to know the secret to a perfectly straight edgestitch or topstitch? Use the blind hem foot as your guide. Set your machine in the left needle position, and sew with the edge of the fabric against the guide on the foot. If your blind hem foot has an adjustable guide, then you have an extra advantage. You can use the guide to perfectly edge stitch or topstitch at various distances from the edge of the fabric.

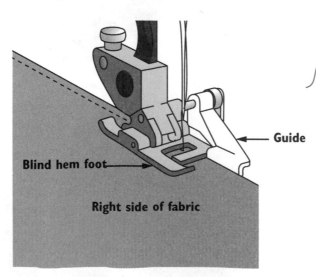

Guide

Blind hem foot

Right side of fabric

Verna Erickson
Singer Sewing Company

Seams Like Velvet

I find that a walking foot is an absolute necessity when sewing with velvet. It's also important to use a 4 mm stitch length. But when a long seam falls on the bias, such as in a cape or full skirt, use a 0.5 mm zigzag stitch for the best results.

Kenneth D. King

Brother Makes Bigger Buttonholes

Brother machines with one-step buttonhole mechanisms often sew only a limited number of buttonhole sizes. But there is a way to get around this so that you can sew bigger buttonholes.

Step 1: Attach the satin stitch foot to your Brother and lower the buttonhole (blue) lever.

Step 2: Place your fabric under the presser foot, but remember the machine sews in reverse to start. When the stitches reach the top of the desired buttonhole length, tap firmly on the back of the blue lever, but don't hold the lever in place. By doing this, you have sent an electronic signal to the machine telling it to begin the next step of the buttonhole process.

Step 3: After you have completed the second line of stitching, tap the front of the lever. Continue tapping the lever for each step.

June Mellinger
Brother International Corporation

Roller Foot

If you have trouble sewing thick fabrics, vinyls, and leathers, try using a roller foot. It keeps the layers together and glides over the fabric, causing less friction. A roller foot stretches the fabric less and ensures that your stitches will be consistent.

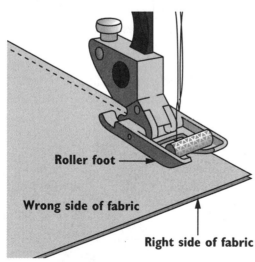

Roller foot

Wrong side of fabric

Right side of fabric

Karen Kunkel

Walk It Through

A walking, or even feed, foot is wonderful for sewing stiff and napped fabrics or when matching plaids and stripes. Your fabric layers will begin and end together, without creeping or slipping as you sew. These feet have a built-in feeding mechanism that pulls the top layer of fabric through the machine at the same rate of speed at which the feed dogs are pushing the bottom layer through.

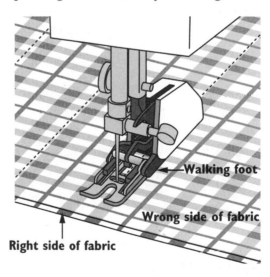

Walking foot

Wrong side of fabric

Right side of fabric

Karen Kunkel

Zip It Up

A zipper foot is not just for sewing zippers. I use it whenever I want to see the row of stitching I'm creating.

Claire Shaeffer

★ Bright Idea ★

To ease the presser foot over a thick seam and eliminate skipped stitches, try using a Hump Jumper between the back of the presser foot and the fabric. Keep your jumper handy by attaching a strip of Velcro to its handle and your machine. Hump Jumpers are available through mail-order sources.

Clotilde

Let's Take a Walk

I use a walking foot for most garment sewing. In a pinch, I use a roller foot because it will keep the layers of fabric together better than other feet.

Robbie Fanning

Rolling Along

When I apply trim to my fabric, I always attach a roller foot with loops to my sewing machine. This type of foot can hook onto the toes of a regular presser foot. To prevent the trim from shifting too much, I baste it in place with strips of fusible web. If you use ribbon trim, always test fuse it to make sure the web and ribbon will bond to your fabric

smoothly. Sew both edges of the ribbon trim in the same direction to prevent diagonal wrinkles.

Janis Bullis

Quick-Covered Piping

Instead of purchasing or making piping to insert into the seam of your project, try this type of decorative piping. It is a cinch to sew because the cording is covered with thread and secured directly onto the fabric in one step. So get out your cording foot and pipe away!

Supplies

- Sewing machine with a zigzag stitch
- Cording foot with a tunnel
- Rayon thread
- Cotton or poly/cotton thread that matches the rayon thread
- Cording

Step 1: Attach the cording foot, as shown in **Diagram 1,** to your machine.

Step 2: Thread the upper part of your machine with the rayon thread and the bobbin with cotton thread.

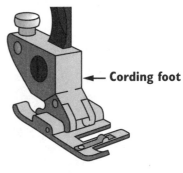

← **Cording foot**

DIAGRAM 1

Step 3: Set your machine for a close, dense satin stitch, making sure the width of the stitch will clear the cording on both sides.

Step 4: Place your fabric under the needle. Begin making your covered piping by feeding the cording under the foot. Zigzag over it directly onto the fabric, as shown in **Diagram 2.**

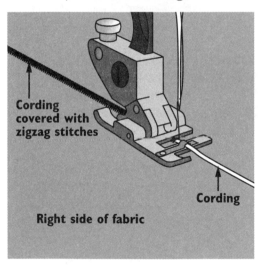

Cording covered with zigzag stitches

Cording

Right side of fabric

DIAGRAM 2

Sulky of America

Blind Appliqué

To give your appliqués a hand-stitched look, use a blind hem foot and a blind hem stitch. Here's how.

Step 1: Turn all of the edges of your appliqué to the wrong side and press them.

Step 2: Use monofilament thread in the needle and all-purpose thread that matches your background fabric in the bobbin. Set your machine for a narrow stitch width and a short stitch length. Adjust your blind hem foot guide so that the straight portion of the blind hem stitch falls on the background fabric and the zigzag stitch catches the appliqué.

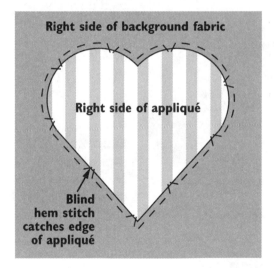

Right side of background fabric

Right side of appliqué

Blind hem stitch catches edge of appliqué

Verna Erickson
Singer Sewing Company

Get in Line

If your presser feet aren't marked with your most frequently used measurements, you can easily customize them using an extra-fine point, permanent, felt-tip pen.

Carol Laflin Ahles

Eyelet Made Easy

You can create delicate eyelet designs with an eyelet plate. If your sewing machine doesn't have an eyelet plate, you can purchase one through your favorite notions catalog or at your local fabric store.

Step 1: Read your machine's owner's manual to find if you must lower the feed dogs and remove the presser foot to attach the eyelet plate. Snap the eyelet plate over the feed dog area.

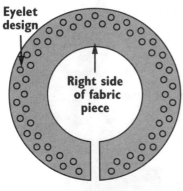

DIAGRAM 1

Eyelet design

Right side of fabric piece

Step 2: Referring to **Diagram 1**, create an eyelet design on your fabric piece.

Step 3: Place your fabric piece in an embroidery hoop and make sure it is pulled taut. With an awl, pierce a hole in the fabric inside the hoop where you want an eyelet, as shown in **Diagram 2**. It is important to pierce only one hole at a time to prevent the edges of the hole from fraying.

Step 4: Position the pierced hole over the eyelet plate prong. Lower the presser bar and set your machine for a narrow zigzag stitch.

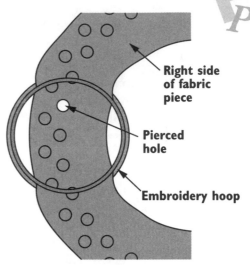

Right side of fabric piece

Pierced hole

Embroidery hoop

DIAGRAM 2

Step 5: Zigzag along the edges of the hole, rotating the hoop as you sew. This will bind the edges of the hole and create an eyelet, as shown in Diagram 3.

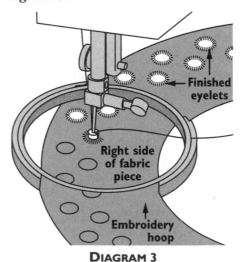

Finished eyelets

Right side of fabric piece

Embroidery hoop

DIAGRAM 3

Step 6: Repeat Steps 3 through 5 to sew eyelets in the rest of your design.

Jane M. Burbach
Elna Inc.

Fringe Benefits

Whether or not you have an Elna, you can create fabulous fringe. For Elna machines, use sole plate B with models 8000, 9000, and DIVA. For other Elna models and other sewing machine brands, use the net/curtain sole plate #494-290.

Step 1: Set your machine for a 5.0 stitch width and a 1.2 stitch length. Change the machine tension to five.

Step 2: Wind trim, such as ribbon, braid, or yarn, around the fringe fork to a width of 2½ inches, as shown in **Diagram 1**. Be careful not to wind the trim too tight. The fork must slide easily.

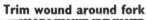

Trim wound around fork

DIAGRAM 1

Step 3: Place your fabric under the fork, with the right prong ¼ inch from the edge of the fabric. Zigzag along the length of the trim for 2 inches, as shown in **Diagram 2**.

Step 4: Lift the presser foot and gently pull the fork forward, leaving some of the stitched fringe on the fork. Continue winding the trim around the fork and sewing until you have made the amount of fringe you need. Remove the fabric from the machine.

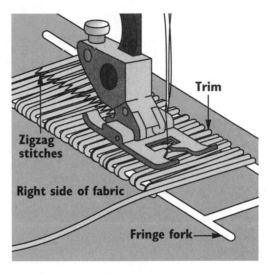

DIAGRAM 2

Step 5: Cut the trim carefully on each side of fork to form the fringe, as shown in **Diagram 3**.

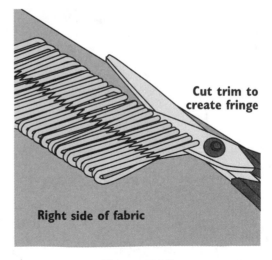

DIAGRAM 3

Jane M. Burbach
Elna Inc.

Pressing

Do you know the difference between pressing and ironing? Do you know how to make your own seam roll in a pinch? The answer to questions like these will help you to perfect your pressing skills. Although there are no shortcuts to pressing, having the proper equipment and knowledge will make your job easier. So whether your garment is brand new or ten years old, it's never too late to learn how to press for success.

Pressed for Time?

To prevent freshly pressed fabric from stretching and wrinkling, wait a minute or two before removing it from your ironing board.

If you can't afford to wait, place a portable fan on a nearby table to speed the process of setting the pressing.

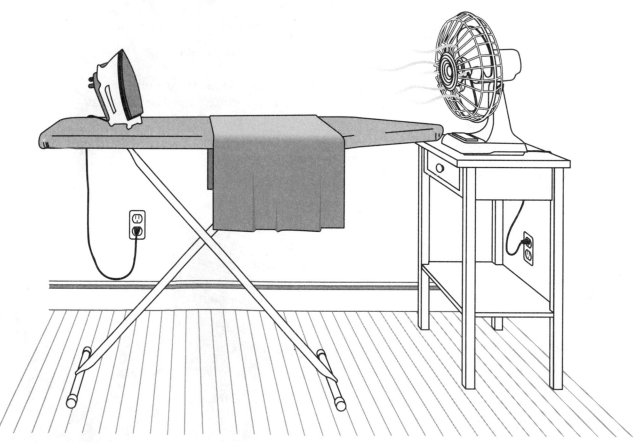

Belva Barrick

The Press Test

Pressing is just as important as sewing. So before you press, ask yourself the following questions about temperature, moisture, fabric weight, water, and pressure to ensure the best pressing results.

- Does the fabric have a glaze? Is the fabric made of synthetic fibers that can melt? Is the fabric very delicate? If so, a very hot iron will melt, glaze, or scorch your fabric. Test a fabric scrap for the optimum pressing temperature. If your iron has ever been knocked to the floor, don't rely on its thermostat.

- Does the fabric react better with or without moisture? Test a fabric scrap to see whether you get the best results from a dry iron with a moist press cloth or from a steam iron and a dry press cloth.

- Does the fabric have a nap that will crush or mat? Does it shine when pressed? If so, don't press on the right side of the fabric without a press cloth.

- Does water cause spots on the fabric? If it does, empty all of the water from your iron and use it dry. If moisture is needed, use a slightly damp press cloth or a mister-spray bottle. Make sure you don't wet the fabric.

- Do you know how much pressure to apply? Never use pressure when pressing fabrics with a nap, such as velvet. Simply hold a steam iron above the fabric's surface and let the steam penetrate the fabric. When a seam allowance or dart is stubborn, simply finger press lightly.

Belva Barrick

SMART SHOPPER

Have you ever wished for the ultimate pressing surface but just don't have the room? Try the Space Board— a 22 × 51-inch padded board that easily transforms any flat surface into a temporary pressing and/or work surface. I use it for everything from pressing to pinning projects.

This unique board is made from the same heat-resistant material used for quality custom-made table pads. It has a gridded work area and felt backing that provides a slip-resistant surface. I find it great for working with silk and satin fabrics.

The best part of owning a Space Board is that it folds in half for easy storage under my bed or in a closet. You can purchase one through Voster Marketing, 190 Mount Pleasant Road, Newtown, CT 06470; (800) 231-1959.

Virginia K. Jansen

Pressing

Iron Safety

If you have a hard time remembering to unplug your iron, purchase a multiple electric outlet strip with an on/off switch. Plug your iron and your overhead light into the same strip. When the light is off, so is the iron. This is a much better reminder than the little light built into your iron.

Kenneth D. King

Press As You Sew!

Never stitch across a seam, dart, or tuck without pressing it first. Sew as many seams as possible at once and then press. This guarantees flat seams without tucks and puckers on the outside of your garment.

Belva Barrick

Short Fuse

If fusible interfacing is not preshrunk, it can shrink as you fuse it to your fabric. To avoid this, lay out the pattern pieces on your fabric. Leaving a border around the edge of each piece, cut out the pieces. Then fuse the interfacing to the fabric pieces. Allow your fabric to cool and then cut the pattern pieces along the cutting lines.

Mary Griffin
Singer Sewing Company

Hot Idea!

Purchase two irons for your sewing room and reserve one for fusing and laminating only. This way you'll never run the risk of smudging and ruining a precious piece of silk or wool with adhesive residue.

Gail Brown

Best Pocket Pressing Tool

A wooden chopstick makes the best pressing tool for reaching into places where my fingers can't. A chopstick is the perfect size for getting into lined patch pockets to smooth out curves and for using as a mini clapper to set in sharp edges. And since the wood is untreated, you can use it with a steam iron without damaging your fabric.

Nancy Erickson

Seams Stubborn

When it seems impossible to set a crease in your fabrics, try this technique. Lay a press cloth over the folded edge to be creased. Then place a steam iron over the press cloth, and use your body weight to apply pressure to the iron for 10 to 15 seconds. Remove the iron and press a clapper or Seam Stick over the folded edge. This will squeeze out the mois-

ture and set in a sharp crease. If necessary, repeat the process. This procedure will give you beautifully creased pant legs, pleats, and lapel edges.

Belva Barrick

Dribbling Iron?

If your iron dribbles water, check the owner's manual to see what kind of water you should use in it. Some irons will leak when filled with tap water. If yours does, it may require filtered water.

Elizabeth M. Barry

Pressing Is Key

I believe pressing is the only way to obtain truly professional results in sewing. Before I sew any seams, I place my fabric with right sides together and press along the seam allowances. This way I am assured of a flat, neat edge as I sew.

Virginia K. Jansen

Quick Press

I always keep a man's cotton handkerchief to use as a pressing cloth and a plastic spray bottle of water near my ironing board for quick pressing jobs.

Elizabeth M. Barry

Pressing Box

I store all of my pressing equipment together in a clear plastic box. Besides my pressing ham, point presser, and seam roll, I also include a press cloth, a small brush for reviving the nap on pile fabrics, and strips of brown paper for pressing seams.

Lynn L. Browne
Coats & Clark

Rub Out Scorch Marks

If you leave a scorch mark in your wool fabric because the iron was too hot, don't despair. Take a nickel and rub it on the scorch. Like magic, the scorch will disappear!

SMART SHOPPER

Seam rolls are easy to make from wooden dowels. I like to keep two of them on hand for pressing different kinds of fabrics. For each roll I purchase a $1\frac{1}{2} \times 36$-inch hardwood dowel. I cover one with felt or cotton twill for pressing smooth fabrics and the other with felt or flannel for pressing napped fabrics. The hard wooden surface won't flatten out the way some stuffed seam rolls do.

Kenneth D. King

Pressing

A Grain of Truth

It's important to press with the grain, not against it; otherwise, the fabric could stretch. To determine the direction of the grain, check the "whiskers" of thread along the raw edge of the fabric. The direction in which they are pointing is the correct grain direction, so press accordingly.

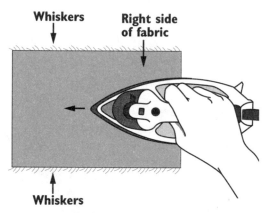

Belva Barrick

Seams Like Pressing

Eliminate seam allowance impressions and an overpressed look on your garment with this pressing technique. This method works great on sleeves, pants, and hard-to-reach places.

Step 1: Set the stitches in the seam of your garment by pressing the seam flat just as it was sewn, as shown in **Diagram 1.**

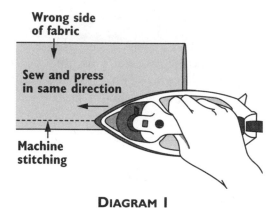

DIAGRAM 1

Step 2: With your garment turned wrong side out, position the seam over a curved surface, such as a seam roll, the edge of your ironing board, a rolled-up magazine, or a Seam Stick, and press it open, as shown in **Diagram 2.** This method allows only the edges of the seam allowance to come in contact with the iron, thus avoiding impressions on your garment.

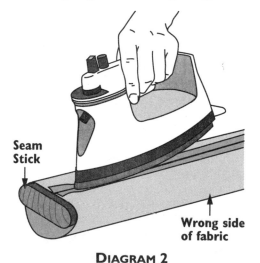

DIAGRAM 2

Belva Barrick

It's Best to Underpress

To avoid a steam-rolled look when pressing collars and facings, I always press lightly first. Then, if more pressing is needed, I do a little at a time. Because garments can be ruined by overpressing, it's best to take your time and underpress.

Belva Barrick

Pressing from the Right Side

When you must press the right side of your fabric, use a press cloth and follow these helpful hints. It will prevent your fabric from acquiring an unwanted shine.

 If you don't have a press cloth, use a piece of lightweight fabric, such as batiste, organdy, or cheesecloth, if your fabric doesn't have a nap. These lightweight fabrics are sheer enough to let you see your fabric underneath.

 If your fabric has a nap, use a piece of the same fabric for your press cloth. Make sure the right side of your press cloth is facing your fabric and that the naps are going in the same direction. This will prevent your fabric from becoming crushed.

 If your fabric has a nap and you don't have enough extra fabric for a press cloth, use a terry cloth towel.

 Use brown kraft paper or tissue paper to prevent seam and dart lines from showing through on the right side of your fabric. Simply place a sheet of paper between the fabric and the seam or dart on the wrong side, as shown, and press away. Then remove the paper when you have finished.

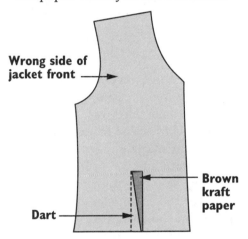

Barbara Fimbel

★ Bright Idea ★

IF A SHINE APPEARS ON DELICATE FABRICS, SUCH AS SILK AND VELVET, AS you press, try rubbing the fabric with a scrap of the same fabric. This technique also works well for removing markings such as tailor's chalk.

Karen Costello Soltys

 ★ **Bright Idea** ★

KEEP A DAMP SPONGE AT YOUR IRONING BOARD AS YOU PRESS. **Use it to evenly moisten an area of your fabric.**

Karen Kunkel

In a Pinch

If you don't have a seam roll handy when pressing, you can quickly make your own. Simply roll up a newspaper or magazine, and wrap it with tape to keep it together. Cover it with a terry cloth towel. With the wrong side of your garment facing up, center the seam over your home-made seam roll and press.

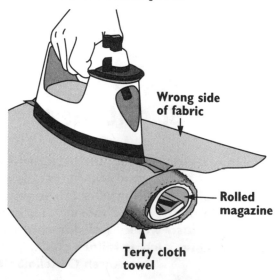

Wrong side of fabric

Rolled magazine

Terry cloth towel

Barbara Fimbel

Pressing Matters

Do you know the difference between pressing and ironing? Pressing is done with an up-and-down motion. Ironing is done with a back-and-forth motion and is used to remove wrinkles. Ironing will stretch seams, so be sure to press them, not iron them. Using the proper motion and correct tools will give you the best results.

Belva Barrick

Cover Your Board in Cotton

Whether you're pressing on a table, sleeve board, or freestanding ironing board, always use a 100 percent cotton cover. Cotton allows moisture to permeate your fabric rather than to bounce back, which intensifies the heat and damages some synthetics. If you are unable to find a 100 percent cotton cover for your ironing board, make one by following these quick-and-easy directions.

Supplies

- ⅝ yard of 100 percent cotton white denim, duck, twill, or canvas
- Padding to place between the cover and the ironing board
- 4 yards of ⅛-inch-wide cording
- Water-soluble or air-erasable marking pen
- 12-inch ruler

Step 1: Place your fabric wrong side up on a clean floor.

Step 2: Turn the ironing board upside down and center it on the fabric. With the pen and ruler, mark a 2½-inch hem on the fabric around the edge of the board, as shown in **Diagram 1**.

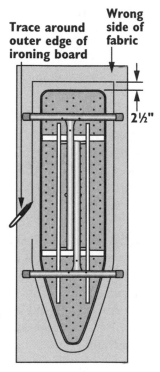

Trace around outer edge of ironing board

Wrong side of fabric

2½"

DIAGRAM 1

Step 3: Remove the ironing board and cut out the ironing board cover.

Step 4: Turn under a ¼-inch hem to the wrong side of the fabric and press. Turn under another ¼ inch and press again. Sew the hem in place.

Step 5: Set your machine for a wide zigzag stitch and a medium stitch length. Leaving a 5-inch tail, lay the cording ½ inch from the edge of your fabric. Zigzag over the cording, making sure not to sew through it, to create a casing, as shown in **Diagram 2**. Leave a 5-inch tail before cutting off the excess cording.

½"   Hemmed edge

⅛" cording

Wrong side of fabric

DIAGRAM 2

Step 6: Lay the ironing board padding on top of the wrong side of the ironing board cover. If your padding is worn and no longer dense and firm, make a new one from an old wool blanket, cutting it 1 inch larger than the ironing board surface. Place your ironing board upside down on top of the padding. Draw up the cording and adjust it until the cover fits snugly around the board, as shown in **Diagram 3**.

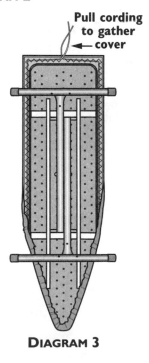

Pull cording to gather cover

DIAGRAM 3

Belva Barrick

Ribbonwork

Whether you love silk ribbon embroidery, bouquets of flowers made from French wire ribbon, or just the addition of a simple ribbon trim on a garment, ribbons allow you to add rich texture and color and to personalize your work. Leaf through these pages for some inspirational ideas from our experts on how to create and care for your ribbonwork.

Realistic Ribbon Flowers

Put leftover scraps of wire-edged ribbon to good use by making decorative ribbon flowers. Stock up on an assortment because they'll come in handy for decorating wrapped packages. If your ribbon has a different shade of the same color on each side, your flowers will have a lovely three-dimensional look.

Step 1: Cut a 15-inch length of ribbon. If the ribbon is wider than 2 inches, you'll need a 30-inch length. Expose the end of the wire on the top edge of one short side of your ribbon, as shown in **Diagram 1**.

Exposed wire

Wire-edged ribbon

DIAGRAM 1

Step 2: Pull the wire to gather the ribbon, as shown in **Diagram 2**.

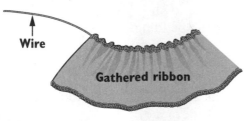

Wire

Gathered ribbon

DIAGRAM 2

Step 3: Expose a tiny bit of the wire on the bottom edge of the same short side. Turn the wire back onto itself so that the gathers don't slip off of the side.

Step 4: Fold one short side of the ribbon ¼ inch over onto itself twice to hide the raw edge. Then pull the gathered edges together as you coil the ribbon around itself into the shape of a flower, as shown in **Diagram 3**.

Top view of ribbon flower

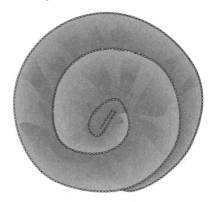

DIAGRAM 3

Step 5: Fold the other short side of the ribbon ¼ inch over onto itself twice and into a triangle, as shown in Diagram 4.

Side view of ribbon flower

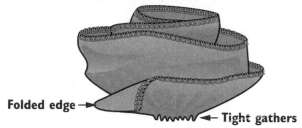

Folded edge →

← Tight gathers

DIAGRAM 4

Step 6: Hold the ribbon gathers in place with a dab of fabric or craft glue. Then place the flower, with the gathered side down, on a small circle of green felt or fabric. Wrap the felt over the gathers and secure in place with small amounts of fabric or craft glue. The ribbon flower can now be used to decorate a package or a garment.

C. M. Offray & Son

Your choice of ribbon and the direction of each stitch will affect the way the ribbon looks on your fabric, as shown in **Diagram 2.** So don't fight the direction in which the ribbon wants to lie. Sometimes it will pull through the fabric with its center perfectly even, and sometimes it will fold softly as it comes through.

Kaethe Kliot

Right side of fabric   **Wooden hoop**

Ribbon flowers →

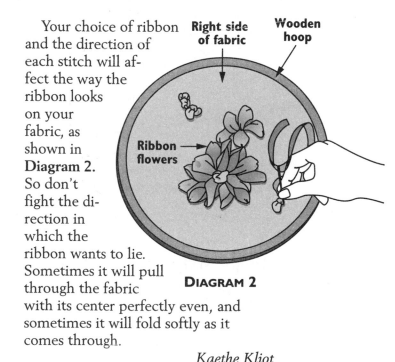

DIAGRAM 2

Sew Lightly

When embroidering ribbon flowers, remember to use a light touch. Don't pull the ribbon too tight at the completion of each stitch. There should be a slight gap between the ribbon and the fabric on both the right side and wrong side, as shown in **Diagram 1.**

Going My Way?

When sewing along the long edges of a length of ribbon, sew both sides in the same direction. This will keep your ribbon from stretching in two different directions.

Right side of fabric   **Ribbon gathers as it goes through fabric**

Ribbon →   **Wrong side of fabric**

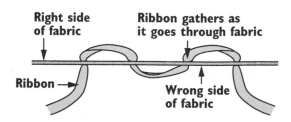

DIAGRAM 1

Sew →   **Woven ribbon**   Sew →

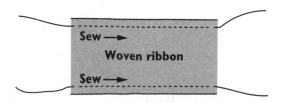

C. M. Offray & Son

Guide to Stitches

Here are the basic stitches you need to know before you begin to embroider. Try the Japanese ribbon stitch for flower buds and the lazy daisy for petals or leaves. For flower centers and other accents, use a French knot. The stem stitch can be used to outline large or small areas, and the coiled rose makes an entire flower. Experiment with other embroidery stitches as you learn what the ribbon can do.

Japanese Ribbon Stitch

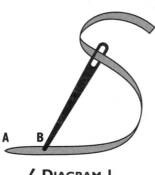

Step 1: Referring to **Diagram 1,** bring your needle up at point A, keeping the ribbon flat. Then push your needle through the ribbon and into the fabric at point B.

DIAGRAM 1

Completed Japanese ribbon stitch

DIAGRAM 2

Step 2: As you gently pull your needle through to the wrong side, the ribbon will curl at one end of the stitch, as shown in Diagram 2.

Lazy Daisy

Step 1: Bring your needle up at point A. Form a loop with the ribbon and insert the needle back into the fabric right next to point A. Bring your needle back through to the right side

of the fabric at point B, making sure the ribbon is underneath the needle, as shown in **Diagram 3.**

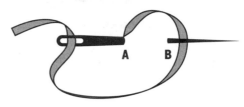

DIAGRAM 3

Step 2: Pull your needle through the loop and insert it into the fabric at point C, as shown in **Diagram 4.** This will produce a small stitch to anchor the loop.

DIAGRAM 4

French Knot

Step 1: Bring your needle up through the fabric at point A. Then wrap the ribbon around the point of your needle three times, as shown in **Diagram 5.**

DIAGRAM 5

Step 2: Hold the ribbon in place on the needle with your thumb and fore-finger of one hand. Push the needle into the fabric near point A, as shown in **Diagram 6.** Gently pull the needle to the wrong side as the ribbon forms a knot on the surface of the fabric.

DIAGRAM 6

Stem Stitch

Step 1: Bring your needle up at point A. Then insert it back into the fabric at point B and bring it up at point C. Insert it at point D and bring it out at point B, as shown in **Diagram 7.** You have completed one stitch.

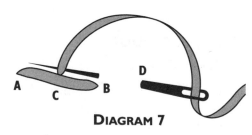

DIAGRAM 7

Step 2: Repeat Step 1 to create a line of stitches, as shown in Diagram 8.

Completed line of stem stitches

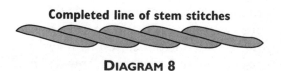

DIAGRAM 8

Coiled Rose

Step 1: Bring your needle up at point A, as shown in **Diagram 9.** Hold your needle straight up and twist it to coil the ribbon tightly, as shown.

Step 2: Hold the coil at the mid-point, and put just the tip of your needle back into the fabric near point A, as shown in **Diagram 10.**

Step 3: Let go of the coil, allowing the ribbon to unwrap into a looser coil, as shown in **Diagram 11.** To smooth any tangles, run your fingers down the double coil.

Step 4: Pull your needle completely through to the wrong side of the fabric, pulling and ad-justing the ribbon until the rose is the size you want, as shown in **Diagram 12.**

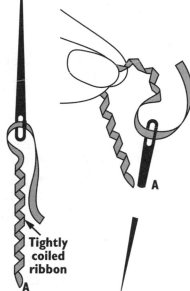

Tightly coiled ribbon

DIAGRAM 9

DIAGRAM 10

Looser coil

DIAGRAM 11

Completed coiled ribbon rose

DIAGRAM 12

The Rodale Sewing Editors

Ribbonwork

The Right Stuff

When embroidering with silk ribbon, I always use a #16 or #18 chenille needle. The large eye accommodates the ribbon without crushing it, and the wide shaft provides a clear course through the fabric, minimizing fraying.

I like to embroider with silk ribbon on loosely woven fabric. The weave allows my ribbon-threaded needle to flow through the fabric easily. It is important that the needle be pulled between the fabric threads and not through them. Otherwise, the thickness of the ribbon might break the thread fibers.

Kaethe Kliot

Treat Silk Ribbon Gently

When embroidering with silk ribbon, work only with a 12-inch length at a time. This will prevent any wear and fraying of the ribbon during handling.

Kaethe Kliot

No Knots, Please

When creating an elegant work of ribbon embroidery, the last thing you want is a lumpy effect caused by knotting the ribbon ends on the back of your fabric! To prevent this, use a crewel needle and a strand of embroi-

dery floss to finish off the ribbon ends. Take a few tacking stitches to secure each ribbon end to the wrong side of the fabric. In order for the tacking stitches not to show through the fabric, position them directly underneath a ribbon stitch that was made on the right side of the fabric.

Kaethe Kliot

The Right Ribbon for the Job

When you plan to use ribbon on a home decorating project or as garment trim, check the fiber content and the care instructions. Some ribbons can be washed; others must be dry-cleaned. Be sure the ribbon you choose is right for the job.

Barbara Fimbel

Caring for Ribbon Embroidery

Launder your ribbon embroidery piece with care, and dry it as quickly as possible. If your piece needs pressing after being washed, steam it with a hand steamer or a steam iron held slightly above the work. Do not press down on the ribbon. If those steaming methods aren't effective, press the work from the wrong side on an ironing board covered with a terry cloth towel. Then

steam the right side to fluff up the embroidery.

Kaethe Kliot

Keeping Silk Ribbon Clean

To keep silk ribbons clean, I place each color in a snack-size reclosable plastic bag. I can flip through the bags when choosing colors without handling the ribbon.

Susan Nester

SMART SHOPPER

If you want to try silk ribbon embroidery but are put off by the high cost of 100 percent silk ribbon, use the inexpensive polyester type. You'll find that it works well, and you won't be afraid to experiment and try new stitches. Invest in the "real" thing only after you've polished your techniques.

Susan Nester

Seams

If you've been sewing seams for years, you can probably do it with your eyes closed. But sewing seams on knits, sheers, and silks takes a little more planning to achieve professional quality. In this chapter, our experts show you surefire seam and seam-finishing techniques for fuss-free, timesaving results.

Bound to Be Easy

To eliminate hand basting or pinning bias binding in place before you sew, use fusible thread. The technique is quick and easy. Once you master it, you can use it when sewing similar binding-type pieces such as the cuffs on a blouse or the waistband on a skirt.

Step 1: Cut a bias strip of fabric the length of the finished binding you need plus a ½-inch seam allowance. Cut the bias strip six times the width of the finished binding you need. With wrong sides together, fold the strip in half lengthwise and press, as shown in Diagram 1.

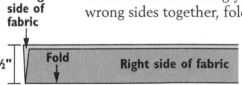

Wrong side of fabric

1½"

Fold

Right side of fabric

DIAGRAM 1

Step 2: Pin the binding to the right side of your garment, making sure raw edges are even, as shown in **Diagram 2.**

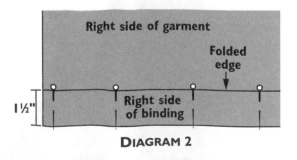

Right side of garment

Folded edge

1½"

Right side of binding

DIAGRAM 2

Step 3: Thread your bobbin with fusible thread and sew the binding to your garment, ½ inch from the raw edges, as shown in **Diagram 3.**

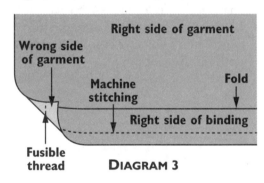

Right side of garment

Wrong side of garment

Machine stitching

Fold

Right side of binding

Fusible thread

DIAGRAM 3

Step 4: Fold the binding over the seam allowance to the wrong side of your garment, making sure the folded edge of the binding extends over the stitching line on the wrong side. The seam allowance will be encased inside the binding, as shown in **Diagram 4.** Use an iron to fuse-baste the binding in place.

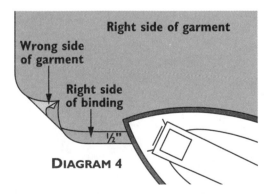

Right side of garment

Wrong side of garment

Right side of binding

½"

DIAGRAM 4

Step 5: Stitch in the ditch on the right side of your garment to secure the binding in place.

Janet Klaer

Silky Seams

The best finished seam is one that is flat and inconspicuous. My favorite seam for silk and silk-type fabrics is a standing felled seam. Made by making one run under the sewing machine, the seam is strong, and the finish is clean.

Step 1: Place the right sides of your fabric together, making sure the bottom layer extends ¼ inch beyond the top layer, as shown in **Diagram 1.**

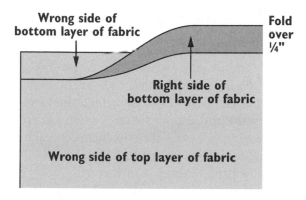

DIAGRAM 2

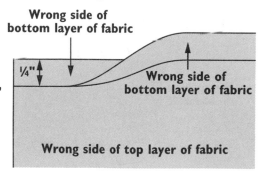

Step 2: Before sewing, fold the bottom layer over the top so that the fold butts against the edge of the top layer, as shown in **Diagram 2.** Make sure the top layer does not fold as you work.

Step 3: Fold both layers ¼ inch one more time, as shown in **Diagram 3,** and edge stitch through all layers, as shown in **Diagram 4.**

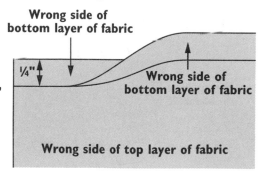

DIAGRAM 3

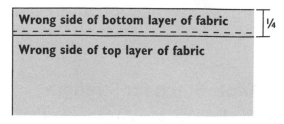

DIAGRAM 4

Claire Shaeffer

Seams

Keep on Sewing

When sewing a number of seams, don't stop between each one. Simply create a bar tack at the end of the first seam, then feed the next seam under the presser foot and keep sewing. Cut the threads between each piece when you are finished. You'll save time, energy, and thread!

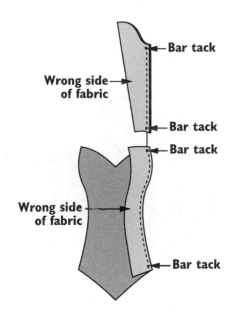

Mary Griffin
Singer Sewing Company

Triple Stitch for Strength

For professional-looking seams on heavy fabrics, such as quilted or upholstery fabrics, you should use a sturdy sewing stitch, such as a triple straight stitch. The needle takes two stitches forward and one stitch backward to ensure a strong seam.

Set your machine for a triple straight stitch, if it's available, and attach a walking foot so that the fabric layers feed evenly under the needle. Make sure the needle is centered within the opening of your walking foot before you begin.

June Mellinger
Brother International Corporation

Seams Silly

Have you ever wondered why pattern companies use ⅝-inch seam allowances on enclosed seams—collars, necklines, cuffs, and waistbands—and then ask you to whittle them down to ¼ inch? I stopped wondering and started saving time by trimming my seam allowances as I cut out my garment pieces. Before cutting, I check the pattern guide for areas that are later trimmed to ¼ inch. Technically, only ⅜ inch should be trimmed away from the ⅝-inch allowance. But I find it easier to cut off half of the seam allowances in the cutting process. Not only do I save time but I also save fabric.

Margaret Islander

Seams Frustrating

To keep threads from wadding up in my machine as I sew, I use a starter fabric. First I make sure I have all of my garment pieces ready to sew. I place a fabric scrap under my presser foot and begin sewing on it, then I move onto my garment. When I'm finished, I cut away my starter fabric and use it for the next seam.

Laurel Hoffmann

Perfect Piecing

For perfect ¼-inch seams, use a blind hem foot. I have an extra one for my machine just for this purpose. I keep it permanently set for this kind of seam. Before I sew my seam, I use a drop of water-soluble fabric glue to hold the layers of fabric in place.

Sharon S. Sullivan
Tacony Corporation

Seams Relaxed

Do the seams on your rayon, silk, or wool jersey skirts or dresses draw up along the sides and cause the hem to hang improperly? To ensure you don't have this problem, use a 0.5 mm zigzag stitch and a regular stitch length. This builds elasticity into the seam so that it can relax when pressed.

Sandra Betzina

Seams Synthetic to Me

Eliminate pins when working with synthetic suede and leather by basting the fabric together with a glue stick. Remember to apply the glue inside the seam allowance only.

Ronda Chaney

Neat and Narrow

Create a ⅛-inch inconspicuous seam on sheer fabrics using a rolled hem foot on your sewing machine. This foot rolls the fabric automatically as you sew, leaving a clean, neat finish. Best of all, it eliminates the time-consuming pressing and pinning tasks!

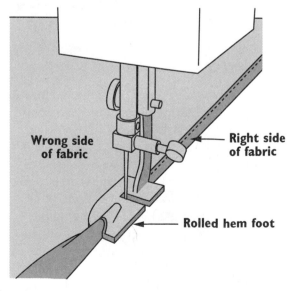

Wrong side of fabric

Right side of fabric

Rolled hem foot

Annie T. Tuley

Seams Smooth as Silk

The seamed edges of silk and silk-like fabrics tend to unravel even after you've finished sewing. To remedy this, try one of these seam finishes.

- Use a liquid seam sealant along the cut edges after you sew your seams.

- After sewing the seam, trim the seam allowance with pinking shears.

- Zigzag the edges of your seam allowances together.

- Serge-finish the fabric edges on your serger.

House of Fabrics
So-Fro Fabrics

Narrow Escape

Try this French seaming technique on lightweight and sheer fabrics to create a narrow seam. Use a rolled hem foot on your machine to seam your fabric with the wrong sides together. Press the seam allowance to one side. Then fold the fabric along the seam with right sides together and press. Using a zipper foot as your guide, straight stitch close to the encased rolled edge. This finish makes a strong seam that is ⅛ inch wide.

Annie T. Tuley

Simple Seaming

Make it a habit to hold the thread ends behind the needle of your sewing machine when you start to sew a seam. I use my left index finger to pinch the thread ends to the needle plate. This prevents jams on any machine I'm working on.

Robbie Fanning

Lovely Lace Seam

If you are cutting out a garment from lace fabric, it is wise to extend the seam allowances to 1 inch because the lace is weaker in areas between motifs. And since lace fabrics do not unravel easily, your seam finish can be chosen for comfort as well as for appearance.

House of Fabrics
So-Fro Fabrics

Serged Flat-Felled Seam

There's nothing like a serger to sew flat-felled seams quickly and easily. Here's how.

Step 1: With the right sides of your fabric together, sew your seam with a straight stitch, as shown in **Diagram 1.** If you want to reduce the bulk of heavyweight fabrics, trim the seam allowance of the bottom layer of fabric to ¼ inch after straight stitching.

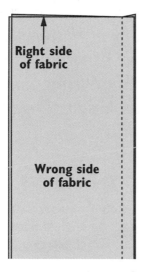

DIAGRAM 1

Step 2: Serge-finish the edges of the seam allowance together, as shown in **Diagram 2.** For heavyweight fabrics, serge-finish the seam allowance on the top layer of fabric only.

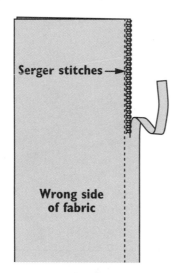

DIAGRAM 2

Step 3: With the wrong side of the fabric facing up, press the seam allowance to one side, as shown in

Diagram 3. For heavy-weight fabrics, press the serged seam allowance to the side over the trimmed seam allowance.

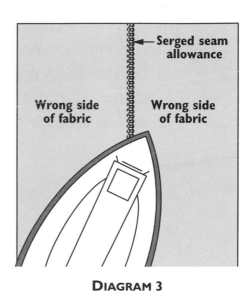

DIAGRAM 3

Step 4: With the right side of your fabric facing up, topstitch next to the seam line, catching the seam allowance in the stitching. Then topstitch again ¼ inch away, as shown in **Diagram 4.** For heavyweight fabrics, follow this step as well.

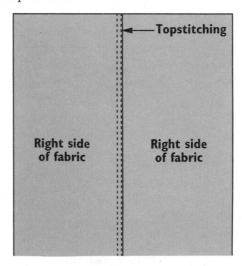

DIAGRAM 4

Lori Bottom

Serging

A serger is one of the most timesaving machines a sewer can own. It has revolutionized the sewing world by operating nearly twice as fast as a conventional machine while performing several tasks simultaneously. Like magic, a serger seams, trims, and binds the edges of your fabric to produce a professional seam finish like those found on ready-to-wear clothing.

Serging On

Here's a fast way to serge your garment together. First make sure you have all of your garment pieces ready to sew. Serge as many edges or seams as you can continuously without raising the presser foot, leaving a 4-inch thread chain between each seam or edge. Clip the thread chains later to separate the sections.

Gail Brown

Thread with Ease

When threading the loopers on your serger with decorative thread, try using dental floss threaders. Simply pull the end of the thread through the loop on the threader, then push the straight end of the threader through the hole in the looper from front to back. These inexpensive threaders can be found at your local drug store.

Thread →

Looper →

Dental floss threader →

Lana Bennett

No Ruffled Feathers

Take the guesswork out of gathering a ruffle with this easy serger technique and a gathering attachment.

Step 1: Cut a strip of fabric three times the finished length you need. Turn under a ¼-inch hem along one short side and press. Turn under another ¼ inch and press again, as shown in **Diagram 1**.

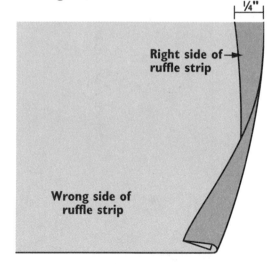

¼"

Right side of ruffle strip

Wrong side of ruffle strip

DIAGRAM 1

Step 2: Using your serger, finish the edge of one long side of the ruffle strip with a rolled hem stitch, as shown in **Diagram 2**.

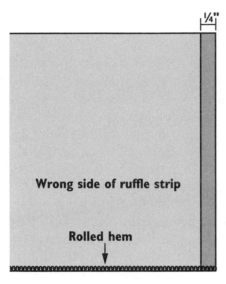

DIAGRAM 2

Step 3: Attach a gathering foot to your serger. Now with right sides together, serge and gather your ruffle strip to your fabric in one operation.

Nancy Bednar

Troubleshooting Tips

Here are some quick-and-easy solutions to common serging problems.

⚉ If your machine doesn't have differential feed, you can prevent seams from puckering by holding the fabric firmly in front of and behind the needle. Be careful not to pull the fabric too much as you sew, or the needle will break.

⚉ When skipped stitches occur, change to a new needle or try a blue Schmetz stretch needle. Pre-

shrinking your fabric, if appropriate, will also help. If your fabric cannot be preshrunk, try dampening just the seam line area before you sew.

⚉ If you are sewing a long piece of fabric to a short one, always sew with the longer layer on the bottom, so that the feed dogs pull the fabric through the machine. The longer your stitch length, the easier it will be to ease the fabric.

Naomi Baker

Quality Counts

Because sergers sew at a fast speed, you must use quality thread to avoid stitching problems. Bargain threads tend to be weak and have uneven twists or slubs that catch in the needle or thread guides, causing breakage. When shopping for serger thread, examine it to make sure it does not

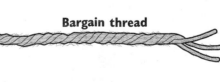

have short filaments and a fuzzy appearance. If a thread is twisted unevenly with thick and thin areas, it's not a bargain!

Lori Bottom

Superfast Gathering

For superfast and accurate gathering by serger, I love to use clear elastic. It works great when I need to gather the sections on a tiered skirt before sewing the skirt together and when I need to gather ruffles on dresses for my young daughters. It even works well on home decorating fabrics when I make pillow ruffles and gathered bed skirts. Here's my technique.

Step 1: Cut out your ruffle strips according to your pattern directions. Then cut a length of clear elastic that's the length of the finished ruffle plus 4 inches.

Step 2: Measure in 2 inches from each end of the elastic. Then divide the elastic into quarters, or eighths for very long lengths, and mark with a fine-point, permanent, felt-tip pen, as shown in **Diagram 1.** Be sure you don't include the additional 4 inches when you divide.

Step 3: Divide your ruffle into quarters, or eighths for very long lengths, and mark it with a water-soluble marking pen along one lengthwise edge.

Step 4: Adjust your serger for a long, wide, balanced three- or four-thread stitch. If you are working with home decorating fabrics, use the more stable three-/four-thread stitch with all-purpose thread. (For a strong, soft finish, use woolly nylon thread.)

Step 5: Place the elastic ¼ inch from the lengthwise raw edge of your ruffle, matching the first set of dividing marks. The serger will trim away the ¼ inch of fabric as you work. Be sure to catch the elastic in the stitches, as shown in **Diagram 2.**

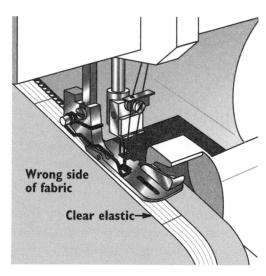

Wrong side of fabric

Clear elastic→

DIAGRAM 2

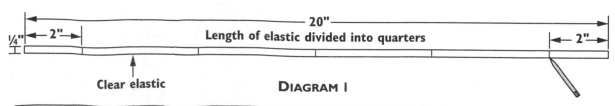

¼" | 2" | 20" — Length of elastic divided into quarters | 2"

Clear elastic   DIAGRAM 1

Step 6: Continue serging, stretching the elastic to match the dividing marks. If you have difficulty stretching the elastic, set your differential feed to a plus setting. This will help ease the fabric to the elastic.

Cindy Kacynski

Ivory thread blends with light-color fabrics, gray thread blends with medium tones, and black, navy, or brown thread blends with dark colors. When only exact colors will do, purchase spools, rather than cones, of all-purpose thread.

Lori Bottom

Stable Shoulders

Quality knitwear has stabilized, or taped shoulder seams, to prevent them from stretching or growing with wear. You can readily duplicate this technique. Many sergers come with a tape guide on the presser foot that feeds the tape under the foot and allows it to be incorporated into your stitches without cutting it. To sew, place a piece of ¼-inch twill tape or ribbon into the tape guide and use a four-thread stitch to serge shoulder seams. If you don't have a tape guide on your presser foot, use a piece of ⅝-inch twill tape or ribbon. The tape will be trimmed as you serge, but the result will be the same as with the guide.

Mary Griffin
Singer Sewing Company

A Better Blend

Instead of purchasing a different cone of colored thread for every new project, try blending different color threads to match your fabric.

Curves Ahead

When serging curves, avoid serging off the fabric by holding the fabric from behind the presser foot at a slight angle and encouraging it to the right rather than straight ahead. This will help the feed dogs keep the curved angle directly under the presser foot.

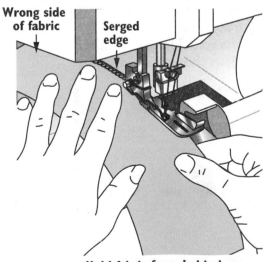

Wrong side of fabric **Serged edge**

Hold fabric from behind presser foot at slight angle

Agnes Mercik

Serging

Gather Round

Quick-and-easy gathers can be created with your serger by increasing the stitch length and tightening the needle tension(s). After stitching, you can further adjust the gathers by pulling up on the needle threads. To quickly spot the needle threads, use contrasting colors.

Lana Bennett

Mock Piping

Here's an easy way to create mock piping when joining two pieces of fabric.

Step 1: With the right side of your fabric facing up, fold the seam allowance to the wrong side. Using decorative thread in the upper looper, serge a rolled hem along the folded seam, as shown in **Diagram 1**.

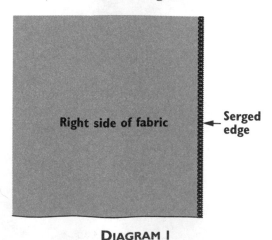

DIAGRAM 1

Step 2: With the right side of the fabric facing up, place the serged fold over the seam allowance of the remaining piece of fabric, as shown in **Diagram 2**.

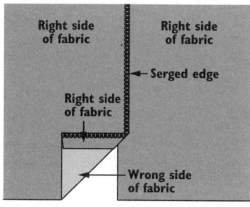

DIAGRAM 2

Step 3: Topstitch close to the serged edge with an invisible monofilament thread on your sewing machine, as shown in **Diagram 3**.

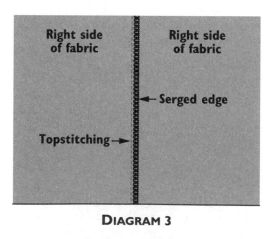

DIAGRAM 3

Agnes Mercik

Get It Write!

Here's a practical way to save testing and adjusting time when serging on specialty fabrics or when using decorative thread. For each fabric or thread type, write down the tension, stitch width, and differential feed on an index card. Then tape a stitch sample to it. Keep your reference cards handy in a small-ring binder or recipe-card box.

Lana Bennett

Serged Blanket Stitching

I use a simple-to-serge wrapped stitch, or mock blanket stitch, to duplicate the blanket stitch look. It not only produces an attractive edging—especially on wool and polar fleeces—but it also is fun to sew with yarn.

Step 1: Use all-purpose thread in the needle, yarn in the upper looper, and woolly nylon thread in the lower looper. Adjust your serger for the longest, widest, three-thread wrapped stitch. Loosen the upper looper tension and tighten the lower looper tension completely so that the yarn will wrap around the edge of your fabric.

Step 2: Test the settings on a fabric scrap to make sure your yarn feeds easily and evenly through the looper guides, or eyes.

Step 3: Serge the edges of your garment, trimming ¼ inch if you're serging along the raw edge. If your garment has a facing along the edge you are serging, don't trim as you serge.

Cindy Kacynski

Stress-Free Tension

Adjusting the tension on your serger doesn't have to be stressful. First check your threading before adjusting any of the tensions. Then adjust only one tension at a time by first loosening any thread that looks tight, instead of tightening a loose one.

Lana Bennett

SMART SHOPPER

Before you begin your quest for the ideal serger, determine your needs and wants. Seek out buyer's guides and comparison charts to help you decide which will meet those needs. *Sew News* magazine produces an annual serger comparison chart that features more than 30 models from top-of-the-line manufacturers. To obtain a copy, write to *Sew News*, PJS Publications, P.O. Box 1790, Peoria, IL 61656.

Karen Kunkel

★ Bright Idea ★

USE YOUR SERGER TO DUPLICATE THE FLATLOCKED SEAM FINISHES OFTEN FOUND ON READY-TO-WEAR SPORTS-WEAR. This kind of seam works best on knit fabrics and those that don't unravel easily. Align your fabric so that half of the stitching hangs over the edge when you're serging. This will allow the seam to pull flat and accommodate the bulk of the fabric.

Karen Kunkel

Learning to Thread

Make learning to use your serger a painless endeavor. Try threading each of the needles and loopers in a different color. This will help you learn to identify each thread and its corresponding tension.

Lana Bennett

Seams Like a Stretch

For seams requiring maximum stretch and a soft touch, such as those on garments made of Lycra spandex, use woolly nylon thread in both the loopers and the needles. The tensions will need to be loosened to allow the thread to fluff up and stretch.

Agnes Mercik

Going in Circles

The challenge of serging an oval or circular shape is sewing it perfectly so that you can't detect the beginning or end of the stitching. This surefire method works every time.

Step 1: With the right side of your fabric facing up, cut a 1½-inch-long notch in the seam allowance of your fabric, as shown in **Diagram 1.**

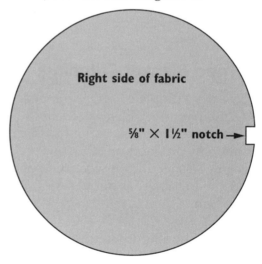

Right side of fabric

⅝" × 1½" notch →

DIAGRAM 1

Step 2: Raise the needle and position your fabric under it so that the edge of the notch is in line with the serger knife, as shown in **Diagram 2.**

Step 3: Serge around your fabric, trimming away the seam allowance as you sew. When you reach the starting point, take one or two stitches over the first few stitches, then stop.

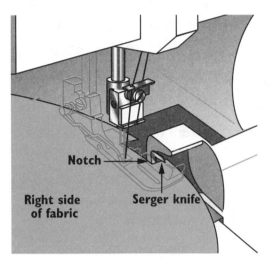

DIAGRAM 2

Step 4: Raise the needle and turn the fabric away from the knife. Finish by serging a 2- to 3-inch thread chain, as shown in **Diagram 3.** Use a tapestry needle to thread the end of the chain through the serged stitching on the wrong side of the fabric, or trim the chain and apply liquid seam sealant to secure the thread ends in place.

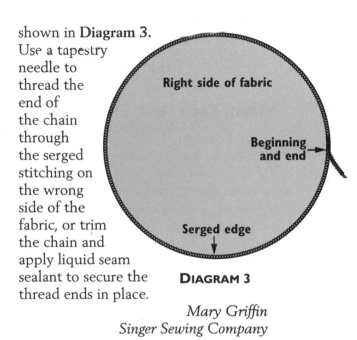

DIAGRAM 3

Mary Griffin
Singer Sewing Company

Sleeves

Whether long, short, or three-quarter length, sleeves are sometimes difficult to set in to a garment. No matter what your skill level, this chapter is bound to bring you increased success as you learn an array of today's best methods for marking, cutting, and setting in sleeves. In addition, you'll find lots of simple shortcuts and practical pointers for custom-fitting sleeves to your garments.

Trim, Face, and Finish Fast

This trim, face, and hem technique works beautifully on sleeves that have elastic at the wrist. To complete these three steps at the same time, use contrasting bias strips on your sleeves. You'll be pleased with the polished and professional-looking results.

Step 1: Cut two sleeves from your fabric. Then measure the wrist edge of your pattern piece to determine the length of your bias strips. To determine the width of the strips, measure from the wrist edge of the sleeve to the elastic placement line and add 1¼ inches. Then use those measurements to cut two bias strips from a contrasting fabric.

Step 2: With right sides together and raw edges even, sew one bias strip to the lower edge of each sleeve with a ¼-inch seam allowance, as shown in Diagram 1.

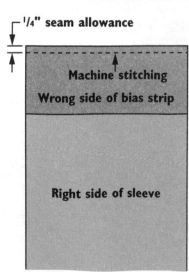

¼" seam allowance

Machine stitching
Wrong side of bias strip

Right side of sleeve

DIAGRAM 1

Step 3: Turn the bias strip to the wrong side of each sleeve to encase the seam allowance and press. On the right side of each sleeve, stitch in the ditch to secure the bias strip in place, as shown in **Diagram 2**.

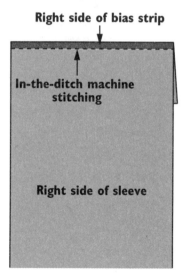

Right side of bias strip

In-the-ditch machine stitching

Right side of sleeve

DIAGRAM 2

Step 4: For each sleeve, measure and cut a length of elastic that fits comfortably around your wrist. Pin the elastic to the wrong side of each sleeve, ¾ inch from the raw edge of the binding, as shown in **Diagram 3**. Then sew the elastic to the sleeve with a zigzag stitch that is wide enough to zigzag over and not through the elastic, as shown.

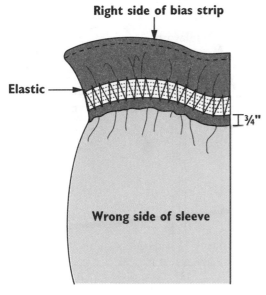

Right side of bias strip

Elastic

I¾"

Wrong side of sleeve

DIAGRAM 3

Step 5: Trim the bias strip close to the edge of the elastic, leaving less than ¼ inch, as shown in **Diagram 4.**

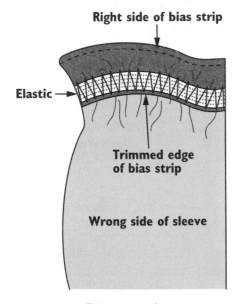

Right side of bias strip

Elastic

Trimmed edge of bias strip

Wrong side of sleeve

DIAGRAM 4

Step 6: Finish sewing your garment according to the pattern directions.
Dorothy R. Martin

Only Half Flat

Whenever the pattern or style allows, I sew sleeves into my garment at the shoulder before I sew them into the underarm. To do this, stitch the sleeves to the shoulders only between the notches. Then stitch the garment side seams and the sleeve underarm seams. Finally, stitch the sleeves to the lower part of the armholes.

Compared to the classic method of setting in sleeves, this is faster, and there is less chance for error. Plus your sleeves will fit more comfortably and hang better than if sewn to the shoulder totally by the flat-construction method.
Sue Hausmann
Viking/White Sewing Machine Companies

SMART SHOPPER

Puzzled as to which type of shoulder pad to purchase for which sleeve? Shoulder pads are available for set-in, raglan, or dropped-shoulder sleeves, and they are available in a variety of thicknesses. Use ¼- to ½-inch-thick shoulder pads for blouses and dresses and ½- to 1-inch-thick pads for jackets and outerwear. When a pattern calls for shoulder pads, be sure to use them. If you don't, your garment will not fit properly due to the amount of fullness allowed for the pads.

Karen Kunkel

Easy Cuffed-Sleeve Placket

With a little cutting and taping of your pattern, you can eliminate facing and binding plackets on straight sleeves and save time in the assembly process. Here's what to do.

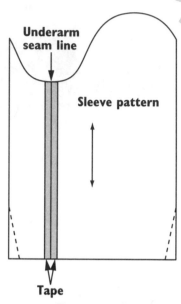

DIAGRAM 2

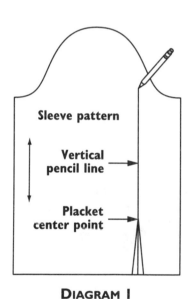

Step 1: With a pencil, draw a vertical line on your sleeve pattern from the placket center point to the armhole edge. Your line should be parallel to the pattern grain line, as shown in **Diagram 1.** Cut the pattern along the vertical pencil line.

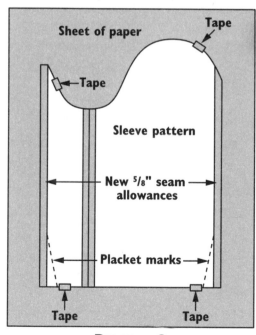

DIAGRAM 1

Step 2: Overlap the two sleeve pattern pieces ⅝ inch, aligning the underarm seam lines, and tape the two sleeve pattern pieces together, as shown in **Diagram 2.**

Step 3: Place your taped pattern piece on a large sheet of paper, taping as needed. Draw a new ⅝-inch seam allowance on either side of the sleeve, as shown in **Diagram 3.** Trace the armhole and sleeve edges, and cut out the new pattern. Using the old placket marking as a guide, draw half of the new placket marking along each new seam line.

DIAGRAM 3

Step 4: Using the new pattern piece, cut two sleeves from your fabric and transfer the placket markings to both sleeves. Make a ¼-inch V-clip into the

seam allowances at the placket center points, as shown in **Diagram 4.**

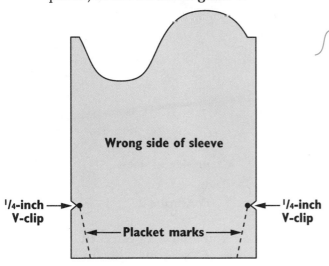

Wrong side of sleeve

¹/₄-inch →
V-clip

← ¹/₄-inch
V-clip

← **Placket marks** →

DIAGRAM 4

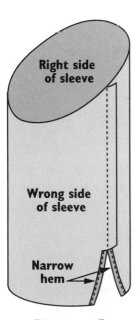

Right side of sleeve

Wrong side of sleeve

Narrow hem →

DIAGRAM 5

Step 5: With right sides together and raw edges aligned, stitch the underarm seams on both sleeves, stopping at the clip marks. Make a narrow hem in the seam allowances below the clip marks, as shown in **Diagram 5.**

Step 6: Finish the sleeves of your blouse according to the pattern directions.

Betty Ann Watts

Keep It Flat

When sewing flat-construction sleeves, make the feeding system of your machine work for you. To ease or slightly gather your sleeves, place the sleeve fabric against the feed dogs. Lengthen the stitch length, and hold back the top layer of fabric slightly as you sew. The pulling action of the feed dogs will help ease the sleeve fabric as it is stitched to the bodice.

Sue Hausmann
Viking/White
Sewing Machine Companies

Ease-y Does It

Sleeves are sometimes difficult to set in to the body of a garment because there is too much ease included in the pattern piece. Instead of fitting smoothly, the sleeve ends up puckered.

To correct this, measure the sleeve pattern along the armhole stitching line. Do the same on the armhole of the bodice pattern. If the sleeve stitching line is more than 1½ inches larger than the bodice armhole stitching line, make a ¼-inch horizontal pleat in the pattern piece above the sleeve cap notches in the same manner shown in **Diagram 1** for "Taming Synthetic Suede" on page 260. This will reduce the length of the sleeve cap by ½ inch.

Karen Kunkel

A Clear Solution

Setting in a sleeve that doesn't have pleats or gathers is a breeze when you use clear elastic. It is fast, and the results are tailor perfect.

Step 1: Measure the armhole of the pattern front and pattern back pieces from the shoulder seam line to the notch, as shown in **Diagram 1.** Add the measurements and cut two pieces of clear elastic to the same length.

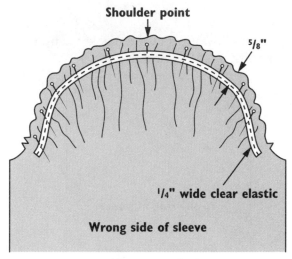

DIAGRAM 2

directions. You'll have a perfect fit with no ease or gathering adjustments necessary.

Karen Kunkel

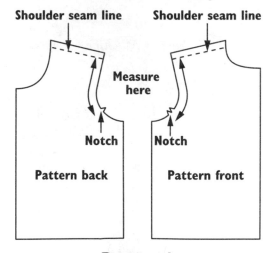

DIAGRAM 1

Step 2: With right sides together and raw edges aligned, sew the shoulder seams of your garment pieces. Then pin one piece of the elastic to the wrong side of each sleeve cap between the notches, stretching it as needed to fit. Next, sew the elastic to the sleeve just inside the seam line, as shown in **Diagram 2.** Finally, sew the sleeve to your garment according to the pattern

Taming Synthetic Suede

It is especially difficult to set in synthetic suede sleeves because the fabric is nonwoven and does not ease well into the armhole. You must adjust your sleeve pattern to remove 1 inch of ease from the height of the sleeve cap to set the sleeve without puckers. Here's what you do.

Step 1: Fold a ½-inch horizontal tuck in the sleeve pattern above the sleeve cap notches, as shown in **Diagram 1,** securing it with pins or tape. The result will be a 1-inch ease instead of the standard 2 inches.

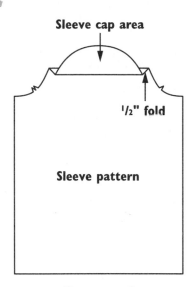

Sleeve cap area

¹/₂" fold

Sleeve pattern

DIAGRAM 1

Step 2: Using your altered pattern piece, cut two sleeves from synthetic suede. Use the sleeve pattern to cut a 2-inch-wide strip of fusible tricot interfacing for the armhole edge of each sleeve. Fuse the tricot strips to the wrong side of the synthetic suede sleeve caps, as shown in **Diagram 2**, to help control the ease.

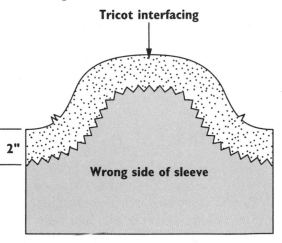

Tricot interfacing

2"

Wrong side of sleeve

DIAGRAM 2

Step 3: Sew three rows of machine basting stitches between the notches on the sleeve cap, positioning the first row on the seam line and the other two rows inside the seam allowance, as shown in **Diagram 3**.

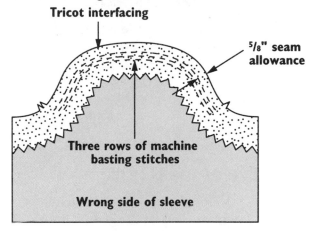

Tricot interfacing

⁵/₈" seam allowance

Three rows of machine basting stitches

Wrong side of sleeve

DIAGRAM 3

Step 4: Finish sewing and attaching the sleeve to your garment according to the pattern directions.

Ronda Chaney

Sleeve Sense

To help fill out the upper sleeve on a tailored jacket, fuse a lightweight tricot interfacing into the sleeve cap—the area from the bottom of the armhole to the shoulder—before constructing the sleeve. Pink the interfacing edges to prevent them from showing on the right side.

Linda Griepentrog

Smocking

Smocking is a decorative method of embroidery made by gathering fabric into small pleats and working over them with embroidery stitches. While smocking is usually associated with children's heirloom clothing, it also looks exquisite on dresses, blouses, accessories, and home decorating projects. You'll find this chapter full of tips and techniques to get you started.

Don't Get Tangled Up

The optimum length of embroidery floss to work with when smocking is 18 to 24 inches. Anything longer may fray and tangle as you sew.

Kathy McMakin

Eye of the Needle

Remove all misplaced stitches with the eye of the needle, not the point, to avoid damaging your fabric. Simply slide the eye under the stitch and gently ease the stitch out.

Kathy McMakin

Going with the Grain

When smocking with embroidery floss, make sure you sew with the grain of the floss and not against it. You can easily determine the grain by the way the floss unwinds. The loose end on the skein is called the "blooming end" and should be threaded through the eye of your needle. The end that you cut from the skein should be knotted. If you've already cut a piece of floss and can't tell which end is the blooming end, don't worry. One end will untwist or unravel more than the other. This is the blooming end.

Kathy McMakin

Count Down

The number of floss strands you should use in smocking depends on many factors. As a rule of thumb, work geometric designs in three strands of floss and pictorials in four strands. If you are lightly smocking on a lightweight background fabric, use only two strands of floss. If you are densely smocking on a heavier-weight fabric such as corduroy or velveteen or if your background fabric is dark, use four to six strands of floss for more coverage.

Kathy McMakin

Picture This

If your project uses lots of colors, thread a bunch of needles at once so you are ready for color changes. This practice is especially helpful when smocking pictorial designs.

Janice M. Giles

Oh, What a Tangled Web

Floss will often twist while you are smocking. To untwist it, hold the end of the floss in your fingers and let the needle drop to the fabric, as shown in **Diagram 1**. Untwist the floss as you bring the needle back up the thread to get ready for the next stitch, as shown in Diagram 2.

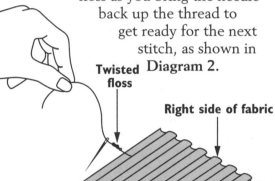

Twisted floss

Right side of fabric

DIAGRAM 1

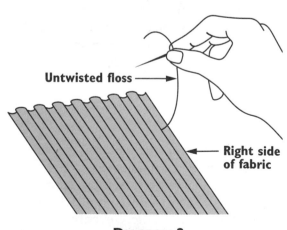

Untwisted floss →

← **Right side of fabric**

DIAGRAM 2

Kathy McMakin

Smocking Pointers

Here are several smocking pointers that will make your smocking time enjoyable and less troublesome.

⊞ For stitches that are smooth, even, and not crooked, keep your needle parallel to the gathering lines as you sew.

⊞ Keep your tension steady as you sew. Don't pull your stitches so tight that the pleats are pulled out of alignment, and don't sew so loosely that they droop.

⊞ When working stitches up from one row to another, as in a trellis or wave pattern, keep the thread below the needle. Conversely, when working down from one row to another, keep the thread above the needle.

Janice M. Giles

Tying Off Holding Rows

I always tie holding rows—the very top and bottom pleating, or gathering, threads—separately by making a big slip knot or by wrapping the threads around a pin. Then when I construct the garment, it is easier to use those threads as gathering threads to adjust the pleats.

Janice M. Giles

Smocking

Knot So Easy

After you've pleated your fabric, pull the pleating threads out of the seam allowance to ease the assembly of the garment later. Here's how to tie a simple surgical knot with your pleating threads so they don't become untied as you smock.

Using one or two threads in each hand, cross the right-hand thread over the left and push it through the opening beneath the two threads, just as if you are tying shoelaces, as shown in **Diagram 1**.

DIAGRAM 1

Do this again. You'll find that the threads lie flat and don't untie. Now, cross the left thread over the right to complete a square knot, as shown in **Diagram 2**.

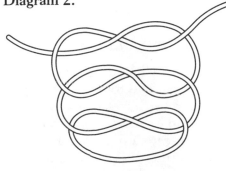

DIAGRAM 2

Janice M. Giles

Long Is Wrong

After fabric has been pleated in a pleater, it has a right and wrong side. To determine each side, stretch out the pleated fabric and examine the length of the stitches closely. The longer stitches will be on the wrong side. You'll never make a mistake if you remember that long is wrong.

Kathy McMakin

Mistakes Happen!

If you make a mistake that is not easily corrected, don't get upset! Put the project aside, walk away for a few minutes, and take a few deep breaths. Now, go back and look at your work. Is it really a mistake that shows? Is it going to affect the design adversely? How much does it bother you? If you decide you can live with it, go on with your work. If you must correct your work, take a longer break and start only when you feel refreshed.

Janice M. Giles

Size It Up

When smocking pictorial designs, use a size 7 darning needle. It creates a large hole, so more strands of floss can fit through. It also keeps the floss flat for a more evenly covered look.

Kathy McMakin

Block Party

To block your smocking, you need to steam it well with an iron. Except for the top row, remove the gathering threads and pin the piece facedown on your ironing board. Use the yoke or neck measurement as a guide for sizing. After you have the piece properly sized, steam it generously by holding your iron 1 or 2 inches above the smocking; allow the piece to cool thoroughly before sewing it into a garment or project.

Janice M. Giles

Proper-Size Bites

Your smocking stitches should take from one-third to one-half of the distance from the top of the pleat to the gathering thread. If you take too big a bite from the pleat, your smocking will not have the elasticity needed when the garment is worn. If you take too small a bite, the pleat will not lay right when the gathering threads are removed.

Janice M. Giles

Proper Flossing

Before threading your needle, prepare your floss in one of these ways to produce a ribbonlike finish.

 Untwist or strip the floss by running it between your thumbnail and index finger.

Moisten the floss by running it through a damp cloth, then press it flat with an iron. A curling iron will also do the trick.

 Run the floss between a folded fabric softener sheet for your dryer or across a cake of beeswax.

Kathy McMakin

★ Bright Idea ★

IN A HURRY TO SMOCK? Try this quick-and-easy machine technique. Run two threads through one needle on your machine, or wind thick thread onto your bobbin. Then sew several rows of decorative stitches in the area to be smocked. If you use two threads through your needle, sew on the right side of the fabric. But if you use thick thread in your bobbin, sew on the wrong side. When you are finished, hand wind the bobbin with elastic thread. Using that bobbin, sew several rows of straight stitches between your rows of decorative stitches. Your fabric will be smocked instantly.

Karen Kunkel

Smocking

SMART SHOPPER

When smocking heirloom garments, purchase the best-quality fabric you can afford, and you won't be disappointed. Use high-quality lace and buttons, as well. Generally, the lace and buttons that you use should be of equal quality to that of your fabric. Avoid using nylon lace and plastic buttons on imported batiste. Mother-of-pearl buttons, although sometimes hard to find, are a lovely accent for hand-smocked garments. Laces from France, England, and Switzerland are usually 100 percent cotton and are easy to gather and sew.

Janice M. Giles

Faux Smocking

Here is an attractive smocking treatment that is perfect for dresses, blouses, robes, nightgowns, and home decoration projects. It's fast and easy to do by machine.

Supplies

- Satin stitch or all-purpose foot
- Sewing thread to contrast with your fabric
- Comb with wide teeth

Step 1: Select the piece of your garment to be smocked. Cut a square of fabric twice the width of the finished garment piece.

Step 2: Attach a satin stitch or all-purpose foot to your machine and set it for a long basting stitch. Thread your machine.

Step 3: To gather or pleat the fabric, position it with the wrong side facing up. Beginning ⅝ inch from the upper edge, sew parallel rows of basting stitches ½ inch apart, as shown in **Diagram 1.** You can sew as many rows as you like.

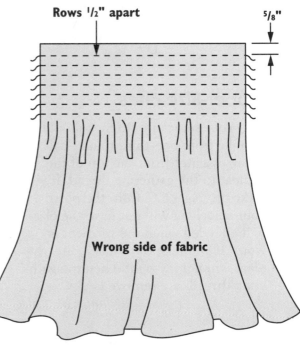

Rows ½" apart

⅝"

Wrong side of fabric

DIAGRAM 1

Step 4: Secure each basting thread along one side of the fabric by wrapping it in a figure eight around a straight pin, as shown in **Diagram 2.**

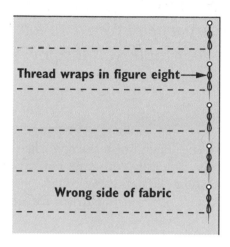

Thread wraps in figure eight →

Wrong side of fabric

DIAGRAM 2

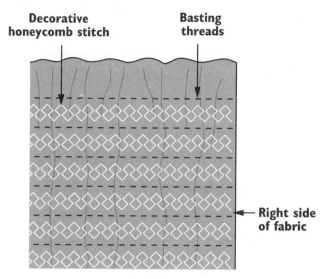

Decorative honeycomb stitch

Basting threads

← Right side of fabric

DIAGRAM 3

Step 5: On the opposite side of the fabric, draw up the basting threads, and gather the fabric just enough to equal the width of the pattern piece. Follow Step 4 to secure the threads in place. Using your fingers and the comb, adjust the gathers evenly.

Step 6: To smock the fabric, select a decorative stitch on your machine that will leave a heavy buildup of thread, such as a feather or honeycomb stitch. Sew across the gathered fabric between the rows of basting stitches, as shown in **Diagram 3.** To keep the stitches even, hold the gathers on each side slightly taut as they feed under the presser foot.

Step 7: Remove the basting threads by pulling them from the right side of the piece. Continue assembling the garment according to your pattern directions.

Dorothy R. Martin

Preparing for Perfect Pleats

As in all sewing, remember to prewash your fabrics before smocking. This step preshrinks the fabric, straightens the grain, and removes any sizing, making it easier to pleat. Most important, you will find out if your fabric is colorfast before you spend many hours smocking it!

Janice M. Giles

Table Toppers

Of all home decorating projects, table toppers are probably the most fun and least time-consuming. You can cheer up a living room end table with a floral chintz, or create a sensational dining room tabletop with luxurious brocade. Coordinating place mats or table runners add a look of luxury when layered on top of a tablecloth. However you like to set your table, you'll enjoy these inspirational ideas.

Two for One

When making a square table topper for a skirted table, make it reversible. It takes no extra sewing time to create two different looks. Choose one fabric for everyday use and a more luxurious type for special occasions. Or select a lightweight floral for the summer and a solid damask for the winter.

Richard M. Braun

Twice the Trim

When finishing the edges of a reversible table topper, add decorative fringe along each side. Just make sure the colors coordinate or blend together. If you glue or pin both trims in place carefully, you should be able to sew them simultaneously.

Robin Rose

Going to Batt for Your Table

If you want durable place mats that protect your table's finish, first back them with prequilted fabric or fabric that has been fused to fusible fleece or batting. Then finish the raw edges quickly and easily with quilt binding in a matching or contrasting color.

Patricia De Santis

Classic Fringe Finish

Fringing is a simple way to finish edges on napkins, place mats, and table runners made from a loosely woven, even-weave fabric. One classic approach is this stitched fringing technique. This example is for an 18-inch-square napkin, but you can use this same technique for any size square napkin.

Step 1: Square your fabric by pulling and removing one thread ½ inch from one cut end along the length of your fabric, as shown in **Diagram 1**. Carefully cut

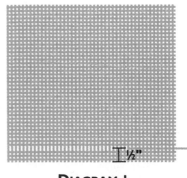

DIAGRAM 1

along the space created where the thread was removed.

Step 2: Cut the remaining three sides of your napkin 19 inches long. Then follow Step 1 for all four sides to ensure a perfect 18-inch square, as shown in **Diagram 2.**

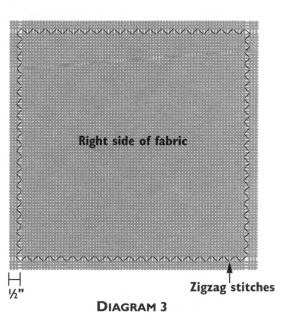

Right side of fabric

Zigzag stitches

½"

DIAGRAM 3

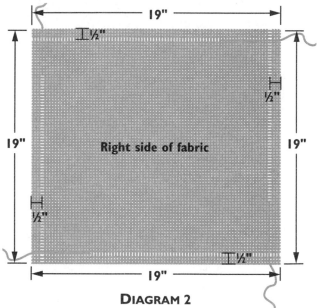

19"

½"

19"

Right side of fabric

19"

½"

½"

19"

DIAGRAM 2

Step 3: For a ½-inch fringe all around your napkin, pull out the thread that is ½ inch in from each new edge.

Step 4: Set your machine for a short stitch length and a medium stitch width. Zigzag directly over the space left by the pulled thread, as shown in **Diagram 3.** This row of stitching will keep the fringe from fraying beyond the finished edge.

Step 5: With a pin or your fingernail, pick at one corner of the square until you loosen the threads. Working with one thread at a time, remove the threads outside of the zigzag stitches to create a fringe, as shown in **Diagram 4.**

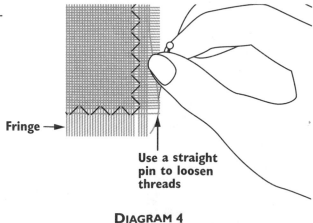

Fringe →

Use a straight pin to loosen threads

DIAGRAM 4

Barbara Fimbel

Table It

Here's a terrific table runner you can make to coordinate with napkins or any other table linens you have on hand. It requires two contrasting fabrics.

Step 1: From the fabric you will use for the top of the runner, cut a piece that is 17 inches wide by the length you need. Cut the contrasting backing fabric 2 inches wider and 2 inches longer.

DIAGRAM 1

Step 2: With a chalk pencil or an air-erasable marking pen, measure and mark the runner top fabric at the center of each short side and 5 inches in from each short side, as shown in **Diagram 1**.

Step 3: Referring to **Diagram 2**, draw a straight line from the center of each short side to the end of the 5-inch lines, creating two triangles along each short side. Cut along these diagonal lines to form a point at each end of the table runner.

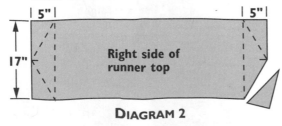

DIAGRAM 2

Step 4: To create a point at each short side of the runner back fabric, repeat Steps 2 and 3, but measure and mark a line 6 inches from the short side of the fabric instead of 5 inches, as shown in **Diagram 3**.

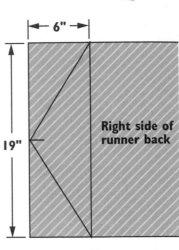

DIAGRAM 3

Step 5: With the wrong side of the runner back fabric facing up, turn under ½ inch along each edge and press, mitering the corners and points. With wrong sides together, center and pin the runner top and runner back together. The runner back will extend beyond the runner top.

Step 6: Fold the runner back over the runner top, forming a binding and mitering the corners and points, as shown in **Diagram 4**. Blindstitch the binding in place. If you like, sew a tassel to each point.

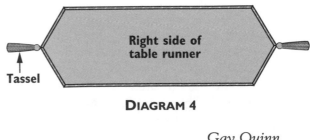

DIAGRAM 4

Gay Quinn

Knot That Fringe

This technique works best for linens that are larger than napkins because it creates a longer fringe. By following these instructions, you can create a beautiful place mat, but the same technique can be used to accent tablecloths and table runners.

Step 1: To get perfect edges on your fabric piece, follow the pulled thread cutting technique in Step 1 of "Classic Fringe Finish" on page 268. In the same manner, cut the remaining three sides of your fabric piece to measure 14 × 18 inches.

Step 2: Press under ½ inch along each 18-inch side of the place mat. Fold in the raw edge to meet the crease, press again, and edge stitch the hem in place.

Step 3: For a 4-inch fringe, pull out the thread that is 4 inches in from each of the short sides of your place mat.

Step 4: Set your machine for a short stitch length and a medium stitch width. Zigzag directly over the space left by the pulled thread. This row of stitching will keep the fringe from fraying beyond the finished edge.

Step 5: With a pin or your fingernail, pick at a corner of the square until you loosen the threads. Working with one thread at a time, remove the threads below the zigzagging to create fringe.

Step 6: Gather together a ½-inch-wide group of threads and tie them loosely with an overhand knot. Slide the knot as close as possible toward the fabric's edge without wrinkling the fabric. Tighten the knot firmly, as shown in **Diagram 1**.

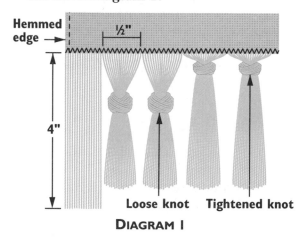

Hemmed edge →   ½"

4"

Loose knot   **Tightened knot**

DIAGRAM I

If your fabric has a woven stripe or a check pattern, you can group like-color threads for knotting instead of grouping them in ½-inch-wide bunches, as shown in **Diagram 2**.

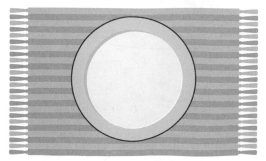

DIAGRAM 2

Barbara Fimbel

Table Toppers

Productive Play Time

If your want to experiment with all of the different stitches your serger can produce, edge a different set of napkins with each stitch. You'll have mastered a new skill and made a variety of delightful accessories. Stitch a small swatch to save for your overlock reference library as well.

Barbara Fimbel

Figure It Round

If you have a round table that isn't a standard size, here's how to determine the amount of fabric you'll need for a tablecloth.

Step 1: Measure the diameter of the tabletop. This will be referred to as A, as shown in **Diagram 1.**

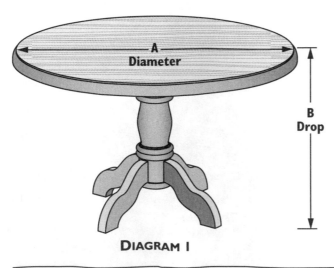

A
Diameter

B
Drop

DIAGRAM I

Step 2: Referring to the diagram, measure from the top edge of the table to the floor. If you don't want the cloth to reach the floor, measure the drop you choose. This measurement will be referred to as B. Add a 2-inch hem allowance. This will be referred to as C.

Step 3: Now use the following equation to determine the diameter of the tablecloth: A + B + B + C + C = tablecloth diameter. For example, if the diameter of your table is 48 inches and you want a standard side drop of 12 inches and a 2-inch hem allowance, the equation would be: 48 + 12 + 12 + 2 + 2 = 76. Therefore, you will need a tablecloth with a 76-inch diameter.

Step 4: To determine the number of fabric lengths you'll need, divide the diameter by the width of your fabric and round the number up to the nearest whole number. For example, if your fabric is 45 inches wide, then 76 ÷ 45 = 1.68. Rounding up to the nearest whole number will give you two lengths.

Step 5: To determine the number of yards of fabric, multiply the diameter by the number of lengths, and then divide by 36. Continuing with our example, 76 × 2 ÷ 36 = 4.2, or 4¼ yards.

Step 6: Referring to **Diagram 2,** cut your fabric in half crosswise. Set one

piece aside. Cut the other piece in half lengthwise.

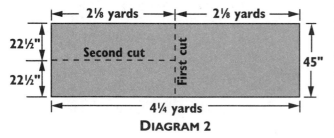

DIAGRAM 2

Step 7: With right sides together and using a ¼-inch seam allowance, sew a narrow piece of fabric to each long side of the wider piece, as shown in **Diagram 3.**

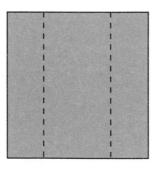

DIAGRAM 3

Step 8: Fold the fabric into quarters. Pin the four layers of fabric together along the edges so that the fabric doesn't slip.

Step 9: If the distance equal to half of your tablecloth diameter (38 inches in our example) is longer than 36 inches, mark that distance onto a wooden stick or a broomstick. If the

distance is 36 inches or less, you can simply use a yardstick. Referring to **Diagram 4,** place the mark on the wooden stick or the yardstick at the corner of the folded fabric with no cut edges. Pivot the stick and mark a curve from one side of the square to the other with a chalk pencil. Cut along the curved line.

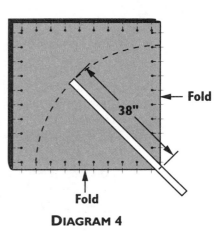

DIAGRAM 4

Step 10: Place the tablecloth on your table to check for the 2-inch hem allowance you already added in. Hem your tablecloth and get ready to entertain!

Julia Bernstein

Pad for Perfection

After you take the time to stitch a new tablecloth, you want it to look perfect. To create a soft edge and elegant draping, cover your tabletop with a leftover piece of thin quilt batting or fleece, a few layers of leftover felt or flannel, a piece of worn blanket, or a section of old mattress pad before putting on the cloth. The padding will round the edge, help to shape the folds, and add to the luxurious look of the finished table.

Carolyn Hoffman

Figure It Oval

If your oval table is not a standard size, here's how to determine the amount of fabric you'll need for a tablecloth.

Step 1: Referring to the diagram below and using the same equation from Step 2 of "Figure It Round" on page 272, determine the width of the tablecloth with the equation A + B + B + C + C. Measure the width (shortest point) of your table. If that measurement is 52 inches and you want a standard side drop of 12 inches plus a 2-inch hem allowance, the equation would be 52 + 12 + 12 + 2 + 2 = 80, so you will need an 80-inch-wide tablecloth.

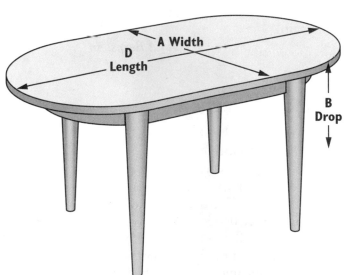

Step 2: To determine the number of fabric lengths you'll need, divide the tablecloth width calculated in Step 1 by the width of your fabric and round the number up to the nearest whole number. For example, if your fabric is 54 inches wide, then 80 ÷ 54 = 1.48. Rounding up to the nearest whole number will give you two lengths.

Step 3: As shown, measure the length of the tabletop. This will be referred to as D. Now determine the amount of yardage you will need with the equation D + B + B + C + C. Continuing with our example, the tabletop is 120 inches long, so 120 + 12 + 12 + 2 + 2 = 148.

Step 4: To determine the number of yards of fabric, multiply the yardage by the number of lengths, and then divide by 36. Continuing with our example, 148 × 2 ÷ 36 = 8.2, or 8¼ yards.

Step 5: Follow Steps 6 through 10 of "Figure It Round" on page 272 to finish your tablecloth.

Julia Bernstein

Calculating the Drop

When making your own table coverings, avoid giving your guests a lapful of cloth! The standard drop on a tablecloth is 10 to 12 inches below the tabletop or 1 to 2 inches above the seat of the dining chairs, whichever is shorter.

Judi Abbott

Fabulous Floral Napkins

Purchase or make plain napkins in a solid color. Fuse leftover scraps of complementary floral fabric to paper-backed fusible web, following the web manufacturer's directions. Cut out a floral motif, leaving about ⅛ inch of background fabric outside of the design area. Fuse the motif in place diagonally at one corner of each napkin. With matching or contrasting thread, zigzag around the edge of the motif and over the background fabric.

Barbara Fimbel

 Bright Idea

DO YOU FIND IT DIFFICULT TO HEM CURVED TABLECLOTHS? Here's a sure-fire solution to easing in the fullness at the hemline. Set your machine for 10 stitches per inch or a 2.5 mm length, and, with the right side of your fabric facing up, sew a row of stitches ⅜ inch from the edge. Using the machine stitching as your guide, turn under the hem and press. Then turn under another ⅜ inch, press again, and sew your hem in place.

Charlotte Biro

Thread

Gone is the day when your only concern about thread was if it matched your fabric. Today, you might choose fabric to match one of the many new threads that are available. Thread has become the inspirational source behind many elaborate wearable art garments. Silk, rayon, metallic, quilting, topstitching, and ribbon thread are just a few of the exciting varieties.

Simple but Significant

Cut thread on the diagonal so that the end will slip more easily through the eye of the needle. Thread the newly cut end into the eye of the needle, and tie the knot on the other end.

Coats & Clark

Terminate Tangles

To prevent thread from tangling as you remove it from a spool, allow the spool to roll loosely in one hand as you draw the thread off with the other.

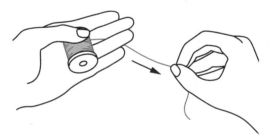

To reduce the possibility of your thread twisting or tangling when you hand sew, use a single strand of thread that doesn't exceed 24 inches in length.

Coats & Clark

Suit the Needle to Your Thread

Whether you hand or machine sew, make sure your needle creates a hole in the fabric that is large enough for the thread to pass through easily. This reduces wear and cuts down on thread breakage.

Susan Rock

Better Basting

When hand basting, use cotton basting thread or regular cotton thread in a light color that contrasts with your fabric. Avoid basting with dark-color thread, which could leave fibers or color behind when it is removed.

Coats & Clark

A Shade of Difference

If you can't find the exact shade of thread to match your fabric, choose a shade that is darker, not lighter, than your fabric. When sewn into the fabric, thread will appear lighter than it does on the spool.

Karen Costello Soltys

Stay Loose

When hand stitching, sew loosely with smooth motions. Pulling the thread tight or jerking it causes it to stretch and then tangle as it relaxes. Every few inches, drop your needle and let it hang free, allowing the thread to untwist.

Coats & Clark

Check the Yardage

If you plan to use thread you already have on hand, check the yardage on the spool to make sure there's enough to complete your project. The rule of thumb is that one small spool is enough for a simple dress, blouse, or skirt. But if you're planning to topstitch, zigzag, or overcast, you'll need extra thread.

Coats & Clark

A Decorative Decision

To create a quick-and-easy reference guide to thread color and texture, double a piece of neutral or white scrap fabric and sew one row of satin stitches for each of your threads. Use a permanent marker to label each row with the thread color number. Now you have a handy thread guide.

Carol Laflin Ahles

Instant Organization

The three-hole punched plastic pages with pockets designed to hold baseball cards make great embroidery floss holders. Keep the pages in a loose-leaf binder, and mark each section divider with the basic color that can be found in the pages that follow.

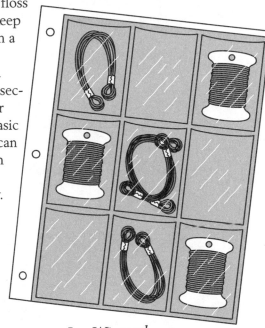

Lee Wiegand

Cool Spool

To restore flexibility to 100 percent cotton thread that has dried out, unwind and remove the first two layers of thread, then store the spool in your refrigerator's produce drawer for several days. Or mist the spool lightly with water, then place it on a shelf in your refrigerator for a few days. Moisture will permeate the thread and make it come alive again.

Susan Rock

Thread

Perfect Cover-Up

Is your thread storage area a jumbled mess of tangled threads? You can fix that with tubular surgical gauze, which is available at pharmacies and surgical-supply stores. Cut the gauze into short lengths about the "height" of your spools. Open the tube and slip it over your spools of thread.

Cross wound

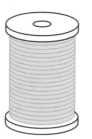

Parallel wound

DIAGRAM 1

lay the spool horizontally in a coffee mug, positioned directly behind your machine and even with the thread spindle, as shown in **Diagram 2.** (Note: Mug is shown to the left of the spindle for illustrative purposes.) This will keep the tension on the thread even and will lessen breakage. If the thread strays, attach masking tape to the machine, as shown, to form a tunnel that will keep it in place.

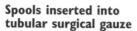

Spools inserted into tubular surgical gauze

Before   **After**

Marinda Stewart

The Proper Position

Spools that are cross wound, where the threads lie diagonally up and down the spool (as shown in **Diagram 1**), should be used in a horizontal position. Spools that are parallel wound, where the threads lie next to one another in parallel rows, should be used in a vertical position.

If your machine can't accommodate a horizontal spool, use a thread stand or

Vertical thread spindle

Masking tape

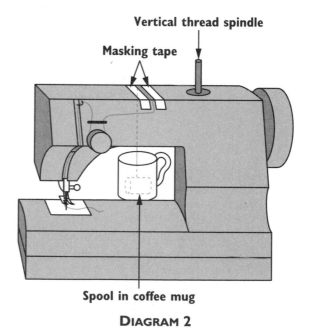

Spool in coffee mug

DIAGRAM 2

Susan Rock

THREADS AT A GLANCE

TYPE OF THREADS	DESCRIPTION	APPLICATION
All Purpose		
Cotton-covered polyester	Most common thread. Core of continuous polyester filament wrapped with cotton. Polyester fibers provide strength, flexibility, and durability. Cotton wrap mercerized for strength and sheen. Wide range of colors. Sews and irons like cotton thread.	All fabrics. Extra-fine version preferable for sheers, lightweight fabrics, and decorative machine work.
100% cotton thread	General purpose. Very little stretch.	Woven fabrics in natural fibers. Not enough strength for synthetics; not enough flexibility for knits. Size 40 for heavier fabrics; size 50 for light- to medium-weight fabrics.
100% polyester	Designed for strength and ability to stretch and recover.	Knitted fabrics and woven synthetic fabrics.
100% silk	Quality thread is one continuous filament; avoid using inferior spun fiber. Soft, resilient stitches.	Fashion and heirloom sewing. Size 50 for natural fibers (silk and wool).
Serger		
General-purpose overlock	Slightly finer version of cotton-covered polyester or 100% polyester thread for conventional machine. Fine texture needed to accommodate three, four, or five interlocking threads. Available on 1,000- to 6,000-yard cones.	All types of sewing.

(continued)

Thread

THREADS AT A GLANCE—Continued

TYPE OF THREADS	DESCRIPTION	APPLICATION
Serger		
Texturized nylon	Multifilament stretch nylon. Bulks or fluffs up when serged. Gives a soft, filled, lustrous look.	Excellent coverage in narrow rolled hems and other overlock finishes. Flexible, soft seam for bathing suits, leotards, and baby clothes.
Specialty		
Basting	Fine 100% cotton. Breaks easily to facilitate removal.	Marking; hand basting. Doesn't leave press marks.
Nylon monofilament	Continuous strand of clear or dark transparent thread.	Crafts, machine quilting, emergency repairs. Softer size 80 for attaching sequin or pearl strands on serger and making rolled-edge hems on metallics and laces. Use in serger needle with decorative thread in looper as embellishment.
Topstitching	Heavier than all purpose. Available in cotton-covered polyester, 100% polyester, and silk. Provides a bold appearance.	Topstitching. Filler cord in machine-made buttonholes; for sewing hand-worked buttonholes. Raised effect in decorative machine stitching.
Fusible	Will melt under heat of an iron.	Substitute for pins and hand basting. Use when matching plaids, attaching trims, and positioning appliqués. Great time-saver.

TYPE OF THREADS	DESCRIPTION	APPLICATION
100% nylon or polyester upholstery	Extra strong. Resists chemicals, rot, and mildew.	Hand or machine sewing of upholstery and other heavyweight fabrics. Excellent for all projects.
Quilting	Fine, strong, glacé-finished cotton. Limited colors.	Hand quilting. Not for use in machine; finish specially developed for hand sewing.

Decorative

Machine embroidery cotton	100% cotton. More lustrous than all-purpose cotton.	Machine satin stitching and embroidery work.
100% rayon	High luster. Size 40 for lighter, utilitarian uses. Size 30 for thickness; fills in quickly and fully. Less expensive than silk.	Machine embroidery and appliqué.
Metallic	Variety of weights, colors, and fiber contents. Adds sparkle and shine.	Machine embroidery, decorative overlock, and hand or machine quilting.
100% acrylic	Static-free. Adds luster and sheen.	Decorative work. Size 40 for flatlocking and decorative overlocking. Size 50 for machine embroidery.
Ribbon	Soft, supple, narrow rayon or nylon/Mylar ribbon. Available in solid colors and metallics.	Decorative accents on garments, crafts, and home items. Can be used in loopers of serger. Not suitable for satin stitching or other dense stitching.

Trims

You don't need to spend a fortune for embellished garments or home decorations when you can design and make your own. You'll be surprised at how easy it is to transform the plainest garment into a unique creation by adding simple trim accents. When decorating your home for summer, trims in clear, bright colors are wonderful, while dark, rich shades add warmth in winter. Silk braids, tassels, gold piping, and fringe add a plush look year-round.

For Your Protection

Most fringed trim has a row of protective stitching along the fringed edge. Leave this intact until your project is complete, then pull the end of the stitching to free the fringe.

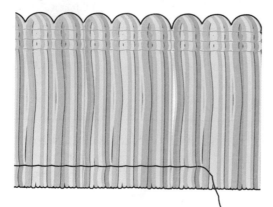

Victoria Waller

Elegant Eyelet

For a more lavish look when ruffling eyelet, buy a wider width than called for in your project directions and place the gathering stitches closer to the eyelet pattern than you would normally. Your finished project will show more of the eyelet design and less of the unembellished fabric.

Patricia De Santis

To Preshrink or Not to Preshrink

Check the trim package. If it isn't marked "preshrunk," you must preshrink the trim. Otherwise, you'll have a puckered mess after the first wash.

Barbara Fimbel

The Right Row

Trims are usually manufactured with multiple rows of stitching in the seam allowance. For best results, place the innermost row of stitching on your seam line and stitch on that inner line. Before sewing around each corner, clip the seam allowance to, but not through, the inner row of stitching, which will allow you to ease the trim around the corner.

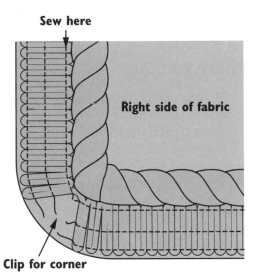

Sew here

Right side of fabric

Clip for corner

At each corner, stop sewing with your needle in the fabric, raise the presser foot, and turn the fabric. Push the trim slightly away from you and toward the needle, easing a little extra trim at each corner into the seam to prevent a puckered corner.

Victoria Waller

Gorgeous Gimp

When using trims edged with gimp, which is a fringe-like seam allowance or heading, you can either let the gimp show or hide it in the seam allowance.

Gimp looks great when you let it show on place mats, table toppers, and along the lower edge of window shades. To attach gimp to a finished edge of your project, pin it well first because it has a tendency to slip as it's being sewn. Then sew one row of edgestitching on either side of the gimp, as shown in **Diagram 1.**

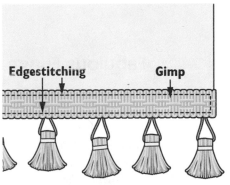

Edgestitching **Gimp**

DIAGRAM 1

To sew gimp into the seams of pillows, reversible table-cloths, and window treat-ments, use a zipper foot and sew along the edge closest to the decorative trim. To ease the gimp when sewing around a corner, clip into it without going through the row of stitching closest to the trim edge, as shown in **Diagram 2.** Only the decorative trim will show when your project is complete.

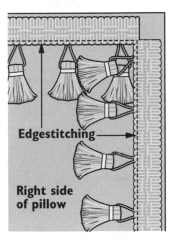

Edgestitching

Right side of pillow

DIAGRAM 2

Victoria Waller

Meant to Be Mitered

Pregathered trim is designed for straight edges, so when applying it around a corner, don't just wrap it. Instead, fold it on an angle and miter it. There isn't enough gathering in this type of trim to fit smoothly around a corner without pulling and looking skimpy.

Patricia De Santis

Fabulous Fringe

You can insert bullion fringe into a seam or topstitch it to a finished project. If you choose to insert it into a seam, clip into the header without going through the row of stitching closest to the fringe as you turn a corner, as shown in **Diagram 1.**

If you are top-stitching the trim, do not clip the header. Instead, miter the header or ease it around the corners, as shown in **Diagram 2.** Secure the fringe in place with a row of stitching near each edge of the header.

Victoria Waller

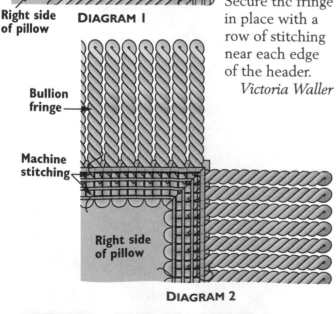

Bullion fringe   **Machine stitching**

Right side of pillow   **DIAGRAM 1**

Bullion fringe

Machine stitching

Right side of pillow

DIAGRAM 2

Where to Start

If your project has corners, start sewing your trim at the center of a straight edge, not at a corner. This way, all of your corners will look even.

Victoria Waller

Seams Easy!

When using pregathered lace, look for the type with a fine net edging. It makes a less bulky seam and is easier to sew.

Patricia De Santis

Make Your Own Tassels

If you can't find a tassel in the right color to match your project, make your own.

Step 1: Cut a stiff piece of cardboard the length of the tassel you want. Select the appropriate color embroidery floss, and wrap it around the cardboard to the desired fullness, as shown in Diagram 1.

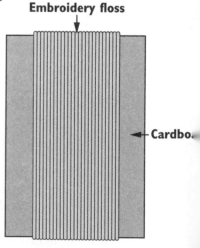

Embroidery floss

Cardboard

DIAGRAM 1

Step 2: To create the tassel head, gather the floss together at one wrapped end of the cardboard with a length of the same color floss, as shown in **Diagram 2,** and tie a knot.

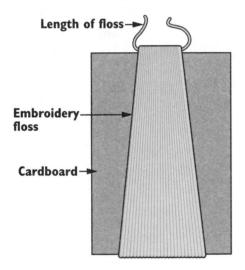

Length of floss→

Embroidery floss

Cardboard→

DIAGRAM 2

Step 3: Gently remove the knotted end of the tassel from the cardboard. Tie another piece of floss ½ to 1 inch below the knotted end. Cut the floss along the opposite end of the cardboard to create the tassel tails, as shown in **Diagram 3.**

Barbara Fimbel

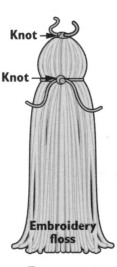

Knot

Knot

Embroidery floss

DIAGRAM 3

Keep It Together

To prevent decorative cording from fraying once it is cut, wrap transparent tape firmly around the area to be cut, as shown in **Diagram 1.**

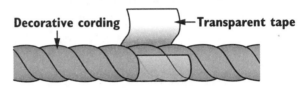

Decorative cording ——— Transparent tape

DIAGRAM 1

Use a piece of tape wide enough so that you can cut through the middle of it, leaving half on either piece of cording, as shown in **Diagram 2.** Leave the tape in place until you have sewn the cording onto your project.

Transparent tape

Decorative cording

DIAGRAM 2

Victoria Waller

Best Foot Forward

To make easy work of sewing most bulky trims, use a zipper foot on your machine. This foot will allow you to get your needle very close to the cording or fringe.

Victoria Waller

A Flawless Finish

Don't be intimidated by edging cushions in fabric-covered cording, known as welting. It isn't hard to achieve a flawless finish if you follow this technique.

Step 1: Always start one end of welting along the side of the cushion front, never at a corner. Position the welting so that the stitching on the casing is on the ½-inch seam line of your cushion front. To round a corner, clip the welting close to, but not through, the casing stitches. Attach a zipper foot to your machine. Sew the welting to the cushion front, leaving a 1-inch unstitched tail, as shown in **Diagram 1.**

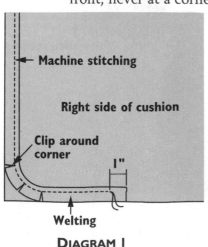

Machine stitching

Right side of cushion

Clip around corner

1"

Welting

DIAGRAM I

Step 2: Stop sewing 3 inches before the starting end of the welting. Cut the welting so that it overlaps the starting end by 1½ inches, as shown in **Diagram 2.** Remove 1½ inches of stitching along the welting casing.

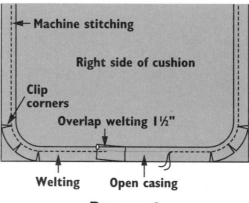

Machine stitching

Right side of cushion

Clip corners

Overlap welting 1½"

Welting   **Open casing**

DIAGRAM 2

Step 3: Open the casing and cut the cording so that it butts against the starting end of cording, as shown in **Diagram 3.** Then fold a ½-inch hem along the end of the open casing and wrap it around both ends of cording. Finish sewing the welting to the cushion front.

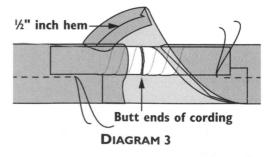

½" inch hem

Butt ends of cording

DIAGRAM 3

Victoria Waller

Surface Appearances

When you want to add a unique decorative effect to the surface of a garment or home decorating project, try using twisted cording. It looks great when added to a pillow or used to create a free-form design on the front of a garment.

To apply ³⁄₁₆-inch or narrower twisted cording, use this timesaving method. Mark the design on the right side of your fabric, as shown in **Diagram 1**.

Cording placement line

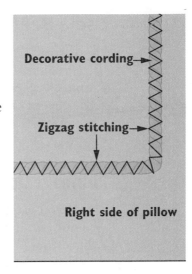

DIAGRAM 1

Then, using an embroidery or cording foot and thread that matches the cording, zigzag over the cording, making sure the swing of the needle clears the cording on either side, as shown in **Diagram 2**. Keep the stitches close to the cording so they won't show on the pillow fabric.

Cording that is ³⁄₁₆ to ¼ inch wide can also be zigzagged. Use a zipper foot or a blind hem foot, and adjust the zigzag stitch width to avoid hitting the foot with your needle. Sew the cording to the right side of your fabric so that one side of the stitch catches the cording and the other side catches only the fabric, as shown in **Diagram 3**. As you sew, push the cording toward the swing of the needle.

DIAGRAM 2

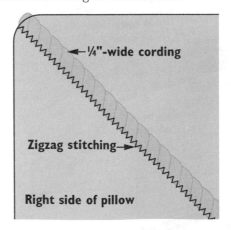

DIAGRAM 3

Cording wider than ¼ inch must be slip stitched by hand or glued in place on your project.

Victoria Waller

Trims

Use a Beefy Needle

Use a 90/100 (size 14 or 16) needle to sew trim to all home decorations. Sew slowly in heavier areas to prevent the needle from breaking.

Victoria Waller

Plump It Up

If you want plump welting but your cording is too thin, try this little trick. Place a layer of batting between the cording and the wrong side of the casing before you sew. Then sew the casing closed.

When you have finished, trim any excess batting before inserting the welting into your project.

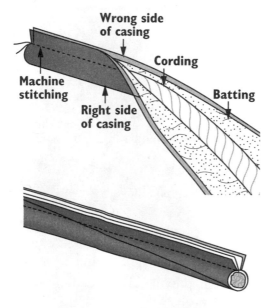

Wrong side of casing

Cording

Machine stitching

Right side of casing

Batting

Barbara Fimbel

Hands-On Solution

Do you get frustrated when you catch the welting casing in the needle of your machine? To prevent this from happening, I guide my work with my right hand while pulling the welting slightly to the left with my left hand. This also allows me to sew closer to the cording.

Victoria Waller

Bullion Basics

When working with bullion fringe, as shown in **Diagram 1** of "Fabulous Fringe" on page 284, be extra careful because the heading unravels easily. Before working with the fringe, secure the heading ends with a row of machine stitching. After sewing bullion fringe to your project, finish the ends by butting them together and not overlapping them.

Victoria Waller

Make It Look Rich

Welting looks fabulous when used in combination with other trims on home decorating projects, and it's easy to apply.

Step 1: Sew the welting in place, as explained in "A Flawless Finish" on page 286.

Step 2: Place fringe, tasseled fringe, cording, lace, or a ruffle on top of the welting, and sew directly on top of the previous row of stitches, as shown in **Diagram 1.** The cording shown has a fringelike seam allowance, known as gimp, that allows you to see the welting as you sew.

Step 4: Don't shy away from adding a third trim if you like the way it looks, as shown in **Diagrams 3** and **4.** Sew this trim on separately, but sew it directly over the previous two rows of stitching.

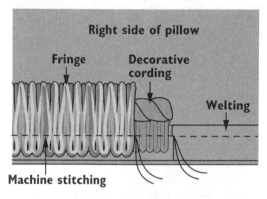

DIAGRAM 3

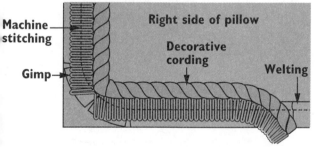

DIAGRAM 1

Step 3: Referring to **Diagram 2,** finish the ends of the cording by overlapping them along the sewing line and trimming as needed.

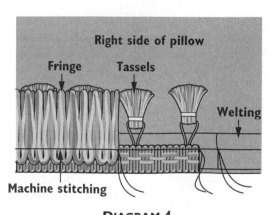

DIAGRAM 4

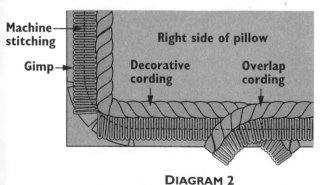

DIAGRAM 2

Victoria Waller

Waistbands

To get a good-looking and comfortable garment, you need a good-fitting waistband. These tried-and-true tips will help you to understand the finer points of stitching a perfect waistband so that you, too, can achieve professional results.

What a Waist!

Use your serger to create this unique-looking elastic waistband.

Step 1: Cut two strips of fabric the length of your waistband plus a ½-inch seam allowance. Cut one strip 3½ inches wide and the other 2 inches wide. Serge-finish the lengthwise edges of both strips with a short and narrow- to medium-width balanced stitch, a shown in **Diagram 1.**

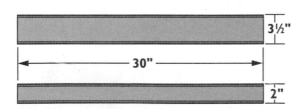

DIAGRAM 1

Step 2: With right sides facing, serge the ends of each strip together, forming two loops, as shown in **Diagram 2.**

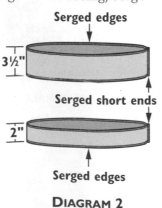

Serged edges

3½"

Serged short ends

2"

Serged edges

DIAGRAM 2

Step 3: Referring to **Diagram 3,** center the wrong side of the 2-inch-wide loop on top of the right side of the 3½-inch-wide loop, matching seams. Straight stitch the loops together ⅜ inch from each serged edge of the 2-inch-wide loop, leaving a 1-inch opening along one of the edges for inserting the elastic.

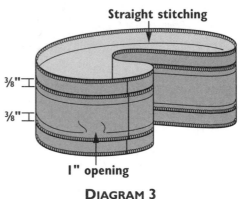

Straight stitching

⅜"

⅜"

1" opening

DIAGRAM 3

Step 4: With right sides facing up, pin the waistband to your garment, positioning the straight stitching along the lower edge of the loop ⅜ inch from the top edge of the garment and matching the loop seam to either a side seam or the back seam on your garment, as shown in **Diagram 4.** Carefully straight stitch over the previous line of stitching, making sure you don't stitch over the opening for the elastic.

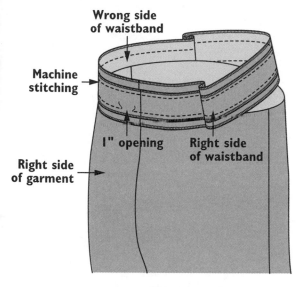

DIAGRAM 4

Step 5: Cut ¾-inch-wide elastic to the same length as your waist plus 2 inches. Insert it into the opening of the casing and pull it until it fits your waistline comfortably. Sew the ends of the elastic together, trimming if necessary, and slip stitch the opening closed.

Ronda Chaney

Get a Serge out of Waistbands

This method of applying elastic to the waist of a garment combines serger and conventional-machine sewing for a ready-to-wear look.

Step 1: Cut a length of elastic 5 inches shorter than your waist measurement.

Step 2: Butt the ends of the elastic together to form a loop, and use a triple zigzag stitch to sew the ends of the elastic together.

Step 3: Divide the elastic into quarters and mark it with straight pins, safety pins, or tailor's chalk. Divide the waist edge of your garment into quarters and mark them. Matching the marks, pin the elastic to the wrong side of the garment, aligning the edge of the elastic with the raw edge of your garment. Stretch the elastic to fit the garment's edge as you serge it in place, as shown in **Diagram 1**, and make sure you don't serge over the pins. If your serger's upper knife blade disengages, you can serge with it in a noncutting position to avoid cutting the elastic.

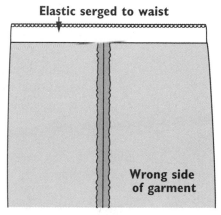

DIAGRAM 1

Step 4: Fold and pin the elastic to the wrong side of your garment, making sure the fabric is taut along the top edge. With a slightly longer stitch length, straight stitch through the serged stitching to secure the elastic band in place, as shown in **Diagram 2**.

Verna Erickson
Singer Sewing Company

DIAGRAM 2

Waistbands

Casual and Comfortable

Good-quality elastic and this technique will ensure that you get a comfortable-fitting waistband every time.

Step 1: Cut your elastic 3 inches shorter than your waist measurement.

Step 2: Stitch the ends of the elastic together, forming a loop. With a fine-point, permanent, felt-tip pen, straight pins, or safety pins, mark the elastic and the wrong side of the waist of your garment into quarters. With the garment turned wrong side out, match the quarter marks on the garment to those on the elastic, pinning the two layers together ¼ inch from the raw edge.

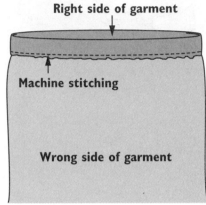

Right side of garment

Machine stitching

Wrong side of garment

DIAGRAM 2

Step 5: Pin the quarter marks again, pinning only through the top layer of the fabric and not into the elastic. Stretch the elastic a bit to distribute the fullness. To hold the elastic in place, sew on top of the previous line of stitching at the quarter marks, as shown in **Diagram 3**.

¼"

Quarter mark **Quarter mark**

Elastic

Quarter mark

Machine stitching

Wrong side of garment

DIAGRAM 1

Step 3: Stitch along the top edge of the elastic, as shown in Diagram 1.

Step 4: Fold the elastic to the inside, making sure the fabric is taut along the top edge. Sew the casing in place by stitching as close to the bottom of the elastic as possible, as shown in **Diagram 2**.

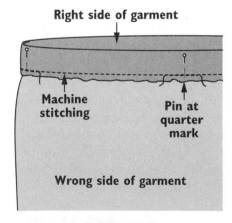

Right side of garment

Machine stitching

Pin at quarter mark

Wrong side of garment

DIAGRAM 3

Step 6: Now sew several rows of top-stitching along the length of the waist-

band, as shown in **Diagram 4.** Use a long stitch length—no more than 9 stitches per inch or a 3.5 mm length—when stitching through elastic. A short stitch length causes the elastic to grow, thus making the waist too big when completed.

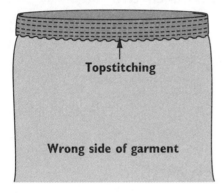

Topstitching

Wrong side of garment

DIAGRAM 4

Step 7: Steam press the elastic to allow it to recover its stretch.

Ruthann Spiegelhoff

Perfect Fit Every Time

If you have trouble stitching fitted waistbands to your garments, try this technique for a professional result.

Step 1: Cut a waistband the width of the waistband pattern piece and 6 inches longer than your waist measurement. This allows you to customize the waistband to fit your body measurements.

Step 2: Interface the waistband with firm, fusible interfacing.

Step 3: Divide your actual waist measurement by four. For example, if your waist is 24 inches, then 24 ÷ 4 = 6 inches. This number will be used to mark the waistband so that you can line up the side seams, center back, and center front of your garment.

Step 4: Mark the seam allowance on one end of the waistband and then make your quarter mark, as shown. Divide and mark the upper edge of your garment into quarters.

Waistbands with an underlap or overlap closure will require extra length. After marking the seam allowance on your waistband, mark your underlap or overlap, then make your quarter mark.

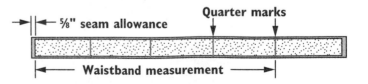

Quarter marks

⅝" seam allowance

Waistband measurement

Step 5: Pin the waistband to your garment's upper edge, matching the quarter marks on the waistband to the garment's seam lines. Trim off the excess waistband length. Complete the waistband according to your pattern directions.

Ruthann Spiegelhoff

 Bright Idea

YOU CAN MAKE A SIMPLE BELT IN LESS TIME THAN IT WOULD TAKE YOU TO BUY ONE. The easiest kind is a tie belt made from the same fabric as your garment or a contrasting fabric.

Wrap a length of ribbon around your waist and tie it into a knot the way you would a belt. Leaving enough length for tails, trim off the excess ribbon. Now cut your fabric to twice the desired width and the same length as your ribbon plus a 1-inch seam allowance.

Press under ½ inch on all sides of your belt. Then, with wrong sides together, fold it in half lengthwise and press. Edge stitch all around, and your belt is finished!

Karen Kunkel

Put the Selvage to Work

If you don't have a serger to finish the inside edge of a waistband, you can still have a finished edge without having to fold under the seam allowance and add bulk to your waistline. Simply cut the waistband with the lengthwise edge of the pattern piece along the selvage edge of the fabric. Sew the cut edge of the waistband to your skirt or slacks. Then fold the waistband over to the inside of your garment, and machine stitch in the ditch of the waistband seam. The selvage edge won't unravel, so you'll have a neatly finished waistband.

Karen Costello Soltys

Get Rid of the Gap

To keep an elastic waistline on a shirtwaist dress from gapping, sew a hook and thread loop at the waistline underneath the front placket.

Elizabeth M. Barry

Waist Not!

The last thing anyone wants is extra fabric around her waist. To reduce the bulk of waistbands and cuffs, don't interface the entire piece. Instead, only interface from one edge to ½ inch beyond the fold line.

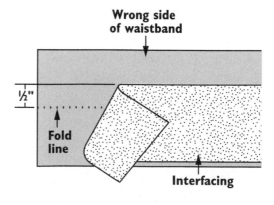

Wrong side of waistband

½"

Fold line

Interfacing

Janis Bullis

Ease-y Waistband

Most waistbands are not made to fit over a tummy, so you should allow for at least 1 inch of ease in the front. To do this, I cut my waistband front 1 inch longer than the back.

Claire Shaeffer

SMART SHOPPER

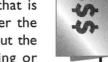

If you often have to alter the waistband of your husband's slacks, make it easy on yourself and buy men's tailored slacks with a waistband that is seamed at the center back. Alter the waistline by taking in or letting out the seam, eliminating tedious piecing or having to remove the band.

Gail Brown

No-Twist Elastic Waist

To prevent the elastic from twisting inside the waistband casings on your skirts, stitch in the ditch at the side seams through the elastic and the casing.

Elizabeth M. Barry

Multiple Rows of Elastic

Run all pieces of elastic through a multiple-casing waistband at the same time so that the elastic doesn't bunch up and twist.

Elizabeth M. Barry

Zippers

Have you ever wondered how people managed without zippers? Perhaps the most timesaving and revolutionary product of its time, zippers are often taken for granted. But they are a part of nearly every garment or home decoration we sew. This book wouldn't be complete without first-rate, timesaving zipper tips. You'll learn how to shorten zippers, topstitch them, and streamline the process of inserting them into your garments.

One Way Only

The secret to inserting a zipper so that the fabric on either side of it aligns perfectly is to sew in one direction only. This works wonders on plaid and striped fabrics.

Start at the bottom of the zipper and sew across the short end. Pivot your garment and sew along one side of the zipper, as shown in **Diagram 1**. Remove your garment from the machine.

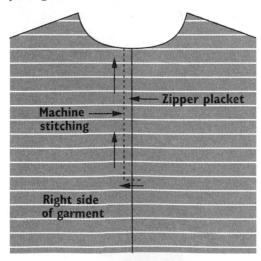

DIAGRAM 1

To sew the remaining side of the zipper, start again at the bottom and sew on top of the stitching across the short end but in the opposite direction. Pivot your garment and sew along the remaining side, as shown in **Diagram 2**.

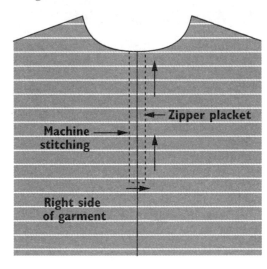

DIAGRAM 2

Coats & Clark

Get the Kinks Out

Get the kinks out of your zipper tape before inserting it into your garment by pressing it with a cool iron and using a press cloth. Press the tape up to, but not over, the zipper's teeth.

Barbara Fimbel

Take It from the Bottom

To shorten a zipper from the bottom, first close the zipper and mark the desired length with a pin, dressmaker's chalk, or an air-erasable marking pen. At the mark, stitch tightly across the teeth eight to ten times with a doubled thread. Cut the zipper off ½ inch below your stitches. Follow your pattern directions to insert the zipper into your garment.

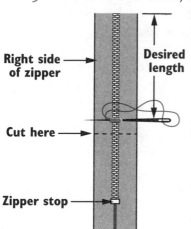

Right side of zipper

Desired length

Cut here →

Zipper stop →

Coats & Clark

Top-Rate Topstitching

If you have trouble topstitching a straight line next to the zipper tab, here's an easy way to do it. Stop topstitching just before you reach the zipper tab, but leave the needle in your fabric. Raise the presser foot, and pull the tab beyond the needle to an area you've already sewn. If necessary, remove the basting stitches that hold the seam closed along the zipper placket or opening. Then lower the presser foot and finish topstitching the zipper in place.

Coats & Clark

 Bright Idea

To make stepping into skirts, slacks, and shorts easier, use a 9-inch-long zipper rather than the frequently suggested 7-inch one. Just leave an extra 2 inches of the seam below the zipper placket open. You'll appreciate the extra ease!

Marinda Stewart

A Neat Neckline

If a neckline edge is to be finished with a facing, install the zipper after the facing has been applied. Position the top of the zipper teeth ⅜ inch below the finished neckline.

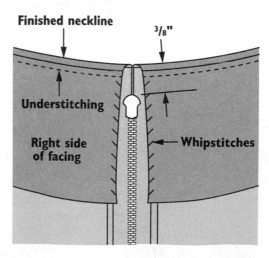

Finished neckline

³⁄₈"

Understitching

Right side of facing

Whipstitches

Barbara Fimbel

Zippers

Template for a Perfect Curve

To topstitch the fly curve perfectly in a pair of slacks, use the zipper package as a template. Trim the curved outer panel of the package to match your pattern stitching line. Use pins or double-faced tape to keep the cardboard template in place on your garment, then topstitch around it.

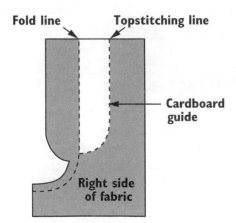

Coats & Clark

Smooth Stitching

If you want to avoid sewing around zipper tabs entirely, use a zipper that is longer than the opening of your garment. Close the zipper so that the tab is at the top. Insert the zipper into the garment, open the zipper, and then shorten it from the top, as described in "Take It from the Top" on page 301.

Coats & Clark

Lapped in No Time Flat

This technique creates a lapped zipper and finishes the seam allowances at the same time.

Step 1: Stitch the seam below your zipper with a $5/8$-inch seam allowance. Trim the seam allowance along the right edge of the zipper opening of your garment to $1/2$ inch. Do not trim the seam allowance along the left edge.

Step 2: With right sides together and the edge of the fabric and the edge of the zipper even, zigzag the right edge of the zipper to the right edge of the zipper opening, as shown in **Diagram 1.**

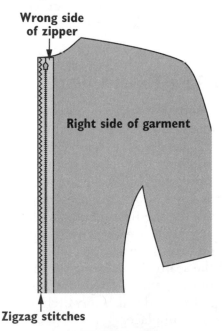

DIAGRAM 1

Step 3: With the right side of the fabric and zipper facing up, roll the fabric toward the edge of the zipper teeth. Using a zipper foot, topstitch the fabric in place close to the zipper teeth, as shown in **Diagram 2.**

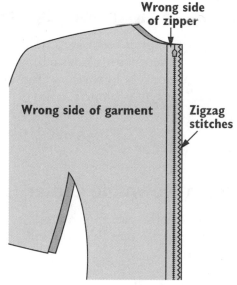

Wrong side of zipper

Wrong side of garment

Zigzag stitches

DIAGRAM 3

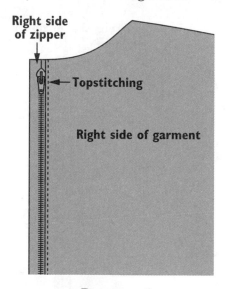

Right side of zipper

Topstitching

Right side of garment

DIAGRAM 2

foot and topstitch the left edge of the zipper in place, as shown in Diagram 4.

Step 4: With the right sides of the zipper and fabric together and the edges even, sew the remaining long edge of the zipper to the left edge of the zipper opening with a zigzag stitch, as shown in **Diagram 3.** With the right side of the fabric facing up, press along the ⁵⁄₈-inch seam line. This will automatically create a lap over the zipper on the right side of the fabric.

Step 5: With the right side of your garment facing up, use a zipper

Topstitching

DIAGRAM 4

Holly Butryn

Zippers

Keep the Zip in Your Zipper

If your zipper teeth are stiff, lubricate them with a nonstaining lubricant, household wax, paraffin, or soap. This will prolong the life of your zipper.

Coats & Clark

Zippin' down the Center

Here is the easiest centered zipper technique that you will ever use.

Step 1: Stitch the seam below your zipper with a ⁵/₈-inch seam allowance. Trim the seam allowance along both edges of the zipper opening to ¹/₂ inch, as shown in **Diagram 1.**

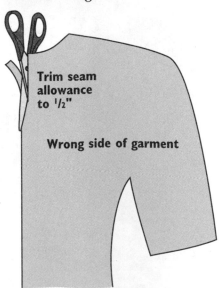

Trim seam allowance to ¹/₂"

Wrong side of garment

DIAGRAM I

Step 2: With right sides together and the edges of the zipper and the fabric even, sew one long edge of the zipper to the left edge of the zipper opening with a zigzag stitch, as shown in **Diagram 2.**

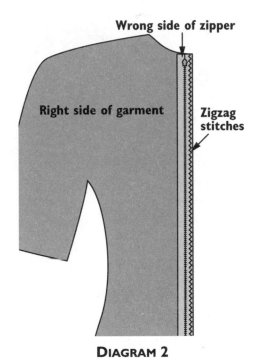

Wrong side of zipper

Right side of garment

Zigzag stitches

DIAGRAM 2

Step 3: Repeat Step 2 for the right edge of the zipper opening.

Step 4: With the right side of the garment facing up, press the zipper placket area, creating two narrow laps centered over the zipper, as shown in **Diagram 3.** Make sure the center of the zipper placket lines up with the seam below the zipper.

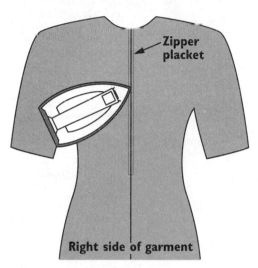

Zipper placket

Right side of garment

DIAGRAM 3

Step 5: Topstitch the zipper in place ³/₈ inch from each edge, as shown in Diagram 4.

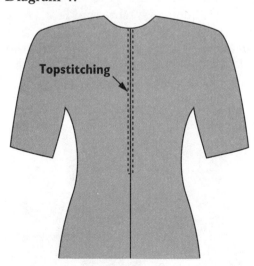

Topstitching

DIAGRAM 4

Holly Butryn

Take It from the Top

If you can't find a zipper in the length you need, or if you already have one but it's too long, you can easily shorten it to fit. This method allows you to shorten the zipper from the top if you are going to insert it into a waistband or a collar, but it is not recommended if you plan to face the upper edge of your garment.

Follow your pattern directions to insert the zipper, allowing the excess amount to extend over the top edge of your garment. Now open the zipper. Limit upward movement of the slider at the top edge by sewing a bar tack by hand or machine over the teeth on each side of the zipper inside the seam allowance, as shown. Cut off the excess tape.

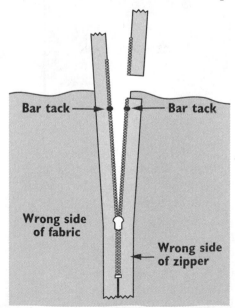

Bar tack ————— ————— **Bar tack**

Wrong side of fabric

Wrong side of zipper

Coats & Clark

Glossary of Sewing Terms

Appliqué. A fabric design or shape stitched and/or fused to the right side of a base fabric.

Appliqué foot. See *Embroidery foot*.

Armhole. The garment opening for the arm and sleeve.

Bar tack. A very short thread reinforcement for stress points. It can be made by hand or machine.

Basting. Stitches used to hold together temporarily two or more layers of fabric. Basting stitches can be sewn by hand or machine, and they should be large enough to see and loose enough to be removed easily.

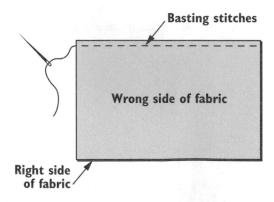

Basting stitches

Wrong side of fabric

Right side of fabric

Batting. A polyester or natural-fleece layer used to back and/or pad a surface. It is also a quilt's center layer or filler.

Bias. A diagonal or oblique line that cuts across the lengthwise and crosswise threads of a fabric. True bias is at a 45-degree angle to the selvage. Bias-cut fabric has the greatest amount of stretch and flexibility.

Bias tape. Bias-cut strips of lightweight fabrics in a variety of widths and colors with prefolded edges. Bias tape can be found in the notions section of your favorite sewing store. It is used on curved hems, facings, or casings where there is not enough fabric or where the fabric is too heavy and will add too much bulk to the finished project.

Binding. The manner in which an edge is finished by encasing it in a strip of fabric.

Blind hem foot. A presser foot that is used for creating a blind hem stitch. It will differ with each machine model, but it will have a separate guide or a

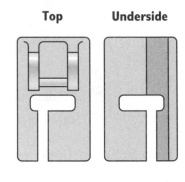

Top   Underside

wide toe on the right and a higher underside on the left that acts as a fabric guide.

Blind hem stitch. This stitch is used to hold up the hem on firm, fairly heavy fabrics and can be done by hand, as shown, or by

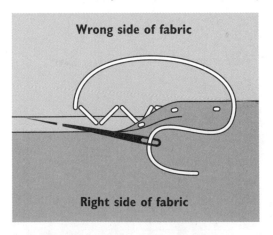

Wrong side of fabric

Right side of fabric

machine. It should not be used when hemming lightweight fabrics because the stitches may show on the right side. A machine-made blind hem stitch is made up of several straight stitches followed by a zigzag stitch to the left of the needle.

Blind stitch. A hand stitch, nearly invisible from either side of a fabric, used to attach appliqués and close turned openings.

Box pleat. Two pleats (lengthwise folds of fabric) facing in opposite directions on the right side and meeting at the center on the wrong side. A box pleat can be edge stitched along the folds to help it retain its shape.

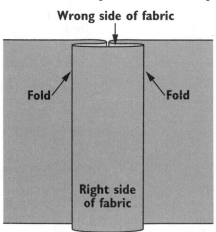

Butt. To place two edges together so that they touch.

Casing. Two layers of fabric sewn together to form a tube into which elastic or a drawstring can be inserted. A casing is formed either by folding over an edge of fabric or by applying a separate piece of fabric. When a casing is applied, it can be sewn either to the inside or the outside of a garment.

Center back. Indicates the vertical line that runs the length of a garment at the center of the back of the body.

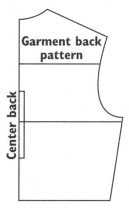

Center front. Indicates the vertical line that runs the length of the garment at the center of the front of the body.

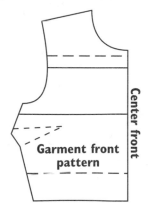

Clean finishing. The treatment of a raw edge of fabric so that it does not fray. Clean finishing can be done by using a straight or zigzag stitch or by serging.

Clip. A small cut made in the seam allowance for the purpose of marking, such as a pleat or dart. Clips are also used along curves to allow the fabric to lay flat.

Glossary of Sewing Terms

Closure. A method or device used to close an opening. Common closures include buttons and buttonholes or loops, hooks and eyes, snaps, hook-and-loop tape, and zippers.

Cording. See *Piping.*

Cording foot. A presser foot that has a wide groove on its underside through which a piece of cable cording or yarn can be fed. It can also be used to attach piping.

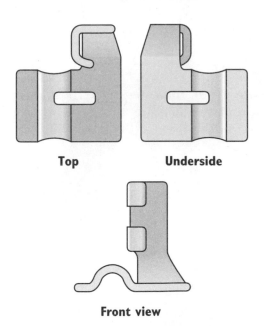

Top   **Underside**

Front view

Crosswise grain. The threads that run from selvage to selvage on a piece of fabric. See also *Grain.*

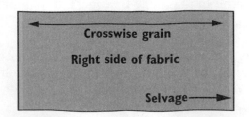

Crosswise grain

Right side of fabric

Selvage→

Cutwork. A method of embroidering fabric in which designs are decoratively stitched by machine or by hand with selected areas of the fabric cut away. Satin stitching is commonly used when cutwork is stitched by machine, and buttonhole stitching is used when cutwork is done by hand. Cutwork is most often stitched in white or ecru-color thread.

Dart. A stitched fold of fabric that is used to provide shaping. A dart is stitched on the inside of a garment and tapers to a point at one or both ends.

Deck. The flat hidden surface under seat cushions or above box springs to which decorative skirts are attached.

Decorative stitching. Machine or hand stitching or embroidery used for ornamentation.

Design ease. The amount of room for movement that a designer incorporates into a garment to make it comfortable to wear and fashionable.

Directional stitching. Stitching with the grain of fabric, usually from the widest point to the narrowest.

Double-fold bias tape. A bias-cut strip of fabric with prefolded edges that is folded in half lengthwise.

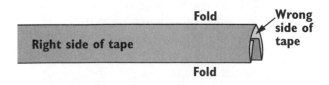

Fold   Wrong side of tape

Right side of tape

Fold

Drapery weights. Square, round, or chain weights used to weigh down curtains or drapes to maintain the shape of pleats and folds.

Duvet. A comforter, usually filled with down or feathers.

Ease. The basic amount of room for movement allowed in a pattern. The amount of ease in garments varies among pattern companies. See also *Design ease*.

Easing. Sewing together two layers of fabric of different lengths so that the fullness of the longer layer is not visible.

Edgestitching. Machine stitching close to a finishing edge or seam line, usually a scant ⅛ inch from the edge.

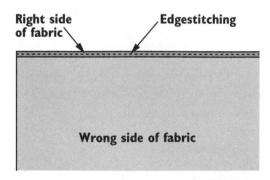

Edging trim. A narrow length of ruffles, lace, decorative banding, or cording that is used to decorate or finish an edge.

Embroidery foot. A presser foot used for machine embroidery and appliqué. It has a wide opening between two long toes that is either open or covered with clear plastic, allowing you to see the stitches as they are sewn. A wide channel on the underside al-lows the foot to ride over the top of the decorative stitches. This foot also can be used for satin stitching.

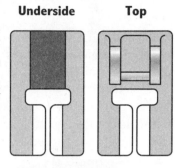

Closed embroidery foot

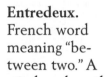

Entredeux. French word meaning "between two." A stitch or lace that features small heavily embroidered holes. Entredeux stitches can be created by using a wing needle and decorative machine stitches.

Open embroidery foot

Even feed foot. A presser foot frequently used by quilters. Also called a walking foot or dual-feeder. It works with the feed dogs to ease either multiple fabric layers or fabric and batting under the sewing machine needle without shifting the layers. This foot also prevents tucks from forming in the top and bottom layers. In garment sewing, this foot is used to match stripes and plaids, as well as evenly feed napped and slippery fabrics.

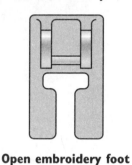

Glossary of Sewing Terms

Even plaid. The spaces and colors of the plaid match along both the lengthwise and crosswise grain of the fabric.

Eyelet. A decorative trim that features small embroidered holes. It is available as a flat trim and in a gathered form.

Facing. A fabric piece usually added to the underside of a garment to finish and support such areas as the neckline, front and back openings, and the armholes of sleeveless garments.

Feed dogs. The teeth under the presser foot that move the fabric through the machine.

Finger press. Using your thumb and index finger instead of an iron to flatten a seam.

Fleece. A dense form of batting used to add loft and resilience to fabric surfaces or warmth to garments. It is also available as a fusible.

Free-motion machine sewing. A decorative sewing technique whereby abstract designs are created on fabric using novelty threads and random stitching. This technique is achieved by lowering the feed dogs, using a darning foot or removing the presser foot, and guiding stabilized fabric by hand. A new trend in this area is sewing directly onto water-soluble stabilizer. The stabilizer is dissolved after dense stitching has been applied, leaving only the new thread "fabric."

Fusible web. Heat-sensitive, nonwoven adhesive fibers placed between two fabric layers for bonding. It is available by the yard, as a sheet, or as tape and with or without paper backing.

Gathering rows. Two or more lines of stitching that can be pulled into gathers to ease uneven lengths of fabric or to obtain fullness.

Gimp. A fringelike seam allowance or heading on many trims used in home decorating projects.

Grade. To trim the raw edges of seam allowances so they are different widths. This will reduce bulk along the seam line. The narrowest grade should be the layer that lies closest to your body.

Grain. The crosswise or lengthwise threads in a woven fabric. Grain is important in creating a garment that fits and hangs well.

Grain line. A double-headed arrow printed on a pattern piece that should be placed on a lengthwise thread of woven fabric, which will run parallel to the selvage.

Heading. Ruffled portion at the top of a shirred curtain. Sometimes referred to as the "header," it is anything that serves as a head, top, or front.

Hemline. The line at which fabric is turned under to create a hem finish.

Hemstitch. A tiny stitch commonly used inside garments to attach an edge of fabric, usually folded, to another piece of fabric. Although this is called a hemstitch, it is rarely used in garment hems, as the stitches would show on the outside surface. See also *Blind hem stitch.*

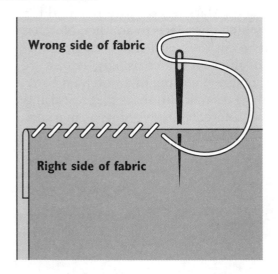

Wrong side of fabric

Right side of fabric

Hook-and-loop tape. A pull-apart fastener with one side having numerous small hooks and the other side having loops. It is available in sew-on and self-adhesive styles.

Insertion lace. Straight-sided lace that can be stitched to the edge of fabric or another piece of lace. This lace also can be stitched to the right side of fabric; then the fabric is trimmed from behind the lace.

Interfacing. A sew-on or fusible fabric piece attached to the inside of a facing or garment to provide shape and support and to increase wear. Interfacing products can be woven or nonwoven and are available in a variety of weights. (See pages 144–147.)

Interlining. The layer of fabric added between a garment's shell and its lining to give warmth and/or shape. This layer can be interfacing.

In-the-ditch stitching. Stitching made from the right side, in a previously stitched seam (the ditch), through all layers. Most frequently used to secure the underside of a waistband or collar.

Knife-edge pillow. A simple pillow made of two pieces of fabric seamed together without a box edge or other side section.

Lapel. The part of the front of a jacket that is turned back onto itself between the collar and the first button.

Layout. The way pattern pieces should be placed on a piece of fabric for cutting.

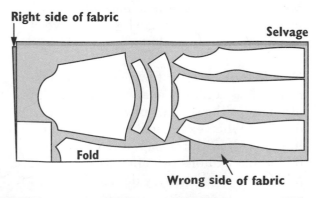

Right side of fabric

Selvage

Fold

Wrong side of fabric

Glossary of Sewing Terms

Lengthwise grain. The threads that run parallel to the selvage. See also *Grain; Grain line.*

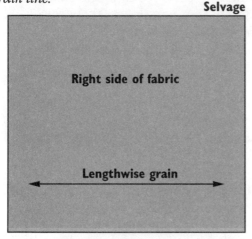

Lining. A layer of fabric used to cover the wrong side of a garment.

Mercerization. The process of passing thread through a caustic soda bath under controlled tension and then through several rinses. This process strengthens cotton thread and improves its luster and colorfastness.

Miter. Diagonal fold made at a corner in an edge finish such as a binding.

Mitered corners. Corners finished with a seam at a 45-degree angle for decorative effect and/or to reduce bulk.

Nap. Raised, hairy, or fuzzy surface on fabrics such as corduroy and velvet that feels different or the shading of which is visibly different when examined in each direction. In patterns, "with the nap" refers to any fabric that exhibits this effect, such as knits, pile fabrics, and one-way designs.

Neck facing. A fabric piece that is attached to the wrong side of a garment along the curved neckline edge. The facing is not visible from the outside and can act as both a partial lining and a finish for the raw edge of the neckline.

Nonwoven fabric. Fabric produced by any method other than weaving or knitting. Such fabrics can be cut in any direction and include synthetic leather and suede, felt, and various interfacings.

Notches. Markings on patterns used for matching one piece to another. Notches can be cut to the outside of or inside the seam allowance. Increasingly, sewers are forgoing the cutting of a notch and are making a small clip in its place or using small colored adhesive, dots as markers. See also *Clip.*

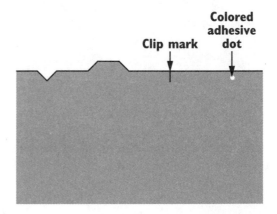

Notions. Small sewing aids or materials such as thread, needles, pins, zippers, marking pens, and buttons.

Overhand knot. A knot created by making a loop in cording or thread and pulling the end through.

Overlock machine. See *Serger.*

Peplum. A decorative piece that is attached to the waistline of a suit jacket, dress, or blouse.

Piping. Cable cording covered with a bias fabric strip that forms a seam allowance. It is used as a decorative trim in seams of garments or home decorating projects.

Placket. A finished opening used to close a garment. It can be located at the lower portion of a sleeve or at the neckline.

Preshrink. To launder, steam, or dry-clean fabric prior to assembling a garment.

Press cloth. A swatch of single- or multiple-ply fabric that is placed on top of a fabric being pressed, thereby preventing direct contact between the fabric and the iron. A press cloth prevents shine and iron imprints. When used damp, a press cloth can help create a sharp crease.

Puddling. Allowing fabric, generally drapery panels or a table skirt, to pool on the floor. Puddling is achieved by making sections longer than the measurement from the top of the curtain or table to the floor.

Raw edge. An unfinished fabric edge that isn't the selvage and that hasn't been serged, edge finished, or encased.

Reinforce. To strengthen an area subject to strain.

Repeats. The vertical distance between identical motifs.

Roller foot. As the name suggests, this presser foot has one or more metal rollers between the toes. The textured rollers allow the presser foot to roll smoothly over heavy or thick layers of fabric.

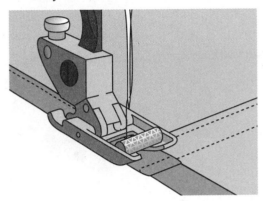

Roll line. The line along which a lapel or collar rolls back onto itself around the neck.

Rotary cutter and mat. A rotary cutter is a sharp circular blade mounted in a handle that fits in the palm of your hand. The rotary cutter is commonly used by quilters to cut patchwork strips and pieces. Many garment sewers are using it to cut pattern pieces from fabric. The mat is a self-healing, flexible cutting surface that must be used with the rotary cutter to prevent the blade from becoming dull.

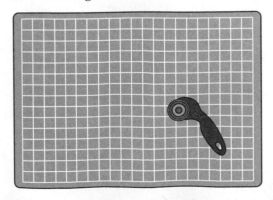

Glossary of Sewing Terms

Satin stitch. Smooth, densely worked parallel stitches. Satin stitches can be worked by hand or machine. When worked by machine, a zigzag stitch is used to create this stitch. See also *Satin stitch foot*.

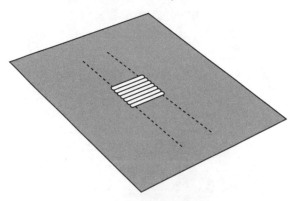

Satin stitch foot. This pressure foot has a wide opening between the toes and a groove extending the length of the underside so the foot can ride over the satin stitches, allowing them to remain even and smooth. In contrast, the groove on the underside of a zigzag foot does not extend the full length of the underside.

Underside   Top

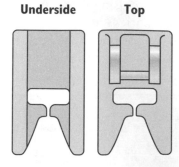

Seam allowance. The amount of fabric extending from the seam line to the raw edge, usually ⅝ inch.

Seam line. The line along which a seam is stitched. It is sometimes printed on a pattern and is usually ⅝ inch from the cutting line.

Seam ripper. A small hand-held, two-prong sewing notion. One of the prongs is half the length of the other and is often covered by a small plastic ball. The gap between the two prongs is sharp enough to cut through taut sewing thread. The seam ripper, as the name suggests, is used to remove stitches from fabric by isolating and breaking stitches.

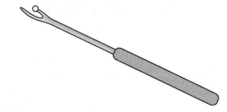

Seam roll. A long, cylindrical cushion used to press seams in narrow areas.

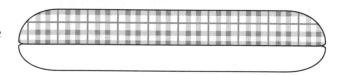

Selvage. The finished edge on all woven fabrics. It runs parallel to the lengthwise grain.

Serge finish. To encase a raw fabric edge with overlocking stitches sewn on a serger. This finish is commonly found on seam allowances and facings.

Serger. A machine that stitches, trims, and finishes in one step. It uses three, four, or five threads and makes up to 1,500 stitches per minute. The term has also been applied to the overlock machine, which produces a similar seam and edge finish but uses two or three threads.

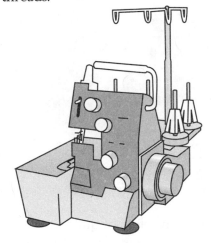

Shank. A button's stem.

Single-fold bias tape. A bias-cut strip of woven material the raw lengthwise edges of which are folded in to meet at the center. It is used to encase raw edges. Folded double, it can be applied as binding. See also *Double-fold bias tape.*

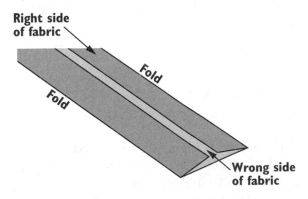

Right side
of fabric

Fold

Fold

Wrong side
of fabric

Sizing. A starchlike finish added by the fabric manufacturer when making some natural-fiber fabrics and rayon. It is water and steam soluble.

Slip stitch. A barely visible hand stitch formed by guiding the needle through a folded edge, then picking up a thread of the fabric underneath.

Smocking. A decorative method of embroidery made by gathering fabric into small pleats and working over them with embroidery stitches.

Stabilizer. A product that temporarily stiffens lightweight fabric so it feeds evenly between the presser foot and feed dogs on a sewing machine. Traditionally, tissue paper, interfacing, or newspaper was placed on top and underneath fabric as it was sewn or cut. Technological advances have led to an array of new stabilizers. Some look and feel like interfacing or freezer paper while others are liquids. Some tear away, while others wash away with water or crumble when ironed.

Stay stitching. Stitching on or just outside of a seam line, before construction, to stabilize curved or angled edges. It is normally used on a single thickness of fabric, but it can also be used to attach interfacing.

Straight grain. Threads in a fabric parallel to the selvage. See also *Grain; Lengthwise grain.*

Swag. A window treatment that falls gracefully from the top of a board or pole, swooping down and then back atop the board or pole.

Tack. To attach one section to another with hand or machine stitches. Tacking stitches can be used temporarily to aid construction or left in permanently.

Glossary of Sewing Terms

Tailoring. A labor-intensive method of sewing classically styled, high-end garments such as suits, coats, and dresses.

Tailor's ham. A very firm, ham-shaped "pillow" used as a pressing surface for curved portions of a garment, like darts and princess seams. One-half of the ham is covered with heavy, napped fabric, while the other half is covered by a smooth linen or cotton.

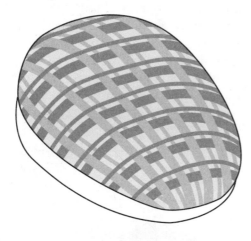

Tailor's tacks. Loose hand stitches used to transfer pattern markings to fabric.

Taper. To gradually reduce in width.

Tension. The amount of strain on the needle and bobbin threads. Stitch tension is normal when the two are balanced.

Tiebacks. Pieces used to hold curtains or draperies back to the side of the window. They can be made from the same fabric as the curtains, coordinating or contrasting fabric, twisted braid, or hardware.

Topstitching. Hand or machine stitching, either functional or decorative, that shows on the outside of a garment, usually ¼ inch or more from the edge.

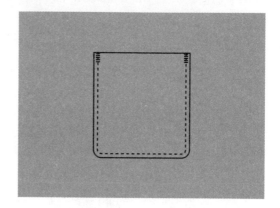

Trapunto. A method of quilting in which a running stitch is used to outline a design area that is then padded from the underside.

Trim. Various fringes, braids, piping, and welting used as an embellishment.

True bias. A diagonal line that crosses the lengthwise and crosswise threads of a fabric at a 45-degree angle to the selvage. Fabric cut on the true bias rather than with the grain has more "give." See also *Bias; Grain; Grain line.*

Tunneling. The formation of thread into a tunnel shape above the surface of the fabric during machine satin stitching.

Twin needle. Two needles attached to a single shank that is inserted into the sewing machine. A twin needle will sew two rows of parallel stitches.

Twisted braid. A braid with or without a header and made of twisted cords. See also *Heading.*

Undercollar. The underside of a collar. On better men's tailored jackets, the undercollar is often made of melton, a smooth but heavy woolen fabric.

Underlining. A second thickness of fabric or interfacing used to add body and shape.

Uneven plaid. Plaid fabric on which the spaces and colors do not match in one or both directions.

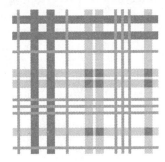

Upper collar. The top portion of a collar.

Valance. A short, decorative window treatment placed over the top of draperies or curtains or used alone.

Vent. A slit in the back of a jacket, skirt, or dress.

Walking foot. See *Even feed foot.*

Water-soluble marking pen. A pen designed to mark fabric temporarily. The marks will dissolve in water.

Welting. Thick piping that is larger than ¼ inch in diameter and covered with bias-cut strips of fabric that form a seam allowance. It is used as an ornamental edging in home decorating projects.

Welt pocket. A pocket with the opening encased in a fabric strip, or welt. A double welt pocket looks like a large bound buttonhole.

Woven fabric. Fabric that is constructed by wrapping or weaving crosswise yarns or threads over and under lengthwise yarns or threads. Woven fabrics have a tendency to fray at cut edges.

Zigzag foot. A presser foot with an indentation on the underside that extends from the front of the foot almost to the back. The zigzag foot is sometimes called an embroidery foot.

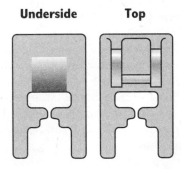

Underside   Top

Zipper foot. A presser foot that can be moved to the left or right so that it does not ride over the zipper teeth. It also can be used for edge stitching.

Top   Underside

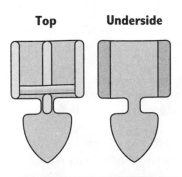

The Sewing Experts

Judi Abbott served as head of public relations for Simplicity Pattern Company, where she handled media relations and contributed to consumer publications. As a freelancer, she has written articles on home decorating for GCR Publishing Group, Inc.

Carol Laflin Ahles is writing a book on decorative machine sewing. She coauthored *Know Your Elna* and teaches sewing courses. She contributes to *Creative Needle* and *Threads* magazines and has created patterns for publication.

Marya Kissinger Amig is an editor of sewing books for Rodale Press and a lifelong sewer.

Donna Babylon runs her own company, Windsor Oak Publishing, which specializes in how-to books on home decorating and quilting. She designs patterns for McCall Pattern Company.

Laurie Baker is editor of *Sewing Update* newsletter and assistant editor of *Sew News*.

Naomi Baker has coauthored ten books on serger and sewing techniques and is a consulting editor and writer for *Serger Update* and *Sewing Update* newsletters.

Belva Barrick, a certified home economist and the author of *As Soon As I Lose . . .* and *Shape Your Shoulders*, is a college clothing and textiles instructor and inventor of the Seam Stick.

Elizabeth M. Barry's work in the sewing, crafts, and needlework industries includes positions at pattern companies and trade associations. She has contributed to numerous publications.

Nancy Bednar is a regular contributor to *Sewing Update* and *Serger Update* newsletters and a freelance sewing specialist for Bernina of America.

Peggy Bendel has written 11 books and is a contributing editor to *Sew News*, an editor of

McCall's Creates craft booklets, and a frequent contributor to *Sewing Decor, Pfaff Club Magazine,* and other publications.

Lana Bennett is a writer and coeditor of a newsletter for Singer Sewing Company and works in the company's training and education department.

Julia Bernstein was assistant art director of Vogart Crafts and assistant creative director for Columbia-Minerva before developing her own line of needlecraft kits. She continues to freelance for Pellon, Simplicity Patterns, B. Blumenthal and Company, Bucilla, and others.

Sandra Betzina writes a syndicated sewing column, contributes to *Threads*, and is author of the books *Power Sewing, More Power Sewing*, and *Couture Cuisine*. Sandra appears in sewing programs on television and lectures nationally.

Charlotte Biro began her career in Coats & Clark's instruction book department. She has been product manager for Talon's yarns, threads, and books and has designed and produced books for American Thread. Charlotte has created fashion and craft designs for many magazines.

Glynda Black, a teacher of quilting and sewing machine arts, is the author of *Creative Pfaff* Programming for the 1471, 1473, and 1475. She owns and operates Glynda Black's Designs, which produces decorative machine embroidery stitches for computer disks for use with the Pfaff sewing machine.

Fred Bloebaum (a woman with a man's nickname) is a consultant and sewing instructor at The Sewing Workshop in San Francisco, Diablo Valley College, and other schools and fabric stores.

Karen Bolesta is an editor of quilt books for Rodale Press. She was formerly on the editorial staff of *McCall's Needlework & Crafts* magazine.

Lori Bottom is a writer for national sewing publications, author of *Taming Your First Serger*, and coauthor of *ABCs of Serging* and *Make It Your Own: Personalizing Patterns for Creative Design*.

Kendra Brandes, assistant professor of home economics at Illinois State, teaches courses in textiles, fashion and costume history, and clothing construction. Kendra is a consultant for PJS Publications, contributes to *Sew News*, and contributed to the book *Sew Much Better*.

Richard M. Braun is a writer and editor specializing in interior design and home improvement. He has been a contributing editor and editor of a number of special-interest decorating magazines.

Gail Brown has authored or coauthored 11 books and hundreds of articles. Her work has appeared in *McCall's Patterns* magazine, *Sew News*, *Singer Sewing Reference Library*, *Woman's Day Super Specials*, and *Vogue Patterns*. Gail is also a regular columnist for the *Serger Update* and *Sewing Update* newsletters.

Lynn L. Browne is manager of educational programs for Coats & Clark.

Janis Bullis is president of Creative Services of Central Valley, New York, her consulting and design company. Janis has written for many how-to publications and women's magazines.

Jane M. Burbach is director of education for Elna, Inc. She has written several books for the creative use of Elna sewing machines and has written for *Sew Beautiful* and *Sewing and Fine Needlework*.

Jan Burns, editor of *Creative Quilting* and a contributor to the *Pfaff Club Magazine*, writes sewing-related articles and project instructions.

Holly Butryn has been a custom dressmaker for 25 years, specializing in evening, wedding, career, and casual wear. She owns Holly Rae Designs and Holly Rae School of Dressmaking in Jamestown, New York.

Roberta C. Carr brings a fashion approach to home sewing in her new book, *Couture, The Art of Fine Sewing*. Roberta has a video series, *Couture Techniques*, and has written articles for *Sew News*, *Singer Sewing Reference Library*, *Threads*, and *Vogue Patterns*.

Diana L. Carswell is an expert in makeup, wardrobe styling, fashion, and sewing. Her beauty advice has appeared in *Mademoiselle*, *Vogue*, *Self*, and *Ladies' Home Journal*. She has written sewing-related articles for *Sew News* and *McCall's Patterns* magazine.

Karen King Carter is an educational consultant for Pfaff American Sales Corporation. She travels, teaching sewing tricks and techniques to Pfaff dealers and their customers.

Ronda Chaney is coauthor of *Make It Your Own: Personalizing Patterns for Creative Design*. Ronda is chairperson and professor of fashion design and textiles at Canada College in Redwood City, California.

Clotilde began her career in 20th Century Fox's wardrobe department and continued to learn designer techniques while sewing for Beverly Hills boutiques. Now owner of the mail-order sewing notions company, Clotilde, Inc., she is also the author of *Sew Smart*.

Anita Collins offers image consulting through her firm, ABCDesign. In addition to teaching sewing classes, Anita has presented workshops at the Fashion Institute of Technology and has written articles for *McCall's Patterns* magazine.

The Sewing Experts

Jane F. Cornell, a decorating, remodeling, and crafts writer, is author of six books, including *Rooms to Grow.* She edited *Sewing Today, Home Decorating Projects* and has written or developed projects for a variety of magazines.

Judi Cull, sewing teacher and coauthor of *Know Your Sewing Machine,* has contributed to a number of books on machine techniques, including *Embellishing Concepts in Sulky.*

Sonja Dagress, a New York–based fashion designer and editor, has been involved with fashion sewing for more than 20 years. She is editor of the *Always in Style Portfolio.*

Patricia De Santis heads the creative/marketing department at William E. Wright Company.

Jackie Dodson, a magazine and newsletter columnist, is the author or coauthor of several books, including *How to Make Soft Jewelry, Twenty Easy Machine-Made Rugs, Gifts Galore,* and two *Quick-Quilted Home Decor* books. She is coauthoring a *Sew and Serge* series.

Joyce Drexler, author of *Thread Painting,* is an authority on machine arts and crafts and has created more than 200 products for the Speed Stitch Company, which she owns. She is the producer and coauthor of the *Concepts in Sulky* books and product coordinator for Sulky of America.

Margit Echols is an artist, author, designer, and nationally exhibited quiltmaker. She has authored five books on quiltmaking and has taught for more than 20 years. Her company, Rowhouse Press, publishes quilting-related materials.

Nancy Erickson divides her energy between consulting for sewing businesses and teaching national sewing seminars. She writes a newsletter for her Fashion Sewing Group and is the author of *Do You Love What You Sew?.*

Verna Erickson is an educational consultant with Singer Sewing Company.

Robbie Fanning's latest book, written with her husband Tony, is *The Complete Book of Machine Quilting* (second edition). For ten years Robbie has been a sewing, quilting, and craft book editor. She also publishes the quarterly newsletter *Creative Machine.*

Eunice Farmer studied fashion design and textiles at Washington University in St. Louis, Missouri, and later in Europe at design houses and with master tailors. With a focus on sewing for fashion, she opened a sewing school in St. Louis in 1961. Seven years later, she established a boutique, Eunice Farmer Fabrics. Eunice has also written the nationally syndicated column "Sew Simple" for 30 years.

Barbara Fimbel, an editor of and contributor to this book, has contributed to such book projects as *Vogue & Butterick's Home Decorating, Christmas Gifts for Everyone,* and several *Better Homes & Gardens* books. In addition, she has edited several crafts magazines, including *Crafts with Simplicity* and *Butterick Make It!*

Glorian Friedel's mail-order novelty pattern business grew out of a pattern giveaway she designed for the Fabric Resale Fairs, which she started in Milwaukee, Wisconsin, in 1985 and ran every six months for eight years. Gloria has written for *Serger Update* and *Country Handcrafts.*

Dianne Giancola is communications and fashion director for the Prym-Dritz Corporation in Spartanburg, South Carolina.

Janice M. Giles is a former book editor and a smocking and heirloom sewing teacher.

The Sewing Experts

Ann Price Gosch, a magazine writer and book editor, specializes in fashion, sewing, and decorating. She has conducted serger seminars and authored *The Serger Idea Book.*

Linda Griepentrog is editor of *Sew News* and editorial director of the sewing division of PJS Publications.

Mary Griffin, sewing consultant to Singer Sewing Company, conducts consumer seminars and training programs for dealers and cowrote the newsletter *From the Singer Sewing Basket.* She has written for *Sew News, Treadleart, Sew Beautiful,* and *Sewing and Fine Needlework.*

Sue Hausmann represents Viking/White Sewing Machine Companies as host of "The Art of Sewing" TV show. Teaching professionally for more than 20 years, she has presented seminars to thousands of retailers and their customers. She has also created many instructional videos for consumers.

Carolyn Hoffman is a well-known Connecticut-based decorator and teacher.

Laurel Hoffmann teaches courses for continuing professional education at Philadelphia College of Textiles and Science. These courses adapt industrial sewing methods for home and cottage industry sewing.

Susan Huxley is a sewing book editor for Rodale Press and a former editor of *Crafts Plus* magazine.

Margaret Islander studied commercial pattern drafting and grading and then worked at a training center for garment workers, mastering all aspects of production sewing. She developed a course based on these techniques, and in 1979, she founded the Islander School of Fashion Arts in Grants Pass, Oregon.

Virginia K. Jansen has created patterns for McCall's and Simplicity and was a contributing editor for *Simplicity's Simply the Best Home Decorating Book.* She is also the author of *I Can't Believe—It's Not Sewn.*

Cindy Kacynski is a freelance writer and editor and lifelong sewing enthusiast. Currently editor of *Serger Update,* she is also writing a serger-troubleshooting book to be published in 1996. Cindy has worked on several editorial staffs for PJS Publications.

Kenneth D. King began his career in window display and evolved into a designer with his own San Francisco studio. His work appears in museums and galleries and on the rich and famous.

Janet Klaer, an authority on sewing notions, writes for *Sew News, Sewing Decor,* and *Sewing Update.* Since 1991, she has been the U.S.-based partner for Klaer Wright International Marketing, promoting the sewing and crafts industry between the United States and Europe.

Stacey L. Klaman is a former editor for Rodale Press.

Kaethe Kliot offers everything for today's lace maker at LACIS, a store in Berkeley, California, that she opened with her husband in 1966. She is an expert in lace restoration.

Gaye Kriegel established a home-based business, Hill Country Interests, for the purposes of sewing professionally, teaching a variety of sewing classes, and writing two self-published books, *All About Appliqué* and *Kiddie Kouture.* Gaye continues to teach, is assistant editor of *Creative Machine* newsletter, and recently coauthored *Affordable Heirlooms.*

Karen Kunkel, an editor of and contributor to this book, is a home economist and sewing con-

The Sewing Experts

sultant who produces educational materials and videos for home sewing and craft companies. She has written for *Sew News, McCall's Patterns* magazine, *Sewing Decor,* and *What's New in Home Economics.* Recently she contributed to a Vogue/Butterick book series.

Jan Larkey is author of *Flatter Your Figure.* She has conducted workshops for McCall's, Singer, Viking, and Elna and has written for numerous magazines.

Claudia Larrabure, a top dressmaker, is often called on by fabric companies such as Waverly and Concord to make samples for use in magazine and print advertising. Many examples of her work appear in the *Singer Sewing Reference Library.* She is also a craft designer.

Libby Lehman is a quilter whose work has been shown and collected nationally and in Japan. She took first place at the American Quilter's Society show in 1993 and third place in 1992. She has coauthored four books on quilting.

Dorothy R. Martin, a sewing designer, educator, and author, has appeared on television news and consumer segments demonstrating the joy of sewing. Her work has appeared in *Sew News, Singer Sewing Reference Library, Erica Wilson's Brides Book,* and *Sew Much Better.*

Kathy McMakin, an internationally known sewing teacher, has written three books: *Picture Smocking, French Sewing by Serger,* and *60 Minute Heirlooms, Serging for Babies.* Her serger techniques have been featured on two PBS sewing programs, and she serves as construction editor for *Sew Beautiful* magazine.

Jill Abeloe Mead is the driving force behind Rag Merchant, a Des Moines, Iowa, clothing pattern company. Jill is a widely published writer and editor.

June Mellinger is education consultant for Brother International Corporation.

Agnes Mercik, a consultant for Bernina of America, lectures at trade shows and dealer trainings and writes and designs projects for Bernina publications. Her latest project ideas are featured in two books, *The Complete Book of Machine Quilting* and *New Creative Serging Illustrated.*

Marian Mongelli began her career designing children's clothes for Cinderella Frocks. Eventually she opened her boutique, Fraises, and for 15 years offered custom dressmaking for women. Now, she offers custom dressmaking from her home.

Susan Nester, a lifelong sewer, owns and operates Susan Nester Originals, offering custom dressmaking and design services.

Nancy Nix-Rice consults on image and wardrobe planning through her business First Impressions, and she is working on a book on the subject. Nancy also runs her own sewing school, has nine sewing videos to her credit, and appears bimonthly as a guest sewing expert on QVC, the cable TV shopping network.

Gay Quinn's fashion and decorating skills helped her become a successful floral designer and shop owner in Shreveport, Louisiana. She puts the same talents to use at an elegant home–furnishings and fine gift shop in Houston.

Judith Rasband, director of the Conselle Institute of Image Management, entered the fashion retailing and styling field in 1960. Eventually she produced a weekly fashion segment for the NBC affiliate in Salt Lake City.

Sharee Dawn Roberts has received international acclaim for her high-fashion quilted clothing and machine art techniques. She is author of *Creative Machine Art* and a contributing editor for *American Quilter* and *Threads*. She owns Web of Thread, a decorative thread mail-order business.

Susan Rock has taught a wide range of needle-art classes throughout the United States, with her chief interest being machine embroidery. Author of *Fiesta Extravaganza*, she's currently writing a book on machine embroidery. Susan is a consultant to Madiera.

Robin Rose served as publicity manager for Simplicity Pattern Company, where she handled media and public relations. She owns The Robin Rose Connection, a public relations firm that serves sewing-related companies.

Donna Salyers set aside her successful career as a syndicated sewing columnist and TV personality to begin Fabulous-Furs. Her product line includes synthetic furs, patterns, and instruction books. Donna has authored six videos and six books.

Jan Saunders, a regular contributor to *Serger Update, Sewing Update, Sew News*, and *Threads*, is author of several books, the most recent being *Wardrobe Quick-Fixes*. She is coauthoring a *Sew and Serge* series.

Claire Shaeffer, author and national lecturer, specializes in adapting fashion industry techniques for home sewers. Her books include *The Complete Book of Sewing Short Cuts*, a collection of industry techniques that revolutionized home sewing, *Claire Shaeffer's Fabric Sewing Guide*, and *Couture Sewing Techniques*.

Lisa Shepard is creative director for Handler Textiles Corporation. She helped found the New Jersey Chapter of the American Sewing Guild. In addition, Lisa has written on sewing and fashion.

Patsy Shields is part of the national teaching staff of Sulky of America. She is a coauthor of the *Singer Sewing Reference Library* book *Decorative Machine Stitching*. She is also a coauthor of *Updated Serger Concepts in Sulky* and a contributor to *Surface Design Concepts in Sulky* and *Quilting Concepts in Sulky*.

Jacquelyn Smyth is a lifelong craftsperson with a particular love of sewing. Her career has included stints as knit and crochet editor at *McCall's Needlework & Crafts*, technical editor for *Vogue Knitting*, and editor in chief for *Butterick Make It!* Her designs have appeared in *Woman's Day* magazine and *Better Homes & Gardens* books.

Karen Costello Soltys, an editor of quilt books at Rodale Press, has been sewing garments for 25 years and has been quilting for 16 years.

Anne Marie Soto, a home economist and sewing journalist, has contributed articles to almost every major sewing magazine. Her credits also include many Simplicity publications and *Vogue's Sewing for Children*.

Ruthann Spiegelhoff is the creator of Great Copy Patterns, which she began in 1989. She has managed Spiegelhoff Fabrics for 22 years. Ruthann is also a contributing writer for a number of sewing publications.

Kathleen Spike owns KS Designs, a custom clothing business and is a consultant to small clothing- and textile-related businesses. She is the author of a business instruction book, *Sew to Success!*, and writes regularly for *Sew News* magazine, *Serger Update* and *Sewing Update* newsletters, and copublishes the *OmniStitch Newsletter*.

Jan M. Steltz, a lifelong sewer, has been quilting for more than 15 years.

The Sewing Experts

Marinda Stewart has her own line of patterns and is the author of four books. Her work has appeared in many publications, and her unique wearable art pieces have been exhibited in Japan, Europe, and the United States.

Sharon S. Sullivan works in research and development for Tacony Corporation, a large sewing machine distributor.

Barbara Wright Sykes is author of *The "Business" of Sewing*, a primer for sewing professionals. Her consulting firm, Barbara Wright & Associates, also serves would-be sewing entrepreneurs.

Cheryl Winters Tetreau is a senior editor of Rodale Press sewing and craft books.

Annie T. Tuley has exhibited her quilting nationally and internationally. Her machine quilting work has been widely published. She sews projects that incorporate new products produced by companies, such as Clotilde, Wright's, and Silkpaint, for use in advertising campaigns.

Victoria Waller, of Victoria Waller Designs, has worked extensively with fabric and decorative trim for more than 20 years, creating home decor, fashion, and craft projects for educational brochures, store display, and national advertisements. As design director for Hollywood Trims, she's an expert on decorative trims.

Betty Ann Watts owns a boutique marketing communications agency, Communication Concepts. She is the former communications director for the American Home Sewing and Crafts Association.

Susan Weaver is a contributing editor to this book and a technical editor for *Simplicity's Quick & Easy Sewing for the Home* series.

Lee Wiegand, in what she calls retirement, makes all of her clothes and upholsters and reupholsters her furniture. She is the author of *The Home Decorating Catalog* and *The Food Catalog*.

Tammy Young, coauthor of 12 books, writes regularly for *Sewing Update* and *Serger Update* newsletters, which she founded and managed until selling them in 1991. She is also an author and consultant for Chilton Book Company.

The editors wish to thank the following organizations and manufacturers and Beth Mauro of AHSCA for assistance.

- American Home Sewing and Crafts Association
- American Wool Council
- Bernina of America
- Butterick Company Inc.
- Coats & Clark, Inc.
- Elna, Inc.
- Handler Textile Corporation
- House of Fabrics, So-Fro Fabrics
- McCall Pattern Company
- Freudenberg Nonwovens/Pellon Consumer Division
- LACIS
- C. M. Offray & Son
- Prym-Dritz Corporation
- Simplicity Pattern Company
- Springs Industries Corporation
- Sulky of America
- Viking/White Sewing Machine Companies
- Wright's Home Sewing